Dr Abdullah Abdurahman

First published by Jacana in 2020

10 Orange Street
Sunnyside
Auckland Park 2092
South Africa
+2711 628 3200
www.jacana.co.za

© Martin Plaut, 2020

ISBN 978-1-4314-3055-0

Cover design by Trevor Paul
Editing by Russell Martin
Proofreading by Megan Mance
Set in Ehrhardt MT Std 11/14.5pt
Printed and bound by Tandym
Job no. 003720

See a complete list of Jacana titles at www.jacana.co.za

Dr Abdullah Abdurahman

SOUTH AFRICA'S FIRST ELECTED
BLACK POLITICIAN

Martin Plaut

Also by the author

Robert Mugabe, Ohio University Press, 2018 (with Sue Onslow)

Understanding Eritrea: Inside Africa's most repressive state, Hurst, 2016

Promise and Despair: The first struggle for a non-racial South Africa, 1899–1914, Jacana Media, 2016

Who Rules South Africa?, Jonathan Ball, 2012 (with Paul Holden)

Unfinished Business: Ethiopia and Eritrea at war, Red Sea Press, 2005, (edited, with Dominique Jacquine-Berdal)

Dedicated to Agnes Cornelia Victoria Jasmine Kronenberg ('Aunty Aggie'), born 10 May 1919, died 20 August 1993 in Genadendal, whose affection, faith and insights have been an inspiration to me all my life.

Contents

Introduction

FROM SLAVERY TO ACCLAIM

A little over a century ago Dr Abdullah Abdurahman and his young Scottish bride, Nellie, disembarked from the steamship RMS *Kinfauns Castle* in Cape Town. It was September 1902 when they landed amid the noise and bustle of the docks. Before them rose Table Mountain, with the city spread out beneath it. He had left Cape Town to study overseas: now Abdurahman was returning home for good, a fully qualified doctor, having graduated from Glasgow University. While there, he had met and married his sweetheart, Helen 'Nellie' Potter James, before going on to further studies in London. It must have been a moment of apprehension as well as ambition: arriving in the city to make it his permanent home after fourteen years, with a white wife whose reception he could not foresee.

Abdurahman returned to the Cape, determined to develop his medical practice and to make his mark in the land of his birth. Born in Wellington,[1] the grandson of slaves, he was keen to take advantage of a city that had blossomed from the economic boom that accompanied the Anglo-Boer War. Cape Town had seen a vast influx of soldiers, horses, artillery and munitions, as men and materiel made their way to the battlefields, and the town made a healthy profit from the trade. It had prospered and invested in its buildings and infrastructure.

Cape Town proved an excellent place to establish a home and a medical practice. Once these were up and running, the doctor looked around to see what else he might achieve. In 1904, just two years after returning home permanently, Abdurahman would be elected to the Cape Town City Council – the first person of colour ever to win public election in South Africa. He was to hold this position, representing Ward Seven in District Six, almost without interruption until his death in 1940. In 1905 the doctor was asked to preside over the African Political Organisation (APO), which would become the pre-eminent party of coloured South Africans for the next three decades.

Abdurahman would later be elected onto the Cape Provincial Council; and he would lead or participate in several delegations to the Imperial Parliament in London on behalf of all black South Africans. His work also included supporting the Indian community in South Africa. In 1926 he was asked to head a delegation to India, to plead their case with the Viceroy and the Indian National Congress. Over time Abdurahman became a figure known across the country, with links around the globe. This was no mean achievement for a man whose family had arrived in the Cape in servitude.

A tall, distinguished-looking man, in later life Abdurahman was seldom seen in public without wearing a suit and a fez. Slight, with deep-set eyes, he had a slender nose and angular cheekbones. As he aged, his face took on the weary, deeply lined appearance of a man worn by years of public service. It is this image that today peers down at visitors to the District Six Museum.

His death in 1940 saw an outpouring of grief in Cape Town seldom witnessed in the city, bringing large parts of the city to a halt, as his funeral cortège processed at walking pace through the streets. Describing Abdurahman's funeral procession, *Cape Times* journalist Willem Steenkamp recalled in his memoir that it was the first funeral that approached the scale and public involvement accorded to Cecil Rhodes in 1902, when twenty-five thousand people had lined Adderley Street.[2] 'Dr Abdurahman', wrote Steenkamp, 'built no huge financial empires, passed no laws that changed the destiny of millions. He was the grandson of slaves, and because he was a man of colour he was almost automatically excluded from the highest forums in the land. Yet … the day he was buried Capetonians flocked into the streets in the thousands in an expression of public grief.'

Abdurahman fought successive white governments, resisting the racist legislation enacted after Union in 1910. He was a founding father of education for coloured children, with schools across Cape Town bearing his imprint. And, as a father, he influenced one of the country's most significant politicians of the 1940s and 1950s, his daughter Cissie Gool. Although they clashed repeatedly in public over political differences, he and Cissie never lost their personal relationship.

There is much that we do know about Dr Abdurahman. His work as a campaigner for justice for all South Africans took him across three continents. It reveals a man of dignity and intellect, someone who could hold his own in any forum. With the backing of a small minority community, he strove to resist white domination and Afrikaner nationalism and the racism associated with them. In so doing he moved beyond the local and onto a national and even global stage. At the same time he was intimately involved in his own community, well known by everyone in District Six as someone who had brought better roads, lighting and health care to the area. He was an orator who could employ explosive phrases and radical rhetoric when he chose to, yet was conservative in his social outlook and in some of his policies. Abdurahman was also an angler, who enjoyed nothing better than standing on the rocks of False Bay, trying his luck. Little wonder that he was a passionate supporter of the Cape Point Nature Reserve, which he worked to protect.[3]

LEADING THE RESISTANCE

How is it that Abdullah Abdurahman – who rose from his grandparents' humble roots to become one of the earliest black doctors in South Africa, who had such a glittering political career – has now receded into the shadows? He was at the forefront of attempts over many years to unite black people as the country drifted ever further into racism. He co-operated with the African National Congress, the South African Indian Congress and the nascent trade union movement. He even worked with the far left, with the Communist Party and Trotskyist groups, when this proved possible.

Why, then, is a political figure of such stature so little known? The answer is partly that he has had no definitive biography so far. There have been several attempts to fill this gap, including very useful work by several previous authors, among them J.H. Reynolds, Yousuf S. Rassool, Mohamed Adhikari, Crain Soudien and Bill Nasson.[4] Richard van der Ross's writing over many years included recollections and references which are difficult, if not impossible, to replicate. Professor Van der Ross knew many of those who were close to the doctor. Finally, there is Gavin Lewis's magisterial work, *Between the Wire and the Wall*. It is an irreplaceable source of information, although it focuses on the history of coloured politics rather than on Dr Abdurahman. Despite the best efforts of these distinguished authors over many years, none has managed successfully to capture the man.

DENIGRATED BY THE LEFT

Perhaps the most important reason for Abdurahman's eclipse has been the hostility he faced from the far left. The African American political scientist and later winner of the Nobel Peace Prize, Ralph Bunche, stayed with Abdullah and his daughter Cissie during his South African travels in the 1930s. He noted that Cissie berated her father, when she hosted parties in her home, as an 'Uncle Tom'. A friend of his daughter's later wrote, 'Dr. Abdurahman, though still pre-eminent in the Coloured community, had discredited himself and his party by clinging to the white liberals ... The younger generation disputed his authority and made a bid for leadership on their own account. Members of his own family led the revolt.' An associate of the doctor's remarked, '[Cissie Gool] was occupying Socialist platforms publicly denouncing her father (the Doctor) and accusing him of having betrayed his people.'

The view of Communist Party stalwarts was equally dismissive. John Gomas, trade unionist and secretary of the Cape Town branch of the Communist Party in the late 1920s,[5] gave an acid assessment. Abdurahman was, in his view, a 'lackey of the white ruling class'.[6] 'This is all that has come of the thirty-four years' record of the APO [African Political Organisation],' Gomas declared. Some later historians have taken a similar stance. Patricia van der Spuy attacked Abdurahman for the lack of success of the Non-European conferences which he led from 1927 until the early 1930s, attributing this to his failure to 'admit confrontational tactics into their repertoire'.[7]

There is, certainly, an element of truth in these assessments. The conferences were not a resounding success and the APO did not halt the tide of racial legislation that the Hertzog government introduced in the 1920s and 1930s. When Abdurahman died in 1940, he left no obvious political successor. His party limped on, soon to collapse. Yet the widespread dismissal of Abdurahman is far too glib. This elite censure of the doctor never trickled down to the streets. Coloured people proved their loyalty to the doctor by faithfully returning him to office election after election. He was loved to the end of his days. From the perspective of the far left, the APO was an obstacle, filling the heads of coloured people with 'false consciousness'. Little wonder that they have been so dismissive.

A fairer assessment is provided by Mohamed Adhikari: 'There are those, usually of liberal persuasion, who revere him as the most distinguished political leader yet to have represented the coloured community, while there are others, mainly adherents of one of the radical political traditions, who dismiss him as an opportunist and a collaborator. Whatever one's ideological position, there can be little argument that in the four decades before his death on 20 February 1940 Abdurahman was far and away the most influential and popular political leader within the coloured community.'[8]

Abduraham suggested to the coloured people that petitions and peaceful protest, accompanied by radical rhetoric and alliances with other groups fighting white domination, might resist the advance of segregation and racism. These tactics signally failed. Yet so too did the tactics of *all* other opposition movements in this period. Whether one considers the campaigns of the ANC (which mirrored the APO's own) or the more radical street protests of the Unity Movement or Communist Party, one has to conclude that all ended in failure. Despite this, few hold these opposition parties to the same standard as they do the APO. While individual campaigns and particular leaders on the left may be criticised, they are not written off as Dr Abdurahman has been. It is – surely – time to reassess Dr Abdurahman's legacy.

This will require the acknowledgement that Abdurahman's career was not without achievements. In reality he was a pioneer of an ideal that was, finally, to rout the forces of racism and oppression. That ideal was non-racism. If there was a passion that drove him on throughout his career, it was the belief that all people were equal, and of equal worth. Abdurahman sought to unite South Africans irrespective of their race or religion. This is to be seen as well in his personal life – his marriage to a white Christian woman, whom he never sought to persuade to take the Muslim faith. It is to be found in his friendships across the colour line: with Gandhi and W.P. Schreiner, with Sol Plaatje and Walter Rubusana. He led delegations abroad which represented not just the coloured people, but the Indian community as well. He strove to achieve his dream of unity with passion to the end of his days. Is it any wonder that he was loved and admired by people far beyond his native Cape Town?

THE MISSING ARCHIVE

Why this discrepancy between the adulation of the public and attempts to denigrate him? The reason is not hard to find. Gavin Lewis suggests that many attacks on Abdurahman have been little more than 'half-truths or … reflections of the self-interest of the authors, or … an ahistorical view of Coloured politics'.[9] They reflect the political currents of the period and the perspectives of the authors, rather than representing an objective judgement. For the far left, Abdurahman was an obstacle to their attempts to win the support of a section of Cape Town society that they believed was theirs by right. Cape Town's communists and Trotskyist groups failed to understand why they made relatively little progress among working-class coloureds, and saw Abdurahman as standing in the way of their progress.

Even today – more than a quarter of a century after the end of apartheid – Dr Abdurahman's many achievements are little known and even less understood. Despite honourable attempts by the District Six Museum to commemorate his life, he is all but forgotten, even by his own community. One is left wondering whether there is not a systematic attempt to erase those who do not fit in with the present ANC government's view that all history should be seen as the clash of two diametrically opposed forces: the ANC (and its allies in the Communist Party), on the one side, and the forces of white reaction, on the other. Other movements, parties or personalities have been systematically ignored. Is it not time to resurrect a more complex, nuanced and varied history, with far more forces and players striving to influence the country's politics?

Correcting these misapprehensions has been hindered by the fact that there are so few original sources available to the biographer. As Gavin Lewis correctly observed: 'The absence of any of Abdurahman's private papers and correspondence hampers investigation of these allegations.'[10] This assessment is almost as true today as it was when Lewis wrote it in the 1980s. No diaries or journals exist. Few personal letters either from, or to, the doctor survive. His manuscript collections are dominated by news clippings, and the remainder by his daughter's papers. Private items in the archives are scarce, and almost no one remains alive today who knew him personally. Research for this book draws on university libraries in London and Cape Town. Material was enriched from archival fragments in Scotland, England and Turkey.

It was only in the last few months of writing this biography that a few precious papers from Dr Abdurahman's own archive finally emerged. They form part of the Dr Edgar Maurice Private Papers, which were partially microfilmed by the University of Cape Town. Unfortunately, much of that microfilm has been damaged and is no longer legible.[11] With the kind assistance of Derek Gripper and Ri'aad Dollie, two boxes of material were discovered. What they contained appeared to be a fraction of what must once have been a very substantial personal collection. Few letters remained – although there was an important and intriguing letter to Sarojini Naidu, a great Indian independence activist, feminist and poet. Much of this material is extremely fragile and appears to consist of evidence to the Wilcocks Commission,[12] which considered the socio-economic conditions of the coloured people, from 1934. Abdurahman sat on the commission (the only person of colour to do so) and helped write critical, dissenting paragraphs for the commission's final report. The rest of the archive consists of cuttings – some from Abdurahman's trip to India for the South African Indian Congress. The remainder is from Cape newspapers and other international publications. Each had been carefully labelled and dated. They provide a tantalising glimpse into Abdurahman's life and his meticulous method of work. No wonder he was able to maintain such an extensive correspondence and workload, alongside his busy medical practice and his political work.

Despite my best efforts, much remains obscure. For example, how did his father – the son of slaves, whose family owned a small shop in Wellington and then another near the Parade in Cape Town – afford to educate his children? How could his family send one son to Al-Azhar University in Cairo to study law, and another son to Glasgow to study medicine? How did his family fund their travels, moving repeatedly as they did between South African and Britain? Ri'aad Dollie, a member of Dr Abdurahman's extended family, has provided this useful suggestion:

> Abdul Rahman, his dad, was quite successful as a scholar. He graduated from Al-Aqsa University in Cairo. He inherited his father's estate which at the time included the grocery [shop], properties and capital that amounted to 5000 sterling. His mother Khadija Dollie's parents were well-off merchants. Her brother Hadji Mohammed Hanif Dollie had a successful fishing business from Granger Bay and Sadick Dollie made his money in property, at one point owning several properties in District Six including a number of buildings on Hanover Street. The Dollie siblings also inherited properties and monies from their mother, Gasilla. So, the Abdurahmans were well off and with further marriages between the Abdurahmans, Effendis, Dollies and Gools, there was generational stability though individuals fluctuated in their fortunes.[13]

This complex family history shines a light on the lives of a South African community. Dr Abdurahman's story reveals the intertwined local, national and international histories within which he operated, and his family's role in the fight for dignity, equality and respect.

CHAPTER ONE

Cape Town, 1900

THE MELTING POT OF SOUTHERN AFRICA

At the dawning of the twentieth century Cape Town exuded an air of self-satisfaction. 'Lofty buildings, palatial shops, crowded pavements, a constant stream of street traffic – what a contrast with the quiet, sleepy, deserted old thoroughfare of but a few years ago, straggling down to the water side,' boasted an illustrated booklet entitled *Progressive Cape Town*.[14]

'Few cities have changed so greatly within the last quarter of a century,' wrote its gushing author. The main thoroughfare, Adderley Street, was declared to be among the finest in the country with buildings that 'would not disgrace a European city twice the size of Cape Town. The Standard Bank, a handsome, well-proportioned structure with a beautiful portico and façade; the General Post Office, built of Colonial stone in a simple and dignified style of architecture ... the various clubs, hotels, theatres, and many other private and public buildings in the principal streets are substantial evidence of the marvellous progress and prosperity of new Cape Town, and of the pluck and enterprise of its citizens.'

These claims were not just an overblown manifestation of civic pride. They reflected the economic progress that had followed the discovery of gold on the Rand in 1886, reinforced by the boom that had been brought to the city by the Anglo–Boer War.[15] Although the city was far from the fighting front, it benefitted enormously as an entrepot for the supplies and materiel as well as British troops flowing through the port. During the war the harbour was so busy that ships had to be double-berthed to offload their cargos.

It wasn't just the new townscape that had changed the face of the city. The city's population had been transformed over recent years by an influx of men and women from around the world.[16] Who were they? The historian Robin Hallett provides a vivid account of their complex origins: 'Afghan mattress-makers, African dockworkers, German private detectives, Italian musical instrument makers, Afrikaner landowners, prostitutes from St. Helena, Chinese laundrymen, Scottish policemen, Italian shopkeepers, Jewish second-hand dealers, restaurant owners from Madeira, English soldiers, as well, of course, as the large amorphous group described in the records as "labourers", whether European or Coloured, and clerks and businessmen and civil servants and clergymen and politicians.'[17] To this list can be added West Indians, some of them working class but also a few middle-class professionals.[18]

Cape Town had become a metropolis, very different from the town of a few years earlier. In a century, it had grown more than tenfold. It was, by the time of the census of 1904, a city of 170,000 people: hardly the sleepy town of 1806 with just 16,000 citizens.[19]

Cape Town was also a city that was more liberal in its relations between the various races and ethnic groups than the rest of the country. This also applied to the workplace. A number of emerging trade unions opened their doors to all. The Typographical Union, for instance, went out of its way to win coloured members, while white tailors tried to get 'Malay' (Muslim) tailors to join a strike, albeit unsuccessfully.[20] The close proximity in which many of the poorer members of the city lived made social (and sexual) intercourse between its varied peoples inevitable, even if this was regarded as shocking by some. A leader in the *South African News* commenting on European artisans in Cape Town said: 'We have been astonished, and from the standpoint of our social prospects, disheartened to find how surprisingly large is the percentage of such settlers who marry coloured women. Let the

2

Imperial Government take a Census on this point in, say, District Six of Cape Town, and the result will astonish them.'[21]

This was not a recent development. The first two formal marriages at the Cape were between freed women slaves and white colonists. Some free blacks (manumitted slaves) were given land alongside whites and attended non-racial schools.[22] Lady Duff Gordon, who visited the Cape in the early 1860s, wrote: 'Malays [Muslim descendants of slaves] are also a mixed race like the Turks – i.e. they marry women of all sorts and colours provided they will embrace Islam. A very nice old [Muslim] fellow who waits here occasionally is married to an Englishwoman, *cidevant* lady's maid to the Governor's wife.'[23]

Despite its appearance of prosperity, Cape Town was a grindingly difficult place to live in for the poor and the working class, most of whom were described as 'coloured', which included the category of Cape 'Malays'. Many lived in District Six, which they shared with poor whites and black Africans. The area had not always been home to the poor. In the second half of the nineteenth century District Six was cosmopolitan and socially mixed, home to everyone from wealthy merchants and tradesmen to labourers and prostitutes. In 1861 the *Monthly Observer* gave an impression of the area:

> It is a rambling, untidy locality. The houses and streets have a newly settled appearance; and the prevailing idea suggested is that of a busy, striving, energetic population having thrown themselves upon the soil, converted into bricks all but a small portion of it, and built houses of every shape and kind on the narrow remainder. Of streets there cannot accurately be said to be any; drains there are positively none, unless it be allowable to regard the whole surface of the earth in that light ... a feeble and paralysed local government is powerless to enforce the most ordinary regulations necessary for the well-being of a rapidly growing town.[24]

But by the end of the nineteenth century the rich had moved out and the poor had multiplied. There was widespread overcrowding and rack-renting.[25] In 1901 bubonic plague arrived in the city. Carried by rats, it spread rapidly in the overcrowded dwellings of areas like District Six. Half of all those infected died. By the beginning of May more than 30 people a week were dying of the disease.[26] The squalor of some of the jerry-built housing in the district was hard to credit. An inspector reported on the filth and overcrowding of a house with African tenants in Horstley Street:

> Not an inch of space went abegging. Lights – very primitive indeed; coarsewick and oil, whose smoke thickened the already dense atmosphere – burned dimly in some of the rooms, and the natives huddled together in their filth and squalor, perfect pictures of misery. Occasionally a scantily-blanketed figure might be vaguely seen darting down the passage into some Cimmerian darkness beyond, but for the most part the 'boys' remained huddled together in this filth of the floor space they had secured. That was the scene with variations in the rooms of dozens of the tenements.'[27]

The depression that followed the Anglo-Boer War began in 1903 and lasted for six long years. It was, declared an economist, the worst in the past century.[28] Soon the city had serious unemployment, with one coloured observer complaining: 'Never during my lifetime has depression been so acute. People with nice houses have had to sell all their furniture and are now living in one room.'[29] The Cape authorities made matters worse by cutting government expenditure on public works. Building contracts vanished and skilled tradesmen found themselves unemployed.

While most coloured people were poor and working class, there was a tiny elite consisting of artisans, small retail traders, clerks, clergymen, teachers and a handful of professionals.[30] Many of them enjoyed the vote in the Cape by virtue of their owning or renting property. It was to this elite that Dr Abdurahman belonged. He was just one of three black doctors in Cape Town at the beginning of the twentieth century and one of just 66 professional 'Malays' listed in the 1904 Cape census.[31]

This, then, was the city in which Dr Abdurahman lived, treated his patients and served his community. It was a vibrant urban environment in which people of many races, ethnicities and countries of origin rubbed shoulders. Sometimes there were sharp differences and bitter strife, but on the whole they got on with each other. As one Rhodesian visitor was to remark, there was a level of social mixing in Cape Town that was quite 'impossible' to imagine back home.[32]

CHAPTER TWO

The young Abdurahman

FROM WELLINGTON TO CAPE TOWN

> Abdurahman, Abdullah (1872–1940), political leader and physician, was born on 18 December 1872 in Wellington, a country town in south-western Cape Colony, the eldest son of the nine children of Abdul Arraman (also known as Rahman), small trader and civic figure, who was a patron of Cape Muslim welfare and burial societies, and his only wife, Kadija Dollie, seamstress. His parents were Cape Muslims or Cape Malays, and his grandparents were imported Dutch East India Company slaves Abdul and Betsy Jemalee, who had managed to buy their freedom and also, following the British occupation, benefited from the friendship and generosity of Lady Duff Gordon.[33]

So begins the crisp entry by the South African historian Bill Nasson in the *Oxford Dictionary of National Biography*. It summarises most of what we know for certain about Abdurahman's early years. Eve Wong has made an admirable attempt to provide greater clarity and detail about his family and parentage in her master's thesis.[34] This includes an extensive family tree garnered from her researches in a number of archives. Yet much remains obscure and much of the family detail has been lost. Reconstructing the early years of Abdullah Abdurahman's life is a little like piecing together the fragments of a badly damaged antique porcelain bowl: a good deal has to be surmised and, unless one is diligent and expert, the repairs are all too visible. Bearing this warning in mind, I have attempted to bring together what is known in a coherent form.

It is often said that Abdurahman was a descendant of slaves, who purchased their freedom. There was, and still is, a belief that at least some of his ancestors came from India and possibly from Bengal. The lawyer and activist Ismail Meer, who grew up in the village of Waschbank, near Dundee in KwaZulu-Natal, certainly thought so. As the editors of his memoirs wrote: 'From discussions at his home and in the village, Mr Meer learnt about Abdullah Abdurahman, grandson of a slave from Bangladesh and a friend of Gandhi, who strove to unite the African, Indian and Coloured people in the struggle for human rights, and was one of the early leaders in the struggle for freedom.'[35] The perception of the doctor as a grandson of Indian slaves was widespread. His own daughter Cissie Gool told the American visitor Ralph Bunche that her father was 'part Indian, part Malay'.[36]

Although I do not suggest that any of this is incorrect, it has proved difficult to trace Dr Abdurahman's ancestry back to Bengal. This is not simply a question of a lack of scholarly effort: the historical record is poor. In a review of the slaves who were brought to Cape Town, Nigel Worden summed up the problem of identifying their origins by comparing the task with the work done to track the ancestry of slavery across the Atlantic. 'It has long been a lament of historians of Cape slavery that we lack information about precisely how individual slaves were obtained. This is a problem for analysis of Dutch slave trading as a whole in the Indian Ocean region, and especially where Dutch trading overlapped with indigenous Asian slaving networks. There are few equivalents to the shipping records of transatlantic slavers, since, in the Indian Ocean, "slaves rarely constituted a special cargo".'[37] Without these detailed records, it has proved almost impossible to trace how slaves and their families arrived in the Cape. The problem is exacerbated by the fact that slave registers also used names that varied over time or simply reflected the place from which the slaves originated.

The first glimmer of a trace of the Abdurahman family comes in the writings of Lady Lucie Duff Gordon, who had come to the Cape in 1861 in an attempt to cure her tuberculosis. In a series of colourful letters home, she described her experiences at the Cape.[38] 'I have a friendship with one Abdul Jemaalee and his wife Betsy, a couple of old folks who were slaves to Dutch owners, and now keep a fruit-shop of a rough sort, with "Betsy, fruiter," painted on the back of an old tin tray, and hung up by the door of the house,' she explains.[39] 'Abdul bought himself, and then his wife Betsy, whose "missus" generously threw in her bed-ridden mother. He is a fine handsome old man, and has confided to me that £5,000 would not buy what he is worth now.' The family offered her some herb tea and they became good friends. She even promised to try to contact their son, who had been sent to study in Egypt.

From this single source one can deduce that although the family had been slaves, they had somehow managed not only to save enough money to purchase their freedom but had also gone on to accumulate sufficient wealth to be very comfortably off, with savings in excess of £250,000 in today's money (or R5 million). How this was achieved from the takings of a 'fruit shop of a rough sort' is neither explained nor is it questioned in later sources. Nor is the fact that Abdul and Betsy say that they could afford to send their son, Abdul Rahman, to study at Cairo's finest university.[40] This tale, perhaps told to impress a visiting English lady, has become the accepted wisdom about the Abdurahmans and has been repeated throughout the literature.[41]

There is one other, perhaps even less plausible, source of information that might suggest where Abdul Jemalee got the funds he needed to purchase his freedom, establish his business and maintain his family. It comes from the pen of R.M. Ballantyne, a popular Victorian author, whose juvenile novels of derring-do across the British Empire made him a household name. He is still remembered for his book *The Coral Island*, which inspired Robert Louis Stevenson to write *Treasure Island*.[42] Ballantyne wrote prolifically, churning out dozens of books. Among them was *The Settler and the Savage: A Tale of Peace and War in South Africa*, which he published in 1877 after a brief visit to the Cape.[43] It contains intriguing references to someone whom the hero of the story meets during his travels in the Karoo: a 'Malay' man called Abdul Jemalee.

Abdul Jemalee, a year or two before, had lived in Capetown, where his owner was a man of some substance. Jemalee had a wife and several children, who were also the property of his owner. Being an expert waggon-driver, the Malay was a valuable piece of human goods. On one occasion Jan Smit happened to be in Capetown, and, hearing of the Malay's qualities, offered his master a high price for him. The offer was accepted, but in order to avoid a scene, the bargain was kept secret from the piece of property, and he was given to understand that he was going up country on his old master's business. When poor Jemalee bade his pretty wife and little ones goodbye, he comforted them with the assurance that he should be back in a few months. On arriving at Smit's place, however, the truth was told, and he found that he had been separated for ever from those he most loved on earth. For some time Abdul Jemalee gave way to sullen despair, and took every sort of abuse and cruel treatment with apparent indifference, but, as time went on, a change came over him. He became more like his former self, and did his work so well, that even the savage Jan Smit seldom had any excuse for finding fault. On his last journey to the Cape, Smit took the Malay with him only part of the way. He left him in charge of a friend, who agreed to look well after him until his return.

Even this crushing of Jemalee's hope that he might meet his wife and children once more did not appear to oppress him much, and when his master returned from Capetown he resumed charge of one of the waggons, and went quietly back to his home in the karroo.

Later in the novel, after the lapse of a few years, 'The Malay in particular – slavery being by that time abolished – returned to Capetown, and there found his amiable wife and loving children ready to receive him with open arms. It is true the wife was somewhat aged, like himself, and his children were grown up – some of them even married – but these little matters weighed nothing in his mind compared with the great, glorious fact, that he was reunited to them in a land where he might call his body his own!'

There is no way of knowing whether this fictional character bears any relation to the real Abdul Jemalee, but the similarity of names and circumstances is intriguing. Is it possible that Ballantyne heard this story during his time in the Cape and adapted it to his purpose? One cannot know, but if it did refer to Dr Abdurahman's grandfather it might give us a clue as to how he made his money. As an expert wagon-driver Abdul Jemalee would indeed have been 'valuable'. He might have used his skills to accumulate enough money to purchase his freedom and then start his 'fruit shop of a rough sort'. This is, of course, entirely speculative.

Beyond this sketch of Dr Abdurahman's grandparents, we have little to go on. His father, also Abdul, was sent to Al-Azhar University in Cairo, Egypt's oldest degree-granting university, with a heritage stretching back over a thousand years.[44] It remains to this day among the chief centres of Arabic and Muslim learning. Abdul remained abroad for ten years, travelling to Mecca and earning the title 'Hadji', as someone who had performed the hajj or pilgrimage to the holy place. On his return he married Khadija Dollie, a seamstress, described as 'the prettiest Malay girl in Cape Town'. They had at least five children, although Abdul may have fathered others.[45] Their eldest son was Abdullah, the future Dr Abdurahman.

There are a few other facts about the family that are certain. One is that Hadji Abdul took his family and settled in the village of Wellington, just north of Paarl. Hadji Abdul worked as a fishmonger, while Khadija was a seamstress.[46] It was here that Abdullah was born in 1872 and received his early education at a Dutch Reformed mission school (1877–80) before going on to the Marist Brothers school in Cape Town, where he received a Catholic training (1881–4). His strongly Muslim parents clearly valued the quality of the education above the Christianity that went with it. He then completed his schooling at the South African College, at that time situated at the top of Gardens in Cape Town (1884–7).[47] He was the first coloured pupil to be educated at SACS, where he was taught by a notable Scottish educationist, Dr John Shaw. Under his tutelage Abdullah excelled, and 'by his diligence and ability, he outdistanced his comrades in almost every branch of school work'.[48] Dr Shaw had been educated at the Glasgow University and, with his help, Abdullah gained entry to its medical school after leaving SACS. He did so as a young man who had grown up in a strongly Muslim environment, surrounded by family members who were steeped in Islam and its traditions, yet also well aware of the tenets and practices of Christianity.

To Britain

In 1888 Abdullah Abdurahman registered at the medical school in Glasgow. Before he left for Britain the imam of the mosque on the Main Road in Claremont held a special service for the young man's 'success and wellbeing'.[49] Abdullah's parents accompanied him to ensure that he settled in well.[50] It has been suggested that his mother and father remained in London for the rest of their lives.[51] This is not the case. Khadija died in London in 1902 and is buried in Willesden New Cemetry,[52] but Hadji Abdul returned to South Africa, although it is not clear when he did so. His death was registered on the 20th of July 1920, aged 88.[53] He died at Dr Abdurahman's home, 7 Mount Street, Cape Town, after suffering from influenza for 14 days. His son signed the death certificate, which names him as Hadjie Abdurahman and described him as a Malay born in the Cape Province.

Dr Abdurahman's sister, Muhsine, did make a home in Britain, providing Abdullah with a useful base when he visited London in 1909. This came about through the family's links with the Ottoman Empire. This involvement in the affairs of the Ottoman Empire is not as extraordinary as it sounds. The relationship between Cape Muslims and the Ottomans dated back to 1861, when the member of the Cape parliament P.E. de Roubaix was appointed the Ottoman honorary consul-general in Cape Town.[54] De Roubaix was not a Muslim and he struggled to deal with religious disputes that flared up among the congregation at the Palm Mosque in Long Street. In the end he appealed for assistance to the Ottoman Sultan, Abdulaziz. The Sultan was the Caliph of Islam and saw his role as being responsible for Muslims worldwide. On 3 September 1862, the Sultan appointed Abu Bakr Effendi to travel to the Cape to disseminate an acceptable form of Islam among the local Muslim population.[55]

Abu Bakr was soon playing an important role in the life of the Cape community, teaching at the school he founded and providing guidance on Islamic issues (which was not always well received) while at the same time representing the Ottoman Empire. He established a family, marrying Rakea (Rukiye) Maker and having two children, only one of whom survived: a son, Ahmet Ataullah.[56] Ahmet Ataullah (later referred to as Ahmet Ataullah Bey, an honorific suggesting his aristocratic status) was educated at his father's school, the Ottoman Theological School on the corner of Wale and Bree streets.[57] From there he went to the Mc Leahlen Academy in Buitengracht Street before travelling with his father in 1876 to Istanbul, where he was introduced to the new Sultan, Abdul Hamid II. Abu Bakr Effendi subsequently returned to the Cape, but he left his son behind to learn Turkish and continue his education. Ahmet Ataullah received his first degree in Istanbul before continuing his studies at the Al-Azhar University in Cairo.[58] After his father's death on 29 June 1880, Atuallah Bey returned to the Cape. He took up residence at 90 Bree Street and married Muhsine, Abdullah Abdurahman's elder sister.[59]

This marriage forged the links between the Abdurahman family and the Ottoman Empire. Following in his father's footsteps, Atuallah Bey went on to serve the Ottomans in several capacities. He opened a school in Kimberley in 1884, supported by the Caliphate.[60] In 1894 he decided to stand for a seat in the Cape Parliament, the first Muslim to do so.[61] Atuallah was unsuccessful and returned to Kimberley before being appointed as consul-general of the Ottoman Empire in Singapore in 1901. He left his wife Muhsine and four children in South Africa. She later decided to take them to London to continue their studies there.[62] In London she established her home in Earl's Court, at 38 Longridge Road.[63] On 11 November 1903, Atuallah Bey was tragically killed in a car accident in Singapore. It must have been a severe blow to Muhsine, but fortunately the Ottoman state decided to step in and take responsibility for the family. Her son's circumcision feast was organised by decree of the Sultan himself – a rare honour indeed.[64] Financial aid followed and from 1905 Muhsine received a stipend from the Ottoman state. The following year bursaries were awarded to the children.[65] When Dr Abdurahman came to London in 1909 to petition the British government, he stayed with his sister Muhsine rather than taking up residence with the rest of his delegation near Trafalgar Square.[66]

The evidence is clear. As Ri'aad Dollie explained in his letter quoted in the Introduction, the family had gradually amassed considerable assets and properties.[67] Over time these took on an international dimension. The Abdurahman family were linked to the Ottoman Empire. Through trade and business networks, and even through grace and favour assistance from the Sultan himself, the family sustained itself and amassed considerable wealth. This may explain how Abdullah Abdurahman was able to receive his medical training at Glasgow University.

CHAPTER THREE

A golden dawn

A Scottish degree and a Scottish wife

Abdullah Abdurahman spent the required five years between 1888 and 1893 studying medicine at the Glasgow University. He was awarded second-class certificates in practical pharmacy, forensic medicine and practical pathology.[68] His graduation schedule showed that he studied chemistry, botany, anatomy, physiology, regional anatomy, materia medica (the history of pharmacy), pathology and clinical surgery. He passed them all, but in two subjects he excelled, receiving marks of 80 per cent in both midwifery and clinical surgery. On 27 July 1893 he graduated. The certificate has the name 'Abdullah Rahman' crossed out, to be replaced with the name by which he would be known for the rest of his life: 'Abdullah Abdurahman'. The doctor had emerged, ready to take on the world.

His time in Glasgow had not only been spent in studies: Abdurahman found time to socialise and fall in love. Here he met his future wife. She was Helen Potter James, universally known as Nellie. We know how they met from an interview Nellie gave in 1948.[69] She spoke to Zelda Friedlander, who painted a vivid picture of her interviewee. 'In an old-world house, tucked away between two buildings, facing the historic Castle, lives Mrs Abdurahman, the grand little white-haired lady of Mount Street – loved and respected by thousands of people in the Mother City for her kindness and long years of service to them – the widow of Dr A. Abdurahman, M.P.C. [Member of the Provincial Council] and a prominent member of the City of Cape Town Council.'

After this introduction Nellie spoke about her meeting with Abdullah as a student.

> Mrs Abdurahman was the only daughter of John Cumming James, a solicitor of Glasgow and well known in his own city as a man who had fought strenuously for free and compulsory education for Scottish children. As a young girl she spent her summer holidays in Forfar, and played in Glamis, the home of the Earl and Countess of Strathmore, the parents of our present Queen [Queen Elizabeth the Queen Mother].
>
> More than half a century ago, while doing electioneering work for the Chancellor of the Glasgow University,[70] Helen James was introduced to young Abdurahman, a medical student, by one of his fellow-students at the University, whose home was also in South Africa.[71]

This does not narrow the search very much. There were sixteen South Africans studying at Glasgow University in Abdurahman's year, or a year above or below him, who graduated in the period 1882–4. Ten were studying medicine, but one stands out: William Anderson Soga.[72] His father, Tiyo Soga, was a famous missionary, preacher and translator, who had spent two periods in Scotland, graduating from Glasgow University.[73] Tiyo returned to South Africa in 1857, arriving in Port Elizabeth with a Scottish bride. 'You should have been with us this day to witness the wonder and amazement with which a black man with a white lady leaning on his arm seemed to be viewed by all classes,' wrote Soga. It was a real novelty, and a triumph for principle, as Soga noted. The Soga family sent their children to Scotland to further their education, with William, the eldest, graduating in medicine in the same year as Abdurahman.[74] Was Soga the fellow medical student who introduced Abdurahman to Nellie Potter? We cannot be certain, but it is worth pointing out that William also met and married a Scot, just like his father.[75]

There was apparently little racial prejudice at the university and students enjoyed a good social life. It seems that the young Abdurahman mixed well and widely, with Scots and with his fellow South Africans like William Soga. There is every chance that they would have discussed the politics back home as well as conversing about the life they were experiencing in Glasgow. Here is the key to Abdurahman: a man at ease with people, irrespective of their race. It was the hallmark of his social and political interactions for the rest of his life.

Zelda Friedlander's account of his meeting with Helen James continues:

> They became friends, and in the home of the James family Abdurahman was spared the loneliness of a stranger in a strange land.
>
> After graduation, and when due to return to the Cape, he asked Miss James to marry him. He warned her of the difficulties that lay ahead as the Scottish wife of an Indian medical practitioner in South Africa, where racial problems and prejudices were much to the fore, but she, unafraid of what the future might hold, married him and so made South Africa her future home.
>
> As she told me about her deep affection for the late doctor, who was South Africa's pioneer non-European medical practitioner, the words of Ruth, one of the noblest characters of the Old Testament, passed through my mind: 'Whither thou goest, I will go … Thy people shall be my people … Thy God my God …' for words similar to these must have been used by her. Throughout her long life in South Africa she has been a crusader, a crusader battling for education and equal rights for non-Europeans.

What happened to the newly qualified doctor and his bride after he qualified is less than clear. Following his graduation in Glasgow in July 1893, Dr Abdurahman went to London, where he married Nellie in 1894 under Muslim law.[76] The doctor returned to Cape Town the following year and registered his medical qualifications, but remained there only temporarily. There then followed seven years during which he moved between London and the Cape. Dr Abdurahman and Nellie only finally embarked for Cape Town in 1902, to settle permanently in the city.

ESTABLISHING A MEDICAL PRACTICE

When he first returned to Cape Town in 1895, Dr Abdurahman immediately set about registering as a medical practitioner, establishing his practice at 99 Loop Street. Soon it was thriving. It is possible to trace the doctor's growing affluence through the *Cape Times* and the adverts that he placed in its pages. He is first mentioned on 6 February 1895, when he appears in a list of licensed medical practitioners.[77]

Within two weeks the doctor was giving evidence in a court case. 'Alleged fiendish cruelty: wife torture extraordinary: charge of murder,' ran the sensational headline in the *Cape Times*.[78] 'Gamat Abrahams and Badaroun, coloured men, who had previously been before the Police Court and remanded on a charge of culpable homicide – the victim being Rosie Badaroun, wife of one of the prisoners – were yesterday morning again brought up before Mr. J.C. Faure, R.M. [Resident Magistrate], when the charge was altered to one of murder ... Naseru Abdol said he saw Abrahams push the deceased to the ground because, he said, she stole his brandy. She fell on her head. A little while afterwards deceased's husband pushed her down a flight of steps ... Dr Abdulha [*sic*] Abdurahman, residing at 69 Bree-street said on the 30th January he was called in to see the deceased, whom he found in a very bad condition. He gave her a certificate for admittance to the hospital. He found a large scalp wound at the back of her head, and she was partly unconscious.'

Dr Abdurahman was making a name with patients as well. In April 1896 an advert appeared thanking him for his 'kind attendance' during the fatal illness of someone's grandchild.[79] As his practice grew, the doctor first hired a 'smart office boy' for his surgery at 99 Loop Street, and then a 'general servant' who had to be able to cook, for his residence at 7 Mount Street.[80] Later there was an advert for a 'boy for stables', then a groom and, finally, a dispenser of prescriptions. All were required to apply to the doctor at 99 Loop Street.[81] Soon children were on the way and there was an advert for a 'Nurse, to look after Child and do a little Housework'.[82] Dr Abdurahman's practice thrived. Finally – and amusingly – the *Cape Times* carried this somewhat tetchy advert on 1 June 1900: 'Small Kerry Cow: horns short and loose; tail white tipped, she ran towards Mountain in Zonnebloem: reward – Dr

Abdurahman, 7 Mount street. Anyone harbouring same after this date will be prosecuted.'

By the turn of the century the doctor was well established and able to extend the range of his work. He provided medical supervision required at the boxing ring. 'Jack Valentine's tournament, held in the Good Hope Hall last night, vied in interest with the best tournament ever arranged by that popular boxing entrepreneur ... Sixth and Last Round: Butler came up looking fresh as a daisy and at once knocked George down. He rose again and was almost a target for Butler, who kept knocking his opponent down, until the latter climbed under the ropes amidst a storm of cheering. Butler was carried in triumph to his drawing-room by his supporters amidst rounds of applause ... George was laid out winded for some time and Dr Abdurahman was called in to bring him to rights amid cheers and thus ended one of the best tournaments ever held in Cape Town.'[83]

On settling in Cape Town in 1902 he and Nellie made 7 Mount Street, just off St Lowry Road, their permanent home. It was described as 'the most prestigious mansion in the whole of District Six'.[84] Dr Abdurahman's growing affluence was indicative of the small but growing black professional class that emerged at the Cape at this time. His reputation soon caused him to be known across town. As a colleague later wrote: 'his name soon became a household word among both Europeans and non-Europeans ... Everywhere one heard people talking about "the clever young Malay doctor".'[85]

During the Anglo-Boer War, Dr Abdurahman remained in Cape Town where, as a doctor, he was inundated with patients from among the many refugees who had fled the Transvaal. The Abdurahman family escaped most of the war's effects, but the doctor would no doubt have been involved in cases of bubonic plague which struck Cape Town in 1901. As a result of the epidemic the Cape government introduced a policy of forced removal of people considered at risk in poor neighbourhoods like District Six. When African residents were relocated from District Six to Uitvlugt and, later, Ndabeni, some of the Muslim community feared they could be next. It has been suggested that during the plague Dr Abdurahman, as a medical practitioner, may have 'acted as an intermediary between the medical authorities and the Muslim community'.[86] John Raynard, who worked for some years as a clerk in Dr Abdurahman's Loop Street practice, recorded the impression Dr Abdurahman made by his fearless opposition to authority for what he felt was right. 'In a dispute between the doctors on the Government and City Council staffs, as to whether a certain patient to whom he was attending, and whom the doctors pronounced to be a plague case, and wished to have removed to the [quarantine] "Camp", "the Doctor" denied the case was one of plague, and won a bet of £200 from these doctors.'[87]

The consequences of the Anglo-Boer War

On 31 May 1902 the war finally ended. With the Boer republics now defeated and British control extended over the whole of southern Africa, it seemed that a new era beckoned. Many coloured and African people had given their support to the British cause, and some had even participated in the fighting on the British side, in the belief that they would be rewarded, that their rights and liberties as British subjects would be strengthened and even extended to fellow coloureds and Africans in the former Boer republics. The British, for their part, had made vague assurances of this kind to retain the loyalty and win the support of black people during the war. But it soon became apparent that in the interests of reconstruction after the war and of reconciliation between Afrikaners and English speakers, Britain had no intention of upsetting the social and racial order.

At the same time, it is important to recognise just how fluid the situation was. The British sought to secure reconciliation with the Afrikaners but they were also aware of their debt to the black population. As London strove to unite South Africa and shed some of its responsibilities, politics entered a period of flux, with the future very much in the balance. Would it tip towards a non-racial settlement for all its peoples, building on the Cape's liberal tradition which had developed irrespective of race since the 1830s? Or would it be drawn inexorably into the racism exemplified by the treatment of black miners in Kimberley and the Rand, as well as by the politics of the Boer republics, which denied anyone but white men the right to vote?

In the Cape at least, coloureds and Africans continued to enjoy the franchise if they were suitably qualified and fulfilled the property qualifications which applied to all, irrespective of colour. By 1904 coloureds represented 3.7 per cent of the Cape's electorate – or 14,836 voters.[88] This was a small number but they made up more than a fifth of the voters in six constituencies, including District Six (35%), Paarl (23%), Stellenbosch (28%) and Namaqualand (25%).[89] Politicians knew the votes of coloured people could be vital, and vied for their support.

The origins of coloured involvement in Cape politics and in forming their own political organisations are difficult to trace. Coloured people had enjoyed the franchise since 1853 when representative government was granted to the Cape and a colour-blind but qualified franchise was instituted. In 1883 the first coloured organisation, the Afrikaner League (Coloured), was formed among miners in the diamond town of Kimberley. The same city also saw the emergence of the Coloured People's Association in 1892, set up to try to resist attempts by Cecil Rhodes to raise the qualifications necessary for voting.[90] The following year a Cape Muslim, Ahmed Effendi, attempted to stand for the Cape parliament but was blocked. Although none of these developments led to a permanent, national organisation, they were indicative of a stirring of political consciousness among the coloured population. Coloured leaders were also prominent in social and sports clubs, including future leaders of the African Political Organisation, which Dr Abdurahman was to head. W.A. Roberts was a vice-president of the Coloured Young Men's Christian Association, while J. Wilson and J. Tobin were both referees and sports officials.[91]

Another significant catalyst in the development of coloured politics was the African and Afro-Caribbean community in the Cape Colony, who numbered nearly 500 by 1904.[92] Many had come as seafarers, serving on the ships that rounded the Cape. Three men in particular had a formative influence on Dr Abdurahman, shaping events that drew him into politics. They were Henry Sylvester Williams, Francis Zaccheus Santiago Peregrino and Rawson Wooding.

Williams, a Trinidadian, is best known as the general secretary of the pioneering Pan-African Conference, which met in London in July 1900.[93] The Conference drew delegates from Britain and across the world and led to the formation of a Pan-African Association, with the famous African American W.E.B. Du Bois as vice-president and officers from as far afield as Jamaica, Abyssinia (Ethiopia), Nigeria and South Africa.

Williams decided to travel to South Africa to continue his work. He said that this decision followed appeals for his assistance from Africans working on the gold mines.[94] In September 1903, Williams sailed for the Cape, leaving his wife and two children in London. There may have been another reason for the decision to make his home in Cape Town: Williams had good connections in the city. He knew of the work of his friend Rawson Wooding, who was from British Guiana.[95] A musician and teacher, Wooding had established a private preparatory school in Cape Town in 1902, which served the children of wealthier coloured families.

On his arrival in Cape Town, Williams established himself (with considerable difficulty) as a lawyer. He then began to fight for black rights, founding a Defence Committee to carry out this work. Williams sought to end restrictions on black ownership of land and the de facto ban on black service on juries, while also protesting against the segregation of public facilities.[96] Alongside this he worked with Wooding, joining the school's board. On the board were five men, including Dr Abdurahman and J.H.M. Gool, a leader of the Indian Association.[97] This may not have been where Williams and Abdurahman became acquainted; but it certainly deepened their relationship.

THE DOCTOR ENTERS POLITICS

The position on the Wooding's school board was among the first public roles that Dr Abdurahman accepted. Education would certainly be a passion that he pursued for the rest of his life. He believed that schools had a special role in preparing pupils for engaging with the world in which they lived: 'The highest ideal which a school could strive for was the turning out of pupils capable of filling all private and public offices.'[98]

Soon Abdurahman was on public platforms himself. In August 1904 he appeared on the stage of the Clifton Hall in Hanover Street, District Six, with Williams, attacking the government's plans to entrench inequality in the provision of education. The Cape parliament planned to make education compulsory for white children, but not for coloureds or Africans. Schools for the different ethnic groups would also receive differential funding, with considerably less per pupil provided for non-white children.[99] Williams led the attack, complaining that as British subjects such children were entitled to equality of treatment. 'Their money was taken to support schools to which they are not admitted … and now they were going to take their money to give compulsory education to all white children.'[100] Dr Abdurahman then seconded the resolution, to loud applause. 'He said that not a day passed that something was being done to them to cause them to raise their voices, and he trusted they would never cease to raise their voices until they had secured their rights.' The doctor was gaining public recognition as an orator and spokesman for the coloured community.

Another African or diasporan figure who was to play a key role in politics at the Cape at the turn of the century and who was to influence Abdurahman was F.Z.S. Peregrino. He is among the most colourful, intriguing and controversial characters to visit and then make Cape Town their home. Born in Ghana, of Brazilian extraction, he was educated in Britain, where he spent 23 years, and married a white American, Ellen Williams.[101] In 1887 he and his family went to Pittsburgh where he took up a variety of occupations, including labour broking. It was to be a practice he would continue in South Africa.

Peregrino was strongly pro-British. He joined the British–American Association in the United States, becoming the 'first colored member', and being described in the local press as a 'fully-fledged citizen of the British Isles and a loyal subject of her Majesty, the Queen'.[102] Peregrino would remain pro-British and supportive of respectable, law-abiding black people for the rest of his life. While he was an outspoken campaigner for black rights, he could also be obsequious before white authority, 'understanding' the position whites took in the American South and prepared to denounce more radical black colleagues to the authorities in South Africa.

Peregrino had personal ambitions: he wished to edit his own newspaper. In the 1890s he launched *The Spectator*, a weekly newspaper, aimed at the black community. The tone of the paper supported the gradualist approach of the 'respectable and observant negroes of the north' and black leaders, like Booker T. Washington, who 'are unostentatiously, but surely and most effectively, solving whatever there is of a race problem'.[103]

In May 1900 Peregrino sailed for London and then, in October, proceeded onwards to Càpe Town. Here he established himself in much the same way as he had done in the United States: as an editor and labour broker. The first issue of the *South African Spectator* was published on 1 December 1900, proclaiming it to be 'The Voice of the People'. Its aim was to 'advocate the cause of the black man ... his progress in America, on the West Coast of Africa, everywhere', and espouse the interests and welfare of 'black people, and also the coloured people'.

Soon Peregrino was at the centre of Cape Town's black political affairs. His paper was actively supported and sold by a local businessman and politician, John Tobin, who ran a restaurant in District Six. Tobin was, for a time, Peregrino's friend and political associate. Having initially promoted in the *Spectator* a Pan-African Society, Peregrino abandoned that idea and established the Coloured People's Vigilance Society, after being mugged by a group of whites. He remained its secretary until his death in 1919. The other organisation Peregrino initiated was the Coloured Men's Protectorate and Political Association. While the Vigilance Society was a campaigning organisation, the Protectorate and Political Association undertook political education. Both were open only to black members and neither had a very large membership. Peregrino's critics suggested that both organisations were little more than fronts for his ambitions.

The *Spectator* supported his political initiatives. Through its pages Peregrino took up the theme of black pride and black unity, rejecting all notions of racial inferiority, while at the same time stressing the need for sobriety and respectability. He cautioned against militancy and said that British rule, 'with all its imperfections ... is so far, and until something better develops, the best form of government for the black man'.[104]

In 1901 Peregrino's friend John Tobin decided that the time was ripe to start a regular series of public discussions for Cape Town's black community on a Sunday. He turned to Peregrino for help. Peregrino wrote to the Cape Colonial Secretary in May seeking permission for the gatherings; this was granted 'as long they are quiet and orderly'.[105] Tobin wasted no time and issued a leaflet inviting people to come together to discuss issues of concern. 'Go to the coloured People's meeting, Sunday Morning at ten', he wrote. 'Learn your political rights. Mr H.O. Ally and other speakers. At the foot of the mountain near St Mark's Church. All are welcome.' The meetings were held at 'the Stone', a landmark at the top of Clifton Street in District Six, conveniently close to the centre of town. There crowds gathered, sometimes in their hundreds. There is a colourful description of the Stone meetings:[106]

> The Stone is a huge grey boulder that squats high on the slope of Table Mountain half-way between the Castle and the Tollgate ... To reach the "Stone" meeting place you start from the heart of District Six – the coloured quarter – and climb through ragged lanes and alleys. Paralytic-looking boarding houses, decayed-looking cottages are on each side of you. As you go higher things improve architecturally and by and bye you find yourself in a network of terraces, which enterprising builders are trailing up the mountain slope ... Once clear of the houses, your way is plain. You cannot fail to see the crowd like a black spot in the distance, make for that as quickly as the boulders and clefts and the gravel will let you.
>
> The 'Stone' is at the top of a circle of smaller stones. These smaller stones are the reserved seats. You have to come very early to secure one of them. The space enclosed is vacant, but outside the circle are gathered some hundreds of coloured men – [Africans], Hottentots [Khoi], Cape boys [coloureds], half castes. They are probably representative of every native race. The majority have come in Sunday clothes – ordinary clothes except the necktie, which is generally alarming, being mostly red, white and blue. There are a few fellows who lack even more than collars and ties – one or two are barely covered. But they are all happy-looking. There is no cold shoulder for the ragged [African], but a nod, a handshake, or perhaps a joke. All crowd together and pass newspapers.

While these debates were taking place, Dr Abdurahman was beginning to make his own presence felt in the city's political life. In 1903 he led a delegation to the Colonial Secretary at the request of the British India League, protesting against restrictions placed on Indian immigration into the Cape.[107] On 8 February the following year Dr Abdurahman accompanied his friend Sylvester Williams, Peregrino and six other coloured men in a deputation to see the Cape's Attorney General, Victor Sampson.[108] They were angry that coloured people were apparently being denied the right to sit on juries. The Attorney General attempted to reassure them: there was 'nothing in the Act which dealt with the laws relating to juries that made any distinction whatsoever between white and coloured men'. At the same time he administered something of a reproach to Dr Abdurahman, saying that he, and some other speakers, 'in their anxiety to right what they considered a grievance … had allowed their feelings to run away with them'. Abdurahman thanked the Attorney General for what he had said, which 'had greatly relieved his mind, but for himself he could not concede that in the past the coloured people had been tried by their peers'. There the matter – as reported by the *Cape Times* – was allowed to lie.

In March 1904 Williams and Abdurahman once again came together and attended a mass meeting to 'protest about the treatment of Coloured People in the Transvaal'.[109] The meeting heard how their fellow citizens were reduced to second-class status under the Transvaal colony's laws, which meant that they could not register property in their names and had to get government permission to sell or transfer their holdings. They also had to carry passes and were required to enter the Johannesburg post office by a separate entrance from whites. Coloureds were barred from parks and the Wanderers cricket ground, and it was illegal for coloured men to live with white women. A flyer was produced to advertise the meeting:

Coloured Men, you are in danger in South Africa
Roll up, and speak your mind.
Speakers: J. Tobin, Dr Abdurahman, Advocate Williams.[110]

Chapter Four

Winning his first election

By 1904 Dr Abdurahman was a respected and well-known figure, and not just among the coloured community. His home – just a stone's throw away from the Grand Parade and the Castle – became what his wife, Nellie, described as 'at the centre of academic and social life' in the city.[111] Abdurahman was also sought out by visitors to the Cape. One of them was W.T. Stead, the influential radical journalist and publisher of the London *Review of Reviews*.

Even in these early days, the doctor was intent on encouraging wider unity among South Africa's black people. After a visit to the Cape in 1904, Stead wrote: 'I made Mr [Sylvester] Williams' acquaintance at Cape Town, and it was in his office that the idea of a federation or league of all coloured races of South Africa was first mooted. This federation was decided upon at the house of Dr Abdurahman, the able and universally respected Malay doctor, who was last year elected to a seat in the municipality of Cape Town. Of this federation Mr Sylvester Williams is president. It includes all natives, [Africans], West Indians, Malays and Chinamen, although the last-named have no regular association as yet.'[112] Stead also witnessed Dr Abdurahman's flourishing career as a doctor. Impressed by what he had seen during his trip to southern Africa, he described how Dr Abdurahman ran his practice, 'visiting his patients in his motor'.[113] Stead concluded that the doctor's success indicated just how far coloured people might progress in the Cape, 'as no less do the lawyers, wealthy merchants, and skilled artisans of that unknown community. There does not seem anything which the coloured man cannot do, nor any position to which he cannot rise.'

As Stead indicates, Dr Abdurahman decided to stand for public office as a member of the Cape Town City Council. At a meeting in District Six, 'on the motion of Advocate Williams, seconded by Dr Forsyth, a vote of confidence (in the candidate) was unanimously passed'.[114] On 31 August 1904 the names of candidates for the City Council election in September were published in the *Cape Times*. Leading the list was 'Abdurahman, Abdullah, Albert Lodge, Mount-Street, Medical Practitioner'. The doctor won the support of the District Six Ratepayers' Association, which expressed the hope that he would help clean up the area, complaining that it 'reeked of filth and vice'.[115]

Dr Abdurahman wasted no time in launching his campaign. On 7 September a crowded meeting was held at St Mark's School in District Six.[116] The *Cape Times* gave a vivid account of what took place.

> Dr Abdurahman had asked [Mr Fremantle] to take the chair at this meeting and he hoped he would be successful in his candidature. (Cheers) ... As a medical man the candidate would be able to give a good deal of advice in the matter of the city's health and sanitary arrangements. Dr Abdurahman was a coloured man, but everyone was 'a coloured' man. (Laughter and cheers) Fortunately, he did not think that it mattered ... Dr Abdurahman said, if returned to the Council he would ensure that it would be his duty to see that every scheme for the betterment of the town had his support. Whatever was in his power to assist in the making of the town, he was now placing in their hands. (Great cheering) ... Advocate Williams moved a vote of confidence in Dr Abdurahman, referring to him as a candidate well worthy of their support. He hoped they would put Dr Abdurahman at the top of the poll, not only because he was one of themselves, but because he had the confidence of Europeans as well ... The vote was unanimously carried.

Further meetings were held. Again they were well attended. Dr Abdurahman had a relaxed manner and was a popular speaker, who knew how to rouse a crowd.[117] But he was not without enemies. Cape Town's far left refused to support him. The Social Democratic Federation, composed of mostly English-born trade unionists working in the city, formed an alliance with the Trades and Labour Council in a Labour Electoral Association to contest the election. On 2 September the Association held a meeting, attended by Tobin and Peregrino, at which they chose three candidates to stand in the elections: Abdurahman was not among them.[118] The Social Democrats, whose members went on to found the Communist Party of South Africa, were dismissive of the doctor. In his memoir, Wilfrid Harrison, an early member of the Social Democrats, remarked that he considered Abdurahman's colour to be only skin deep, since 'it was known that the Doctor favoured, if he did not give direct support to, the white man'. In 1904 and again in 1916 Wilfred Harrison stood against Abdurahman as a Social Democratic candidate, and on both occasions the latter defeated him, without much trouble.

The *Cape Times* also criticised Abdurahman, but from a very different perspective. A debate was then under way about how best to augment the city's water supply. Abdurahman believed any new investment was not required, since it was – in his view – based on inaccurate information, which had been skewed by the abnormally high population in the city as a result of the Anglo-Boer War. He believed there was already an adequate provision. The editor of the *Cape Times* disagreed. 'Dr Abdurahman, we notice, declares that the whole agitation for more water is ridiculous, contending that in 1902 "there was a large superfluity of population in Cape Town, and that it was quite reasonable in that year that the consumption of water was abnormal",' the paper explained on the eve of the election.[119] Abdurahman had said that the 'time has not come to consider the matter'. But the paper declared in opposition to his view: 'Let the ratepayers to-day by their votes show that they have done with the policy of procrastination which has been the curse of the city in the past.'

Despite all this, Abdurahman was elected. The backing of the District Six Ratepayers' Association helped carry the day.[120] Indeed, he received 2,782 votes and was the second most popular of the six men standing in the ward to win office.[121] His supporters were delighted. 'Dr Abdurahman, who was received with cheers, expressed his deep thanks for the confidence they had placed in him. He would endeavour while in the Council to do his duty faithfully. He had made them certain promises, and it would be his duty to carry them out.'[122]

To be elected to the Cape Town City Council was an extraordinary accomplishment for a black man at the time. Abdurahman held the seat until his death in 1940, with the exception of a brief period from 1913 to 1915. He would add to this achievement by being elected to the Cape Provincial Council in 1913, also remaining a member until his death. In just a few years the doctor had shown himself an astute politician and adept orator, capable of mobilising ordinary citizens in the area of the city in which he himself lived. In the years ahead he was to become one of the best known, and most widely respected, South Africans of his generation. This is not to suggest that all sections of the coloured community supported him. Nevertheless, he made an indelible mark on the politics of the Cape and beyond.

MAKING A MARK

With his election behind him, Abdurahman got down to serving his community on the City Council. Within weeks he was being reported in the press for opposing a proposal that the Council should hold Sunday concerts in District Six.[123] It might have seemed an odd issue to choose to make a stand. Sunday concerts had been very popular in De Waal Park at the top of the city, so why not give them a try in District Six? It seems Abdurahman's real objection stemmed from his belief that the money could be better used to serve the poor. He argued: 'that at a time when so much distress prevailed, they could better employ money in relieving the hunger of the poor than by giving concerts. He thought that the Council should give the money spent on band performances to the Salvation Army, who would use it to far better purpose. District No. 6 did not want music, they wanted food.'[124] It was a good point: the depression that followed the end of the Anglo-Boer War had hit Cape Town hard. Unemployment was high and many families were struggling to survive. So severe was the situation that by 1906, at the height of the post-war depression, unrest swept Cape Town in the form of the 'Hunger Riots'. Thousands took to the streets, shop windows were smashed and the rioters plundered what they could.[125]

This was just one of a range of issues Abdurahman pursued – sometimes as a lone voice – carefully scrutinising the proposals put before the Council. Following a tour of Cape Town in late 1904, for example, he was the only councillor who refused to express their satisfaction at the state of the roads.[126] In these early debates, Abdurahman was staking out his territory: he was going to fight for the poor of District Six.

National issues also attracted his attention. The idea of bringing in Chinese labour to work on the gold mines had been raised even before the war, but afterwards the question of how to get the mines up and running again became pressing.[127] In 1903 the shortage of labour was discussed at the annual meeting of the Chamber of Mines and a proposal was made for importing Chinese labour. This was hotly contested in the wider society. Trade unions were strongly opposed and anti-Asian leagues were mobilised to resist the suggestion. Much of black opinion was also hostile. John Tengo Jabavu, the influential editor of *Imvo Zabantsundu*, angrily rejected the scheme in his paper.[128] Abdurahman took a similar stand. He opposed the importation of Chinese indentured labour, believing it would undermine the Cape's carefully preserved franchise.[129] Despite this opposition, over fifty thousand Chinese were working on the mines by 1907. However, the election of the Liberal Party in Britain in 1906, which had resisted the scheme from the start, put a hold on any further importation of indentured labour. Finally, the scheme was cancelled by the Transvaal legislature in 1907 and the Chinese sent home.[130]

In 1905 Abdurahman showed just how persistent he could be. While most of the City Council seemed perfectly happy to spend £500 to help endow a new professorial chair in electronics at the South African College, forerunner of the University of Cape Town, he was not.[131] Why, he asked, should his ratepayers contribute to an institution when it did not allow coloured children into the school that was associated with the college? He described the governing body as comprising 'immoral men – yes, intellectually immoral men' for refusing to accept coloured children as pupils. Abdurahman was one of the very few coloured pupils that SACS had accepted. There followed a sharp discussion on whether or not this was indeed the case. It concluded with the mayor saying that 'as a member of the S.A. College Council, he might say a few words. He thought that they were all agreed that the Council should not give a penny to any institution which drew a line of colour.' With this assurance, the matter was allowed to drop. Clearly Abdurahman was making a name for himself: unafraid to speak out in defence of his community, even if it meant being distinctly awkward.

FOUNDING THE AFRICAN POLITICAL ORGANISATION

The pressing need to help shape the future of their country now that the Anglo-Boer War was over weighed on the minds of leading members of the coloured community. There was a ferment of ideas at the time among the black population, from the Pan-Africanism of the Cape's small but influential Afro-Caribbean community and the notions of African pride and self-reliance fostered by the African Methodist Episcopal Church, to the debates generated by the Stone meetings. This was a conducive environment for the formation of a new movement.

Late in 1902 these influences came together in the founding of the African Political Organisation (APO), which was aimed primarily, but not exclusively, at the coloured people. According to the historian Gavin Lewis, eight men attended a meeting in a house in Claremont on 30 September 1902.[132] Two of the eight were white liberals, T. Searle and J.W. Jagger. The rest were coloureds, but exactly who was present is not entirely clear. Lewis says those in attendance included J.W. Tobin, café owner and friend of Peregrino; W.A. Roberts, a local welfare and religious leader and businessman; P.J. Eksteen, employee of a local German firm of booksellers, who was elected as secretary of the new organisation; and the Rev. W. Collins, a lay preacher from the African Methodist Episcopal Church, who chaired the meeting and who was asked to assume the presidency of the APO.[133] Lewis says that the lawyer Henry Sylvester Williams was there too, but he cannot have been, since he had not yet sailed from England. One person who almost certainly did not attend was Dr Abdurahman, since he was in England on family business. Peregrino reported on 25 October: 'Dr Abdurrahman had the misfortune to lose his mother by death in

London in September last, and he has the sympathy of a large circle of friends and well-wishers.'[134]

Richard van der Ross confirms there was a meeting on 30 September, but describes it as a public meeting held at the Mechanics Institute in Claremont.[135] He says the meeting came about after a letter was issued 'addressed to members of the Coloured community telling of the formation of the APO and inviting people to join'. The letter declared the APO's objectives as follows: 'Our chief aim and objects are ... to promote unity between the Coloured races of South Africa and to obtain higher education for our children.'[136] The letter went on to explain that the meeting had been called 'by the Coloured portion of the community for the purpose of starting an organisation to be called the African Political Organisation'. At the meeting the Rev. W. Collins spoke of the need of coloured people to be represented in parliament.[137] Coloured people were only valued at elections, when their votes were sought, he said. Apart from these occasions, 'the members of the Assembly [parliament] seldom stood up for, or even pretended to stand up for, the Coloured races'. It was time to have a 'Coloured man' to represent their community.

The APO was to retain the same name until its 1919 conference, when it was renamed the African People's Organisation. It is worth noting that from its birth the APO appeared to embrace two rather different uses of the term 'coloured'. On the one hand it talked of the 'Coloured races of South Africa', yet it also spoke of the 'Coloured portion of the community'. While the first suggests an appeal to all black South Africans, the second appears to narrow it to the coloured (creole) people. This lack of clarity was to remain largely unresolved throughout the APO's existence.

As Van der Ross commented: 'It is noticeable that John Tobin, originator of the Stone Meetings, did not sign this letter; some of the differences among its signatories had already begun to show.' This is true. What appeared at first to be a minor question of tactics soon became a chasm that divided opinion within the coloured community. This was an apparently simple question: since the coloured people formed only a relatively small section of the Cape's voting population, whom should they look to as allies? Should they attempt to obtain support from Afrikaners or from the English? Tobin was clear. He believed that

Afrikaners were fellow 'sons of the soil' and had a common interest in opposing British imperialists and financiers. 'Africa for the Africans, white or black,' was his slogan.[138] This meant supporting the Afrikaner Bond and their associated political organisation, the South African Party. Tobin and the Stone movement received regular publicity in the Afrikaner party's paper, the *South African News*.

This angered men like Peregrino, who were wedded to British ideals. Peregrino felt Tobin was being 'disloyal' and even needed to be carefully watched. A rift opened up between them. Tobin was by no means the only one to experience the rancorous Peregrino's wrath. The latter had a habit of taking out his anger in underhand ways, by informing the white authorities on anyone who, in his opinion, stepped out of line or might be considered anti-British in any way. These included some of the most revered black political figures of the time, from his former friend and associate Sylvester Williams to the first leader of the African National Congress, John Dube.[139]

In reality both positions – favouring the Afrikaners or supporting the British – had their merits. Coloureds shared a common ancestry with Afrikaners, as well as a common culture and language (even if whites were often reluctant to recognise these obvious facts). Both ethnic groups were 'sons of the soil' and in the rural areas in particular they shared much in common. On the other hand, the British had brought to the Cape a form of liberalism which, despite its limitations, had conferred real benefits on African and coloured people. Slaves had been freed; the vote had been extended to all racial groups, albeit subject to restrictions; and British missionaries had provided local people with education, even if it was only delivered to a minority. In theory at least, all British subjects were equal, although it turned out that in practice some were more equal than others. It was a problem that infuriated black leaders, from Gandhi to Abdurahman.

A GROWING PARTY

The APO's first annual conference in February 1903 was a considerable success. W. Collins, as APO president, told the gathering: 'this is the first time in history that we are meeting to discuss our own affairs.' The following month the party went on to chalk up another success for the community. A delegation to the mayor of Cape Town was assured that coloureds would not be subject to the residential segregation that was now being enforced on Africans. His response reassured the APO members that it was a party of 'civilised', respectable people, who could justly take their place alongside their white compatriots.

By the time of the 1904 general election in the Cape, the APO had developed a branch network and a solid membership: indeed, by the following year the party could claim 10,000 members.[140] So which white party should its members support? Would the leadership back the South African Party, as Tobin and his Stone supporters pushed for; or would they support the pro-British Progressive Party, as Collins and Peregrino wished? In the end the 1904 APO conference sat on the fence. It was decided that its supporters would be instructed to back whichever candidate promised to advance their interests, regardless of party. Tobin urged coloureds to participate: 'your votes are your guns,' he explained.[141] At the APO conference of that year Collins was re-elected president and Tobin vice-president.

It seems then that the differences within the party had been smoothed over for the moment but divisions remained. The organisation was soon in danger of being torn apart by the tension over which white party to back. By the time of the 1905 conference, things had reached such a state that the APO general secretary, Matt Fredericks, decided he had had enough. Both Collins and Tobin were expelled and the organisation turned to a fresh leader, the newly elected Cape Town City councillor, Dr Abdurahman.[142]

CHAPTER FIVE

Whom to trust?
The initial battles

D r Abdurahman's first task was to rally his party. This he achieved with remarkable success. By 1910 the APO had developed a network of branches across the country and claimed a membership 20,000 strong.[143] It was then the largest black organisation in the country.[144] Abdurahman, and his party, had become a force to be reckoned with. He was in the lucky position of being able to build on the ferment of political discussion that had been initiated by the Stone gatherings and the work of men like Peregrino, Tobin and Williams. At the time it seemed to many that there was an evident threat confronting the coloured community: the increasing racism that was emerging as white South Africans assumed the reins of power. This also worked in Abdurahman's favour: the APO could call on the people to resist a clear and immediate danger. The doctor's skills as a leader and his oratorical abilities, together with the clarity of his writing, propelled him to the forefront of a movement for coloured (and sometimes black) rights.

At his first conference as APO leader, Abdurahman laid out his stall. The conference was held on 2 January 1906 in the Bethel Institute, on the corner of Hanover and Blythe streets in District Six. An educational institution offering primary and secondary education to local pupils, the Institute had been founded by American evangelists of the African Methodist Episcopal Church.[145] When he rose to speak, Abdurahman addressed the party for no less than an hour and a half.[146]

The speech was a careful blend of angry rhetoric, stirring phrases and calls for cool reflection. Were they satisfied with the prevailing conditions? he asked. Did these inspire in them hope for the future? To this there were cries of 'No, no!' There was, Abdurahman said, a growing feeling of discontent. The pre-eminent threat lay in the racist policies towards coloured people adopted in what he called 'the dark days of ignorance', but they would challenge these, even if they were described as disloyal. The hall erupted in loud cheers. He attacked the colour bar that was being practised in the Transvaal and Orange River Colony, saying that it was shocking that such things were being done in the name of the British Empire. Coloured people had fought for Britain (shouts of 'Sorry we did!') and therefore had reason to believe they would be fairly treated. But thanks to what Lord Milner, the British High Commissioner, was permitting, they were 'treated like the barbarous native', Dr Abdurahman concluded with a rallying cry. They should 'unite and be firm, and, above all, unite their children, and in the end justice would be done to them'. There followed – as the minutes recorded – long and prolonged cheers. Abdurahman had clearly struck a chord with his audience.

Dr Abdurahman's speech contained key elements that he would return to time and again throughout his career. He expressed widespread feelings of anger and bitterness about the treatment of the coloured people. They had been loyal and served the British; now London turned its back on them. He knew full well how to stir up their anger and resentment, yet his solution was moderation itself. Stand firm and united; educate your children and lead upright lives; and in the end the authorities will listen to reason.

Perhaps this reflected the influences in Abdurahman's life. He had, after all, received a superior education at mostly white schools in which a British ethos and influence had been strong. He had spent a long time in Britain, qualifying as a doctor and finding a Scottish wife. While he was likely to have experienced British racism, he had also made friends and would have known too of the activities of organisations like the

Anti-Slavery and Aborigines' Protection Society and other radical movements campaigning for black rights. There was also the example that all people of colour knew full well in the north: the treatment of black people in the Orange Free State[147] and the Transvaal, where they had few rights and were deprived of the vote.

Just how strongly Dr Abdurahman felt about this can be gauged from a speech reported in a British paper in February 1906.[148] 'Perhaps they, as coloured people, in approaching the questions, would be called disloyal. The British Empire had a population of 400 millions, 84 per cent of whom were governed in a more or less despotic manner … And even now, in the name of the Empire, a form of labour, differing not much from slavery, had been introduced into South Africa.' Here he was attacking indentured Chinese labour on the gold mines of the Transvaal. He continued: 'A small but unfortunately powerful section of the men in the North had returned to the days of slavery … They had to judge by actions, and the actions of a small section sprung from a spirit to rule and govern, which again was the result of race pride and greed for gold. This was carried under the cloak of Empire and with the flag in hand … Men whose object was gold and whose god was Mammon. If they wished to see what excess despotism and power to rule led, when inhumanity and ungodliness walked hand-in-hand through the country, they should go to the Orange River Colony and the Transvaal.' The British were far from perfect, yet at least they embraced a liberal tradition and held out the hope of a better life for all. By contrast, the former Boer republics held out little prospect of anything positive for the black population, despite being nominally under London's control.

Dr Abdurahman was by this time a well-regarded member of the Cape Town elite. He was comfortable rubbing shoulders with statesmen and politicians, visiting journalists and the business community. The early APO also drew on the African American influence which had been developed by Pan-Africanists like Peregrino and the African Methodist Episcopal Church. The organisation's newspaper quoted from the ideas and philosophy of the African American campaigner Booker T. Washington, whose programme of self-help was held up as a model to emulate. 'Like Washington, the APO believed that a pragmatic strategy of incrementally improving the socioeconomic condition of the Coloured people would break down white prejudice and eventually win them civil equality within the dominant society.'[149]

Despite the fact that most coloured people spoke Dutch or Afrikaans, the party newspaper, launched in May 1909 (also called the *APO*), was published mostly in English, with a Dutch section confined to the back pages. Editorials and some important articles appeared in both languages. Edited and largely written by Abdurahman, it was dismissive of the language most of the coloured working class spoke, as Mohamed Adhikari has pointed out.[150] He quotes from an *APO* editorial of May 1910, urging coloured people to 'endeavour to perfect themselves in English – the language which inspires the noblest thoughts of freedom and liberty, the language that has the finest literature on earth and is the most universally useful of all languages. Let everyone ... drop the habit as far as possible, of expressing themselves in the barbarous Cape Dutch too often heard.'

This suggests an elitist perspective, yet Abdurahman retained the common touch. Living in the vibrant, sometimes sleazy, environment of District Six, this is perhaps no surprise. As one visitor recalled after his death: 'Dr Abdurahman in his greatness was so simple. He loved his home dearly. His friends were always welcomed with open arms and were never allowed to leave without a long talk and tea, and departed with sound words of advice.'[151]

Although he could address politicians and statesmen, he could speak without difficulty in the language of ordinary people. He could rouse a crowd with his rhetoric, but his most popular writing was not the carefully crafted articles he published in the *APO*, but his earthy column *Straat Praatjies*.

Written in the Afrikaans spoken by the ordinary people all around him, they were the tales told by a fictional Piet Uithalder and his friend Stoffel Francis.[152] Both had migrated to Cape Town from the Kat River Settlement in the Eastern Cape, but while Piet was street-wise, Stoffel was a bit of a rural bumpkin. *Straat Praatjies* – written anonymously, but almost certainly by Dr Abdurahman – allowed the author to mercilessly lampoon his opponents in the paper, whether in the coloured community or in parliament. At times the attacks bordered on racism, including a portrayal of Peregrino as a monkey. They were peppered with tales of local folk and references to the food of the coloured working classes: 'gebakte snoek', 'kweper sambal' and 'gars kofe'. The doctor had a good ear for the language of the streets, and the column was enormously popular.

It is hardly surprising that he knew the local patois: he lived among people who spoke it. So did most of his patients, as his practice was just below the Malay district of Bo-Kaap and Schotsche Kloof, at 99 Loop Street.[153] Dr Abdurahman was also very much part of local communal life, going to the cinema over the weekend, sometimes to see a film, but also for his City Council work: 'the bioscope was used during the weekends for meetings and for Council meetings as well,' recalled the daughter of the owner of one of the District Six cinemas. She had a clear memory of the doctor: 'Dr Abdurahman always wore a black fez with a lassie [tassel] hanging down; he was very smartly dressed. He always looked spick and span and immaculate.'[154]

Northern rights

Coloured people hoped (many had assumed) that their support for Britain during the Anglo-Boer War would be rewarded. They had backed the British cause, whether as town guards, armed auxiliaries or muleteers.[155] As one folk song began:

> We Cape men of the farms,
> Stand with the khakis and their arms,
> we are spies ...
> We are scouts, we are dogs
> We bark for Boer blood.[156]

But they were soon disabused of their assumptions.

With the end of the war, London's primary objective was to make its peace with Afrikaners in the Transvaal and Orange Free State. This was complex and difficult enough, especially at a time when the ruined farms and stagnant mines had to be made productive again.[157] From the British perspective, the coloured community in these territories was little more than an insignificant impediment to progress. The Afrikaners for their part were determined to put the black people back 'in their place'. They saw it as a priority to maintain the whites-only franchise and to prevent its extension to anyone of colour. Britain, exhausted and almost bankrupted by the conflict, had agreed at the peace negotiations to allow the Afrikaners to decide on the issue of the franchise only after self-government had been returned to them. In this way black South Africans were sacrificed on the altar of realpolitik, even if it took several years for this fact finally to sink in.

As early as 1903 – a year after peace was declared – there was the first indication of things to come: the British decided that the franchise for municipal elections in the Orange Free State and Transvaal would be restricted to whites only. Dr Abdurahman protested, but to no avail.[158] In March 1905 a draft constitution for the self-government of the two former Boer republics was published. Again, only white men were to be given the vote. Realising that this was now a clear trend, black and coloured people drew up petitions and sent deputations to meet Lord Selborne, the new High Commissioner for South Africa. But Selborne argued that there was nothing he could do since 'the franchise as it existed was part of the terms of surrender at Vereeniging and that these terms must be regarded as a whole'.[159]

Aware that a federation of the four South African colonies was on the cards, and understanding the urgency of the issue for the coloured community, Dr Abdurahman made the issue a central plank of his address to the APO conference in 1906. He attacked Lord Milner, pointing out that under his stewardship the municipal vote had been denied to coloured people in the former republics. 'Was it right that the rights of coloured people should be handed over to such unscrupulous men?' he asked.[160] The conference agreed to send a delegation to the northern colonies to protest at the denial of the franchise, as well as at other racist restrictions. They also backed a petition that Abdurahman had drawn up, appealing to the King.[161] The petition pointed out that coloureds moving to the northern colonies would be deprived of their right to the vote, a right they enjoyed as British subjects, and also argued that the Treaty of Vereeniging applied only to 'aboriginal natives, and not to ... coloured subjects'. The petition – having made this distinction – appealed to the King to ensure that coloured people would not be deprived of their right to vote in any future measures of self-government.

Gavin Lewis has argued that this distinction between 'aboriginal natives' and coloured people is not proof (as some historians have claimed) that Abdurahman and the APO were attempting to win coloured rights at the expense of Africans, or that they were supporting 'segregation of a kind'.[162] He points to Abdurahman's attack on British policies – including their treatment of Africans on the gold mines – as well as his subsequent commitment to non-racialism.

Lewis's argument carries some weight but is not entirely convincing. It would appear, rather, that Dr Abdurahman was primarily a politician representing the coloured community, and he naturally put their interests first. In so doing, he was no different from other black politicians. Gandhi sought to represent the Indian community and has been criticised for doing so to the exclusion of seeking wider black unity. Yet John Dube, the first president of the ANC, took just the same stand. He fought fiercely for African rights, while doing little for other communities. He was not above attacking Indians for taking away what he regarded as African land. In 1912 Dube told a large gathering of Zulu chiefs that 'people like coolies have come to our land and lorded it over us, as though we, who belong to the country, are mere non-entities'.[163] Perhaps we can conclude that each political leader fought for his own people, to the best of his abilities. Sometimes this involved taking stands that appear narrow or unsatisfactory with hindsight. After the Union of South Africa came about in 1910 Dr Abdurahman modified his attitude. He began to work far more closely with Africans, having learned painfully that there was little to be gained from attempting to win rights for coloureds at the expense of Africans. But most South African whites refused to recognise distinctions within the black community, and Britain would not confront their white allies in the run-up to the First World War, or thereafter.

In January 1906, just when South African policy appeared settled, there was an abrupt change in British politics. A general election saw the Liberals oust the Conservatives in a landslide and return to office. Many Liberals had been strongly critical of the Anglo-Boer War; now was their opportunity to mend fences with the Afrikaners.[164] At the same time the Liberals were more favourably disposed towards the country's black community. For the new prime minster, Sir Henry Campbell-Bannerman, it was an opportunity for a fresh start.

Jan Smuts, aware that a new government might come to power in

Britain, saw his chance. He set off to London, determined to try to win self-government for the Transvaal. He arrived in the British capital on 6 January 1906, even before a new administration had been formed.[165] He understood how vital it was to act before policy towards his country was firmly established. Smuts believed he had to remind the British of the promises they had made at the Peace of Vereeniging that whites in the northern colonies would be able to determine their own fate. It was not until the last week in January 1906 that the new Liberal government was ready to receive him. But Smuts made little progress. He met Winston Churchill – in charge of Britain's colonies – and was about to return home, in despair.

Smuts decided on one last throw of the dice. He sought a final meeting with the newly elected Liberal prime minister. Years later Smuts recalled his meeting on 7 February 1906 with Campbell-Bannerman.

> My mission failed with the rest, as it was humanly speaking bound to fail. What an audacious, what an unprecedented request mine was – practically for the restoration of the country to the Boers five years after they had been beaten to the ground in one of the hardest and most lengthy struggles in British warfare. I put a simple case before him that night in 10 Downing Street. It was in substance: Do you want friends or enemies? You can have the Boers for friends, and they have proved what quality their friendship means. I pledge the friendship of my colleagues and myself if you wish it. You can choose to make them enemies, and possibly have another Ireland on your hands. If you do believe in liberty, it is also their faith and their religion. I used no arguments, but simply spoke to him as man to man, and appealed only to the human aspect, which I felt would weigh deeply with him. He was a cautious Scot, and said nothing to me, but yet I left that room that night a happy man. My intuition told me that the thing had been done.[166]

Smuts was right. On 8 February 1906, Campbell-Bannerman held a cabinet meeting and overcame the doubts of his colleagues by arguing that the time had come to trust their former enemies, the Boers. Smuts had won self-government for the Transvaal.[167] He retained a deep affection for Campbell-Bannerman all his life: a portrait of the British prime minister hung in Smuts's study to the end of his days.

In 1906 the Transvaal was granted self-government, to be followed in 1907 by the Orange River Colony. Just five years after the end of Britain's most costly colonial conflict, London had devolved considerable control over the former Boer republics they had fought so hard to defeat, to the Afrikaners. The decision paid almost immediate dividends. In his first speech as prime minister of the Transvaal, Louis Botha promised that 'British interests would be absolutely safe in the hands of the new Cabinet'.[168] As a mark of reconciliation the Transvaal bought and presented to King Edward the largest diamond yet discovered – the 3,106-carat Cullinan – for inclusion in the Crown jewels.[169] The gem was, in truth, a lavish bribe in return for a loan. After some hesitation, and at the prompting of Churchill, London decided it would allow the King to accept the gift. The Transvaal, so long a thorn in British flesh, was becoming an integral part of the Imperial system.

The real losers in this reconciliation were the black population of the two former Boer republics. Dr Abdurahman wrote to the West-Ridgeway Committee, which was considering what constitutions should be given to the northern ex-republics, calling for an extension of the colour-blind Cape franchise to the Transvaal and Orange River Colony.[170] His pleas – and those of others – had little impact. Although the committee apparently studied the arguments carefully, they ruled that the term 'native' in the Treaty of Vereeniging was regarded by most Afrikaners as including coloureds. Since the treaty had been signed with the Afrikaners, it was their interpretation that carried weight. Only whites would be given the vote. Understanding just how critical the situation was, the APO decided to make a stand.

THE 1906 DELEGATION TO LONDON

Clearly something had to be done if the political trend in South Africa was to be resisted. The Cape's non-racial vote was precious and – in Dr Abdurahman's view – it was vital that it be extended to the other colonies. In February 1906 the APO in the Transvaal decided to send a deputation to England, 'praying for "extension of British justice and liberty" to coloured subjects residing in the Transvaal and the Orange River Colony'.[171] The following month there was a 'big demonstration' in Cape Town, with Abdurahman as the chief speaker.[172] 'He said the coloured people of the Transvaal and Orangia wanted the same political rights as they enjoyed in the Cape Colony. Instead of restrictions being taken off the coloured inhabitants of those Colonies, they had increased.' The Reuters report continued: 'They would implore the British Government not to put their seal upon the inhumanities and barbarities in the North in the name of the British Empire. They (the coloured people) wondered whether they were on the earth or in hell (cries of "Shame"). He urged that the terms of the Vereeniging Compact did not include the Cape coloured people in the new colonies. A resolution approving of the petition and sending a deputation to England to convey the same was carried.'

By July 1906 the delegation was in London. W.T. Stead, who had written so enthusiastically about Abdurahman and Sylvester Williams in his *Review of Reviews* during his tour of South Africa in 1904, welcomed the visit. 'There is to be a deputation from the African Political Organisation formed during my visit to Cape Town two years ago, which, under the able presidency of Dr Abdurahman, has now 8,000 members, with seventy branches covering all the South African colonies. They are especially desirous to see to it that the Cape coloured boys who have votes in the Cape Colony should not be deprived of the franchise if they migrate northwards.'[173]

There was nothing novel about African residents and visitors in London. By the time of the First World War around fifteen thousand people of African origin and descent lived in Britain. More than a third lived in London, with the rest scattered across the country.[174] As early as 1895 a London newspaper wrote: 'All roads, even that from Africa, lead to London. Any day you can hardly walk down Piccadilly without rubbing shoulders with an Afghan, a Zulu, a Hottentot, or a foreigner of some kind.'[175] It was in this year that the first delegations came from southern Africa, with three Tswana kings arriving in London.[176] Almost all the delegations that came from the colonies sought redress for the wrongs done to them by British expansion. But what they lacked – apart from a willing interlocutor – was a permanent organisation in London that could coordinate their activities and introduce them to sympathetic movements (like the Aborigines' Protection Society) and individuals (in parliament and outside it). Indians had created just such an organisation in the late 1880s. A British Committee was formed in London to represent the interests of the Indian National Congress.[177] It may have been a plodding, bureaucratic body, but it provided a permanent presence in London. By contrast, every southern African deputation that arrived in Britain in the late nineteenth and early twentieth century had to begin building a support base anew.[178] They had to rely on the contacts they had established before leaving home, assistance from allies in the churches and missionary societies, or from southern Africans already living in Britain. In this respect Dr Abdurahman was perhaps unique: he knew his way around the city. He had ties of family and friendship from his time in London that he could rely upon.

Before setting sail from Cape Town, Abdurahman reached out to the most obvious source of support, the Aborigines' Protection Society. Founded in 1837, it had spent the next seven decades lobbying the Colonial Office, colonial governors and British MPs and kept up a series of well-informed public campaigns against the treatment of the native populations over which Britain ruled. Over the years South Africa had been a central interest of the Society, which had worked to expose the injustices perpetrated against the Zulu, Basotho, Griqua and Tswana peoples.[179] These campaigns frequently involved criticising the brutality which the black population had suffered at the hands of the Boers.[180] During the Anglo–Boer War the Society was divided over whether to support the British war effort and at its 1901 annual meeting it finally agreed on a general motion calling for 'constant vigilance' for the 'treatment of natives in that part of the world'.[181]

The Society's activities were widely reported in newspapers across the Empire. It was highly regarded by black South Africans, who turned to it for support. In 1887 John Tengo Jabavu wrote to the Society's secretary, Henry Fox Bourne, describing himself as 'writing from the depths of obscurity' and calling for the Society's assistance to prevent the passage of a law that would restrict the African franchise at the Cape.[182] 'We are marshalling local forces to defeat the measure,' Jabavu said; 'but, with a Dutch majority in the Cape parliament the battle will have to be fought out in England, and that by your useful Society.' Other black activists from South Africa turned to the 'useful Society'. Allan Kirkland Soga, the editor of *Izwi Labantu* (Voice of the

People), asked Fox Bourne in 1906 for support in publishing his book *The Problems of Black and White in South Africa*.[183]

In 1906, before setting out from Cape Town for London, Dr Abdurahman appealed to the Society for support for his campaign for coloured rights.[184] This was, Abdurahman pointed out, in line with the promise Britain had given in the 1850s at the time representative government was being extended to the Cape. '[Then], in answer to colonial demands for an exclusively white franchise, the Duke of Newcastle, the Secretary of State for War and the Colonies, declared it to be "the earnest desire of Her Majesty's Government that all her subjects at the Cape, without distinction of class or colour, should be united in one common bond of loyalty and common interest".' In response to Abdurahman's appeal, the Society agreed and took up the issue vigorously.[185]

In August 1906 the secretary, Fox Bourne, wrote a long article in the Society's journal, *The Aborigines Friend*, explaining how black people were being deprived of the vote in the Transvaal. He recalled the 'Hottentots' Magna Carta' of 1828 [Ordinance 50] and the promises made at that date that 'free persons of colour ... had the right to become burghers and to exercise and enjoy all the privileges of burghership'.[186] The same edition reported on petitions to the government and the King: one from the APO, signed by Dr Abdurahman, another from Tengo Jabavu, editor of *Imvo*, and a third, from the Rev. James Henderson, principal of Lovedale College in the Eastern Cape. The journal also mentioned petitions from the South African Native National Congress and the Transvaal Native Congress. Fox Bourne wrote to the British Colonial Secretary, calling for the non-racial franchise to be extended to the Transvaal, even though he acknowledged that 'comparatively few Transvaal or Orange River natives are now, or are, perhaps, at present likely to be, in a position to acquire the franchise', since it was property-based.[187]

Once he arrived in London, Dr Abdurahman wasted no time. He contacted whoever he believed had influence. This included the Labour Party leader, Keir Hardie. The party – recently formed in 1900 – had just 29 MPs in parliament. It was a minnow when compared with the Liberals (397 seats) or the Unionist official opposition (156). Nevertheless, Labour had been openly opposed to the Anglo-Boer War, and its general secretary, Ramsay MacDonald, had made an extensive tour of South Africa just three months after the war ended in 1902.[188] It is possible that MacDonald met Dr Abdurahman during his visit, although there is no proof that he did. Certainly, MacDonald was deeply critical of the racism he had experienced in South Africa, and came out in favour of extending the Cape's non-racial franchise to the whole country.

> To extend the Cape system throughout British South Africa would no doubt meet with much opposition; the racial prejudices and the parochialism of the Natal majority would oppose it, so would the majority of Rhodesians, and so would a majority of the Dutch in the new Colonies [Transvaal and Orange River]. Nevertheless the Imperial authorities ought to make a point of persuading the Federation [the impending Union of South Africa] that this is its best policy, and should not hesitate, if need be, to retain in a very definite and effective way sovereignty over all native affairs unless the franchise is granted.[189]

Here was a party that Dr Abdurahman could work with, and he didn't miss the opportunity. Writing to Keir Hardie from the Bedford Hotel on Southampton Row where he was staying, he enclosed a copy of the petition to parliament that he had had printed.[190] He asked Hardie for his support for 'the Coloured People in attaining their Civil Liberty; for without equal law and equal liberty for all, South Africans as a whole cannot expect to reap greatest benefit and enjoy the greatest happiness'. Abdurahman explained that he was 'convinced that the possession of the franchise by the Coloured people is not only consistent with the performance and security of the States as component parts of the Empire, but without a due recognition of our rights and liberties and by placing power in the hands of one section, and denying to others the constitutional means of self-defence, a system will be established which will end in servitude and bring ruin to us all.' He concluded: 'Our chief aim is to become durable Citizens, to work harmoniously with others; and by fulfilling our obligation assist in making South Africa a powerful member of a mighty Empire. To withhold from the Coloured people the franchise would be inflicting upon a self-respecting and intelligent section of men a most disastrous wrong.'

Abdurahman succeeded in getting a hearing with members of the governing Liberal Party. On 11 July he was heard by a meeting of Liberal MPs, presided over by Sir Charles Dilke, who was renowned for his interest in and knowledge of international and Imperial affairs.[191] Described by Sir Charles as 'a medical man, who holds the position of Chairman of the Health Committee on the Cape Town Council', Abdurahman explained that his mission was to 'urge that due recognition of citizens' rights be extended to coloured British subjects in the Transvaal and Orange River Colony'. He had a sympathetic reception and several MPs promised to raise the issue in parliament.

The petition that the APO had brought to London was, indeed, formally received by parliament on 14 June.[192] Dr Abdurahman also managed to ensure that his delegation met Lord Elgin, the Secretary of State for the Colonies. Abdurahman and his colleagues are said to have received a 'satisfactory assurance', as Gandhi noted in his paper, *Indian Opinion*.[193] But warm words were all they would be given. On 13 July the Transvaal constitution was debated in the House of Lords.[194] Lord Elgin opened the debate by saying that the constitution restricted the vote to adult white males. He said he knew that this would deprive Africans of the franchise, but then, as he put it, in Africa 'a very small number of whites [lived] in the midst of an overwhelming number of blacks' and they were fearful of being overwhelmed. 'I make these observations because I regret that the terms of the Vereeniging Treaty confine the franchise to white subjects.' Lord Elgin continued: 'I regret it, because I am of the opinion that a reasonable representation of natives would give strength and not weakness to the Government of the country, and I cannot but hope that this will be recognised in some time to come.'

As far as coloureds were concerned, Elgin said he had received their appeals, in which they asked to be treated differently from Africans, but he added that he could not support their case. 'I have seen representatives of their number, men of intelligence and education, who argued their case moderately and well.' White opinion in the Transvaal and Orange River Colony was against them being granted the vote, despite their being 'coloureds' and not 'natives'. Others in the House of Lords disagreed (including Lord Milner), but Elgin refused to alter the text of the constitution. As a result, coloureds, along with all other black people, were deprived of the vote when the two former Boer republics regained self-government – the Transvaal in 1906 and the Orange River Colony in 1907.

Despite the goodwill expressed by so many, and supportive mass meetings held in Cape Town during their visit,[195] the mission had come to naught. A Reuters telegram summed up the position in a sentence: 'He saw a host of Parliamentary leaders, also the Colonial Secretary, who promised to consult his colleagues, but Dr Abdurahman afterwards learned that nothing had been done as regards the coloured franchise question.'[196] The delegation from the APO had been brought face to face with the stark reality of the situation. Britain was determined to make friends and allies with the Afrikaners and nothing would dissuade them. 'The African Political Association last night welcomed Dr Abdurahman on his return from a mission to England with the object of obtaining the franchise for the coloured population of the Transvaal and Orangia in the new constitutions', the *Grahamstown Journal* informed its readers. 'Dr Abdurahman said he was a disappointed man because his mission was unsuccessful. He said the Colonial Secretary had promised to consult the members of the Cabinet. Abdurahman afterwards heard nothing had been done, but still thought there was hope.'[197]

It was a brave stand: in reality the prospect was bleak. As whites pressed forward with plans to unite the four colonies into a Union of South Africa, black interests came under threat. What chance was there that the Cape franchise allowing any man to vote – irrespective of race – as long as he had sufficient income or wealth, would survive? A new approach was clearly required.

CHAPTER SIX

New allies, fresh challenges

A FINAL APPEAL

The failure of the 1906 delegation to Britain led Dr Abdurahman to reassess his strategy and seek out fresh sources of support. The attempt to assert a coloured identity as a means of convincing London (or the former Boer republics) that they should be granted the vote, even if it was denied to other people of colour, had failed. Abdurahman – whose inclination had always been to co-operate with other groups – now actively courted African support.

This was vital. The Cape's non-racial vote was clearly under threat. There was a great deal at stake: the very status of people of colour as citizens. This was, of course, at least as much a concern for African politicians and activists. By the time the draft constitution of a united South Africa was completed in 1909, Africans made up 4.7 per cent of the Cape electorate (6,633 voters) while coloureds (including Malays, Indians, Chinese and Khoikhoi) formed 10.1 per cent of the electorate, with the remaining 85.2 per cent of the registered voters (142,367) white.[198] Between them, African and coloured men made up nearly 15 per cent of the electorate – a not inconsiderable number. White politicians were well aware of this. The Port Elizabeth *Telegraph* argued: 'If the Afrikaner Bond is to be well beaten it will have to be done with the assistance of the black vote. The Dutch in the colony are to the English as two to one and if they combine they can outvote us and inflict upon us all the absurdities of their national and economic prejudices.'[199]

'AS FAR AS HELL IS FROM HEAVEN'

The starting gun for the debate about how to unite the four British colonies was a memo published by Lord Selborne, the High Commissioner of the territories, on 3 July 1907.[200] The British government pressed for a federation or union. Everyone knew how critical this was. Dr Abdurahman was fearful that the Boer republics would take the political lead in a new South Africa, particularly on race relations. As he told the APO annual conference on 7 October 1907 when they met in Oudtshoorn, coloured people who enjoyed the right to vote in the Cape were deprived of it when they went north to the Transvaal or Orange River Colony.[201] This was by no means the only racism they encountered. Laws forbidding white men to marry coloured 'girls' meant they could 'ruin' them, and then claim they could not be wedded. 'Mr Winston Churchill had likened the Orange River Colony to a "Model Republic",' he told a political meeting, but it was 'as far from that as Hell from Heaven'. The Boer republic was, he said to cheers, a 'Black prison'.

The British government was not unaware of these issues. In his letter to the Governors of the four colonies and of Southern Rhodesia, dated 7 January 1907, Lord Selborne laid out the dilemma in words which could almost have been spoken by Dr Abdurahman.[202] 'What is going to be the policy of South Africa in respect of immigration of Asiatics? What is going to be the policy of South Africa towards coloured people? What towards the natives?' Pointing out that each colony's racial policies differed from the others, Lord Selborne declared that the black population could not understand why this was the case. 'They know that each of the Colonies in which they live owes allegiance to one King; they know that the white men regard South Africa as one county; but yet, every time one of them passes the unseen boundaries which divide one Colony from another, he finds himself subject to different treatment, he finds that he is to expect a different set of rules.'

The High Commissioner then dealt with the specific situation of the coloured population, warning that if their views were not accommodated, they might turn towards the African majority for support.

> The coloured is a son of the soil. In varying degrees he possesses white blood. He is permanently conscious of the fact that the infusion of that blood differentiates him completely from the natives who surround him. He feels that he has a right to a definite place in the social structure of South Africa, and he is embittered by finding that no such place is accorded to him ... South Africa, as such, does not recognise him. And he, who ought to be a permanent support to influence white rule, is tempted to turn his face backwards to a more sympathetic understanding with that of the native population from which he is, in so large a part, derived.

The APO and other black organisations understood that they also needed to act. As the editor of *Izwi Labantu*, Allan Kirkland Soga, remarked: 'when we remember that those people who are shouting so loudly for federation are the same gentry (the capitalists) who ... strove to upset the orderly legislation of half a century and to throw the native franchise to the dogs ... – woe betide the people.'[203]

Despite the threat they faced, African movements were as divided as the coloureds had become. Once again this expressed itself as a question of which white party to support. The divisions were deep and longstanding. On the one side was the influential journalist and editor of *Imvo*, John Tengo Jabavu. He, and those who backed him, were allies of the South African Party, which provided funding for his work. They had obtained assurances from the party that the latter would support the African's right to the franchise at the forthcoming National Convention to consider the question of Union.[204] In the other corner were African leaders who had associated themselves with the South African Native National Congress, established on 31 December 1891. They included men like Walter Rubusana and A.K. Soga, and their efforts received support in the latter's paper, *Izwi*. Their white allies were the Progressives, including Jameson and (until his death)

Rhodes, whose slogan was 'equal rights for all civilised men' south of the Zambezi.

In August 1907, African leaders were planning the annual conference of the South African Native National Congress. Aware of the scale of the crisis, they decided to hold a much more extensive meeting. They invited all African and coloured organisations to attend a conference to consider the question of Union. This was held in Queenstown on 27 and 28 November. It was the first time that African and coloured organisations had come together. As André Odendaal concludes, the conference was a landmark in African politics.[205] Dr Abdurahman accepted the invitation enthusiastically. He argued that the best hope of the black electorate was to advocate a federation, rather than a union, since otherwise 'the rights and privileges of the Cape coloured people would be handed over to one centralised Parliament', which would leave them at the mercy of illiberal northern politicians.[206] Abdurahman believed the 1908 Cape general election would be an ideal occasion for voters to 'extract pledges from candidates and parties' on the 'question of federation and the non-whites' place in it'.

Since federation was the policy of the Progressive Party, Dr Abdurahman urged African and coloured voters to support them. These politicians were – he declared – 'men with liberal views akin to the old Cape traditions', whose manifestos included the 'most liberal provisions for the maintenance of the rights of the Coloured people'.[207]

It is not difficult to see why Dr Abdurahman chose the Progressives. Their leader, Leander Starr Jameson, like Cecil Rhodes, accepted the concept of a qualified, non-racial vote for all South Africans. Jameson, prime minister of the Cape from 1904 to 1908, had insisted it should be given 'to all civilized Natives, yes, certainly!'[208] He made his views plain in a letter to Dr Abdurahman's brother-in-law, Ahmed Effendi. 'Education – compulsory where possible, and free where necessary. This applies absolutely to everyone – White or Coloured and of whatever race. "Equal rights of all white men" – absolutely, again to both White and Coloured. It is only the aboriginal Native we consider uncivilized. Reading and writing is not the test. The Malays in this country are British subjects and as such there is no prejudice against them, and they should have equal rights with the Whites.'[209] The Progressives had also reached out to try to win over coloured people, encouraging the formation of branches specifically aimed at recruiting coloured voters.[210]

Unsurprisingly, the decision to back the Progressives led to further divisions within the coloured community. Tobin, believing that the South African Party of the liberal John X. Merriman and others was a far better guarantor of black rights, came out in its favour.[211] He embarked on a tour of the Cape to drum up support for the party, which paid for his expenses.[212]

WHITES DEBATE THE BLACK VOTE

Tobin's support for Merriman was not irrational. Merriman had engaged in a lengthy confidential correspondence with Smuts, then Colonial Secretary of the Transvaal and deputy leader of Louis Botha's party, Het Volk. The subject of their debate was the franchise within the envisaged Union constitution. Merriman sought to have the Cape's qualified, but non-racial, franchise extended to the whole of South Africa. His interchanges with Smuts in 1906 went a long way to deciding the issue. Despite being a leading liberal, Merriman couched these private letters in a language he believed would appeal to Smuts. On 16 March Merriman wrote to Smuts, saying: 'God forbid I should advocate a general enfranchisement of the Native barbarian. All I think is required for *our* safety is that we shall not deny him the franchise on the account of colour. We can then snap our fingers at Exeter Hall [where missionary societies met] and Downing Street, and experience teaches me that there is no surer bulwark for all the legitimate rights of any class or colour than representation in Parliament ...'[213]

Later that month Merriman wrote to Smuts again, urging that Africans should have the vote, although he believed there should be a high qualification built into it. Again, Merriman made his argument in terms of the security of whites.[214]

In the Native case we are fettered by the notion which all of us entertain that the Native is a schepsel [creature]. But he is a human being, though an undeveloped one, and my contention is that the only *safe* way of management is to give him a chance to acquire political rights if he shows himself fit to manage them. Therefore I confess I dread what you call manhood suffrage. In my humble opinion this is a country for a high franchise and for a property qualification.

Speaking for the Transvaal, Smuts refused to accept the argument, insisting, with the Orange River Colony, that there should be a whites-only franchise for the Union.[215] He pointed out that it was simply impossible for him to argue publicly that poor whites should be deprived of the vote they currently enjoyed by introducing a property or wealth qualification. Whites as a whole, and Afrikaners in particular, regarded the franchise as their right and would not abandon it.[216]

> We have had to go in for manhood suffrage, not only because it existed among burghers before the war, and seems a democratic principle ... but also because even the low franchise of Milner's constitution [residence on premises worth £100 or producing £10 rental a year, or receipt of £100 salary p.a.] resulted in the disenfranchisement of some 10,000 bywoners [tenant farmers or squatters] and grown-up sons on farms, the loss of whom we cannot afford.

For a white politician of this era it was an irresistible argument. Smuts could not go to ten thousand citizens and suggest to them that they be deprived of their democratic right so that a small number of prosperous, educated Africans could be given the vote. The alternative was to propose a universal franchise, without qualifications of any kind. In the early 1900s that was simply inconceivable for most whites.[217]

Merriman continued to put his argument but made no progress. In February 1908 he wrote to Smuts once more, this time suggesting that the Cape might keep its non-racial franchise, while the other provinces retain a racial franchise. At the same time he called for the Cape's arrangement to be safeguarded against amendment by insisting that any change could only be made if agreed to by a two-thirds majority in the Union parliament.[218] This compromise Smuts finally accepted. On this basis the two men reached an agreement, and these terms became the foundation for the Union franchise.

Merriman thought that the compromise was a significant victory. He had fulfilled his promise to secure the Cape franchise, but he knew it had required difficult negotiations and that the arrangement was fragile. Attempts to alter it were dangerous, in his view, since the entire deal might unravel. This explains his resolute opposition to the pressure from Dr Abdurahman and others for the non-racial vote to be extended to the whole of the Union.

THE NON-RACIAL FRANCHISE AND THE UNION OF SOUTH AFRICA

Black politicians, unaware that this private dialogue was under way, gathered in Queenstown in November 1907 for their historic conference. Dr Abdurahman attended enthusiastically, as did APO delegates from Cape Town, Kimberley and Port Elizabeth.[219] Jabavu, however, refused to participate. He dismissed the gathering as a 'pantomime' with 'crusted old Progressives' as players, and held a rival conference in its stead.[220] John Tobin also refused to attend. Speaking to the conference, Abdurahman stressed the importance of a federation rather than a union. If the latter was adopted, the sound policies of the Cape would be submerged, he argued, to the detriment of black people.[221]

In his speech Dr Walter Rubusana, a central figure in African politics,[222] said he hoped the conference would mark the beginning of greater unity between Africans and coloureds. While they all complained about being discriminated against, there had long been a colour line between them, he declared.[223] After a full day of discussion, a resolution was unanimously passed on behalf of 'the coloured people and natives of the Cape Colony'. It called for federation rather than union, for the Cape franchise as the basis of a federal franchise, and for the exclusion of the territories of 'Swaziland, Basutoland and British Bechuanaland' from a future South Africa.[224]

The Cape general election was scheduled for two months' time, on 21 January 1908. Dr Abdurahman told a meeting just ahead of the poll that the Progressive Party was the party to support.[225] John H. Raynard, who worked as a clerk in Abdurahman's practice, described the campaign: 'I personally, under the Doctor, organised both the European and the non-European vote of the Coloured districts of Cape Town. As a result, all the seven Progressive candidates … who stood were returned. Cape Town went delirious with rejoicing.'[226] But the coloured community was not united. Tobin and his Stone colleagues rallied behind the South African Party and its leader, John X. Merriman. For his part, Merriman courted the African vote, touring constituencies in the Eastern Cape in which the African vote was strong and making speeches confirming the sanctity of the 'Native franchise'.[227]

In the event it was Merriman who emerged victorious, ousting Jameson and the Progressives. Dr Abdurahman and his allies had backed the losing side. In the weeks and months ahead, they would be disappointed by the stand that the South African Party took, but their influence over Merriman could hardly have been strengthened by the fact that they had been his political adversaries.

WHITES WRITE THE UNION CONSTITUTION

A National Convention was held from 12 October 1908 until 11 May 1909 to decide on how best to unite the colonies. Only white politicians participated, to the intense frustration of Africans and coloured people. Black groups sent petitions to the Convention attempting to influence its proceedings, but to little effect. In the end the outcome in respect of the franchise was much as agreed during the Merriman–Smuts correspondence. The future Union of South Africa would be one in which only white men would be allowed to vote, except in the Cape. There the Cape qualified franchise would apply, and this was to be protected. Any change would require a two-thirds majority in both houses of parliament. There was, however, one further restriction. Only white men would be eligible to stand for or sit in the Union parliament. Previously, at least in the Cape, any voter could become an MP though in fact no black person ever sat in the Cape parliament. This possibility was now ended. The draft went to the parliaments of each of the four colonies for ratification.

These proposals were not what coloureds and Africans had called for. A.K. Soga expressed the frustration they felt: 'This is treachery,' he wrote. 'It is worse. It is successful betrayal, for the Act has virtually disenfranchised the black man already.'[228] Even Jabavu described the draft as introducing 'immoral colour distinctions among the King's subjects'. In the Cape a former prime minister, W.P. Schreiner, brother of the author Olive Schreiner, led the attack on the proposed constitution when it came before the Cape parliament. Schreiner declared that the colour bar was 'narrow, illiberal and short sighted in concept'.

Among those who watched the debate in the Cape parliament was Olive Schreiner. She met Dr Abdurahman and his wife, Nellie, on 8 April 1909 and established an immediate rapport with them. 'It was a great pleasure to meet you and your wife yesterday,' she wrote from Tamboers Kloof. 'I trust that our brief acquaintance may ripen into sincere friendship.'[229] Olive promised her support for their cause. The issue was debated in parliament the same day and she provided a vivid description of what she saw taking place from the gallery in a most moving letter to her brother.[230]

> That scene in the house yesterday, was without any exception the most contemptible from the broad human stand-point I have ever seen in my life, which has been pretty long & varied. It seemed as though the curse of the serpent had fallen on them all – 'on thy belly shall thou crawl & dust shalt thou eat.' I hardly know what was the most awful thing: Jameson's face, so much worse than it ever used to be, even that with an uncomfortable leer on it, – or dear old [F.S.] Malan looking like a lost soul – for he has a soul & a noble one! And as they squirmed & lied, & each one giving the other away, & all gave away principle, all the while there was Abdurahman's drawn dark intellectual face looking down at them. Men selling their souls & the future – & fate watching them. One sees strange things from that gallery!

Schreiner won some support but most MPs, determined to push through an agreement that had been so carefully hammered out, voted in favour of the draft constitution. Abdurahman and the APO responded as never before. On 5 March 1909 the APO organised a mass meeting in the Cape Town City Hall. Presided over by the mayor and with other whites on the platform, it heard from Dr Abdurahman. He described the draft constitution as 'wicked', 'unjust', and 'un-British'.[231] The APO held similar meetings in sixty other towns, passing resolutions critical of the proposed constitution.

In March 1909 Walter Rubusana and other African leaders called a South African Native Convention in Bloemfontein to discuss the draft

Act. Dr Abdurahman wrote to *Izwi* stating that he had advised all APO branches to attend, 'for it matters not who initiates the movement so long as we attain our object'.[232] The Native Convention passed a number of strong resolutions, appealing to the Imperial and colonial governments, and addressing the white National Convention. There were also tentative moves to found a permanent organisation to monitor developments and for the executive to organise a deputation to Britain to act on their behalf. It was decided to ask W.P. Schreiner to assist them.[233]

APPEALING TO BRITAIN ONCE MORE

The following month sixty APO delegates met in Cape Town. They adopted a resolution favouring 'a lasting Union of British South Africa … founded upon the eternal rule of order and justice', but deploring the exclusion of people of colour from the Union parliament and calling for permanent protection for the Cape's non-racial franchise and for the franchise to be extended to 'all qualified coloured persons in the contemplated union'.[234] The APO resolved to open a fund to 'protect the interests of the coloured people as affected under the draft South Africa Act, including the sending of a delegation to England if necessary'.[235] The APO declared 'that the time has arrived for the co-operation of coloured races in British South Africa, and that the executive of the APO is hereby instructed and empowered to communicate with the executives of all the various organisations to act unitedly to protect the rights of all coloured races and secure an extension of civil and political liberty to all qualified men irrespective of race, colour or creed throughout the contemplated Union.'[236]

Many people contributed to the APO fund, but perhaps the most poignant was the contribution from Cape Town fishermen. They met on 8 June 1909 to hear an appeal from Dr Abdurahman, who had helped found their association four years earlier.[237]

> The Doctor explained that they had just over a hundred pounds; that he had bought a Post Office Savings Bank certificate of one hundred pounds, which was produced, and that he had four or five pounds besides.
> He pointed out to the fishermen that instead of keeping the money they might assist the rest of the coloured people who were fighting

for the political rights of all men. The Draft South Africa Act he said deprived the coloured people of their political rights, whether they were fishermen, carpenters, or masons, and he felt sure that the fishermen would do their duty ... The oldest fisherman then moved that the association contribute eighty pounds towards the Draft Constitution Fund to send the delegates to England. This was unanimously adopted.

It was a generous donation and the doctor thanked them profusely. The APO did not just raise money for their own delegates: £100 was donated towards the expenses of the African delegates who went to London.[238]

Dr Abdurahman, eager to obtain the widest support for the campaign, wrote to W.P. Schreiner on 11 May, updating him on its progress. He explained that he had told two key African political leaders, A.K. Soga and Tengu Jabavu, about the proposed delegation.[239] Soga, he informed Schreiner, 'thinks a delegation to England imperative'. Jabavu, who had been away from King Williams Town, had not yet replied. Abdurahman proposed to call on Schreiner later in the week and said he was 'preparing a petition which might be sent either to the King or parliament, or both. By tomorrow's mail I am sending a letter to *The Times*.' Abdurahman was determined to do all he could to make the delegation to London a success, appealing to the authorities as well as the British media. To get Cape opinion behind the initiative, he told Schreiner that his party was starting a newspaper of its own: 'I wonder whether you would honour it with a contribution to the first issue.'

In May 1909 the official National Convention, taking no heed of black protests, approved the draft constitution unaltered. The white politicians dispatched it to London for final approval and sent a delegation to accompany the draft with strict instructions to ensure it should be passed by the British parliament without amendment.[240]

For black South Africans, London remained the last hope. The British people, the APO declared, would 'never be dragooned into bartering away the glorious reputation won by their ancestors as lovers of freedom and asserters of the rights of humanity'. With these stirring words the APO selected Dr Abdurahman, Matt Fredericks and D.J. Lenders to join a delegation of coloureds and Africans to be convened by W.P. Schreiner.

The intransigence of the white politicians had, unwittingly, united the black opposition. By drawing up a constitution that excluded black South Africans outside the Cape, they had brought together African and coloured parties from across the political spectrum. Even the difficult relations between Rubusana and Jabavu had been smoothed over. These parties had done all they could to petition and lobby for an extension of the franchise to the whole country. They had W.P. Schreiner on their side. He had intervened repeatedly when the draft was debated in the Cape parliament, but without success. Now the matter would be placed in British hands.

A community divided

Despite the urgency of the issue, dissent continued to plague the coloured community. Tobin opposed the deputation, arguing that the previous mission in 1906 had been a complete waste of money.[241] He was joined in his opposition by F.Z.S. Peregrino. Although wishing to advance black rights, Peregrino was a conservative, stressing the need to avoid violent confrontational tactics. 'To resort to violence is but to invite disaster and well-merited punishment upon the heads of the offenders, embarrass those who are grappling with a difficult and trying problem, and add to the burdens of the innocent and offending sufferers,' he argued.[242] Rather, he believed that grievances should be laid before the relevant authorities. Peregrino was an influential voice in Cape politics, even though he did not join the APO.

Just as the Schreiner delegation was about to set sail for Britain, Peregrino and Tobin decided to join forces in a bid to derail the appeal to London. They went to see the influential Cape Afrikaner politician Jan Hofmeyr, presenting him with a 'humble tribute'.[243] Hofmeyr, as leader of the Afrikaner Bond, had persuaded the Cape Town branch of his party to condemn the colour bar clauses in the draft Act. Hofmeyr reiterated his support for a qualified non-racial franchise, as long as it did not endanger white rule. But Hofmeyr warned Tobin and Peregrino that, given the hostility of many white politicians, the survival of the Cape franchise required that the coloured people should act with care. Their success 'greatly depended on the moderation and wisdom of which your and other representative bodies of your people may give proof in their acts and utterances in connection with the draft Constitution and the National Convention'. This was exactly what Merriman had feared.

With this warning ringing in their ears, Tobin and Peregrino attacked the Schreiner deputation, arguing that 'agitation' might worsen the plight of black people. They told Hofmeyr that they rejected 'any scheme whereby an appeal shall be made to any party outside South Africa on behalf of our people for the redress of such grievances'.[244] Hofmeyr was presented with a statement laying out their position in no uncertain terms. The document was widely circulated and the *Cape Times* published it in full under the heading 'Mr. Hofmeyr's Mandate: A Coloured Deputation: Deprecates Appeal to England'.[245] Claiming to speak on behalf of coloured people, they rejected appeals to the British, instead expressing 'confidence and trust in our friends in South Africa who have consistently and steadily defended our cause, and whose efforts will, we believe, ultimately be crowned with success'.

Dr Abdurahman was furious. Matt Fredericks, secretary of the APO, denounced Peregrino and Tobin's approach to Hofmeyr, declaring that they were 'self-appointed' and did not represent the community.[246] A meeting of the Malay Association, held on 12 July, was reported to have attacked those who went to see Hofmeyr with cries of 'Shame!' and passed motions of support for Dr Abdurahman and his deputation.[247] The protests were in vain. Hofmeyr had already sailed to England, as part of the official delegation, and was soon making sure the British authorities were aware of the resolution. Writing to Tobin and Peregrino from London, Hofmeyr explained that their resolution had been put to good effect.[248] 'I had the pleasure of handing a copy to Lord Crewe [Secretary of State for the Colonies] of the address with which you honoured me on the eve of my departure for England,' he told them. Hofmeyr said that Lord Crewe had appeared to sympathise with their stand, and promised to provide a written reply.

In reality the British didn't need Hofmeyr to deliver the message in person. They had known about the Peregrino–Tobin initiative for some time, having been informed of it by Peregrino himself, who had written to Merriman, as Cape prime minister.[249] Merriman then drafted a minute to the Governor on 8 March 1909, drawing attention to Peregrino's letter and describing him as someone 'who is widely known as a man of education and ability and of much influence with the coloured community'.[250]

The next few weeks in Britain would be vital for the future of South Africa: the Union constitution would be settled. So too would the country's role in the Imperial system. On the shoulders of the African and coloured politicians rested the hopes and fears of their communities. Much money had been raised to send them. What if they failed? An official white delegation was also in the process of making their way to London to ensure the British did not alter the text which the National Convention had agreed upon. Their mandate was clear: veto any major alteration to the constitution. Much was at stake and much would be decided before any of them saw Cape Town once more.

The Tobin–Peregrino denunciation was damaging to the Schreiner delegation's chances. As soon as they arrived on British soil, Schreiner found himself attacked for not really representing the interests of the black community. *The Times* carried a report on Schreiner in which he was described as 'claiming a right to express the views of the South African natives'. [251] This the paper disputed, reporting that 'A large section of the coloured people definitely repudiate him.' This perception was reinforced by Merriman. Interviewed on board the *Kenilworth Castle* en route, Merriman described Schreiner's position as 'entirely inexplicable'.[252] The Cape prime minister told *The Times*: 'the agitation can have nothing but the worst possible effect ... I think Mr Schreiner's present mission is one of the most unkind things ever done to the natives.' It was hardly the start that Schreiner, Abdurahman and the others might have hoped for.

The Schreiner delegation brought together white, coloured and African politicians. Dr Abdurahman was joined by two of the APO's most senior members, Matthew Fredericks, its general secretary, and Daniel Lenders, the organisation's vice-president and a well-known cricketer. Other delegates included Walter Rubusana, the president of the South African Native Convention, and his former rival, John Tengo Jabavu, editor and president of the Cape Native Convention. Thomas Mapikela represented Africans from the Orange River Colony. John Dube, the Zulu teacher and preacher, was also in London to support the delegation, but had to keep his head down, since pressure from the Natal authorities restricted his participation. In addition to Schreiner himself there was Joseph Gerrans (who was also white), who had been asked to represent the senior chiefs of Bechuanaland (Botswana).[253] The delegates were an immensely impressive group. It was perhaps the first time a truly representative delegation of South Africans had come together to fight on a common platform before an international audience.

Mahatma Gandhi was also in London at the same time, asking Britain to improve the conditions of Transvaal Indians. Although not part of the Schreiner delegation, he met them and offered what support he could to their cause. Gandhi had little confidence that London would intervene. As he put it in a letter requesting a meeting with Schreiner: 'I am personally more concerned with satisfying South African statesmen as to the justice of our aspirations than with agitating for relief from the Imperial Government.'[254]

The London campaign

Dr Abdurahman was at a distinct advantage in being in London: he was almost on home turf. He had lived there after qualifying in Glasgow, had family members in London and had visited the city repeatedly. He knew the metropolis and how it operated. While the white members of the delegation – Schreiner and Gerrans – also knew London, few of the other delegates had been there for more than a brief period. Schreiner, with his credentials as a Cambridge graduate,[255] a London-trained lawyer and former Cape prime minister, was uniquely qualified to influence the British elite. At the same time, he knew he had to refute claims that he did not truly represent the black population. Throughout the visit he kept in constant contact with the black delegates, ensuring that it was their voices that were heard.

Schreiner and his family made their home at the Morley Hotel on Trafalgar Square (the site of today's South African High Commission) and most of the other delegates found accommodation nearby. Dr Abdurahman was an exception. He stayed with his sister, Muhsine, at 38 Longridge Road, in Earl's Court.[256] She had turned it into a boarding house. The 1911 census records her as a widower from the Ottoman capital, Constantinople.[257]

Schreiner worked hard to give the doctor and other black members of the delegation every opportunity to meet British opinion-formers and to speak at the various gatherings they attended. This is clear from Schreiner's correspondence. On 6 July he wrote to Sir Charles Dilke, the most prominent and well-informed foreign policy expert in the House of Commons and, as a Liberal MP, a vital source of support.[258] Schreiner urged Sir Charles to meet the black members of his delegation since they were important representatives of 'upwards of a million natives and coloured persons in Cape Colony and Natal alone, and their mission is also in a sense representative of the natives and coloured folk of the ORC [Orange River Colony] and Transvaal'. Schreiner described Dr Abdurahman as 'a prominent Member of the Cape Town Corporation, Moslem, cultured and very able'.

There then followed an intense six weeks of public and private meetings with British opinion-formers, as well as the government. No stone was left unturned. A discussion for members of parliament was held at the House of Commons on 13 July. This was arranged by Dilke, who told Schreiner he was pleased to do so, adding that he 'knew Dr Abdurahman well and should be glad to meet him again'.[259] The meeting was evidently a success. The doctor was pleased with his discussions with Dilke. 'I have had a long chat with Sir Charles Dilke,' he wrote to Schreiner.[260] 'He, of course, fully understands our cause and sympathises with us; but he is somewhat pessimistic as to being able to allow any material alteration in the D.S.A. Act [Draft South Africa Act] in its present form. As to the series of meetings it is intended to convene at the House, there appears to be a slight difficulty, as the Conservative men have to obtain the sanction of the party leaders. Mr R. MacDonald [the Labour Party's general secretary] who has the matters in hand will tell me how they stand.'

On 22 July, within two weeks of their campaign getting under way, the deputation succeeded in securing a formal meeting with the Colonial Secretary, Lord Crewe.[261] Schreiner recorded the encounter in the cool, measured language of the day. This was probably a statement agreed with the Colonial Office, since it was reported in exactly these terms by Reuters and carried by *The Times*:

> The Right Hon. Secretary of State for the colonies this morning received at the Colonial Office the delegation on behalf of the native

& coloured inhabitants of South Africa. Dr. A. Abdurahman, the Rev.
W. Rubusana, & Messrs. Mapikela, Lenders and Fredericks attended.
They were accompanied and introduced by the Hon. W.P. Schreiner.
They explained their object & the amendments for which they pressed
in the proposed Act of Parliament to establish the Union of South
Africa. The Secretary of State received them courteously & responded
sympathetically, but without giving any assurance that the desired
amendments would be made.[262]

This was followed by a large public breakfast at the Westminster Palace
Hotel, on 27 July, organised by the Aborigines' Protection Society. The
meeting was widely reported.[263] Sir Thomas Fowell Buxton, president
of the Society, opened the proceedings by saying that he hoped South
Africa would become what he called a 'real Union, not only of States,
but of races'.[264] Dr Abdurahman was at the breakfast, as was his deputy,
Matt Fredericks, and the other black delegates. Abdurahman explained
just how deeply he had been wounded by the inclusion of the words 'of
European descent' in the terms of the draft constitution for eligibility
to stand as an MP. It was clearly racist. 'The people of England cannot
expect coloured men to sit down quietly under that insult. The native
and coloured population felt it very hard that the Imperial Parliament
should now be asked to attach its seal to documents which would make
them feel like outcasts and men without political and civil rights.'[265]
The meeting adopted a resolution, regretting that the draft constitution
did not provide for all races to participate in the proposed parliament
and that the black and coloured franchise of the Cape Colony was not
adequately safeguarded.[266]

July 1909 marked a high water mark for the deputation. Schreiner's
letter had been printed in *The Times* on the 27th. This was followed by
another from Dr Abdurahman the very next day.[267] He told readers of
the paper that the proposed Union abrogated assurances dating from
1852, and embodied in the Cape constitution, that guaranteed equal
rights to all subjects. He attacked the assertion that their rights in the
Cape were secured by the requirement that the Union constitution
could only be changed by a two-thirds majority in a joint sitting of
both houses of parliament. Abdurahman said Botha and Smuts had
made public statements on 24 February promising to end the 'native'

franchise, even in the Cape. He quoted Smuts as saying, 'On the first occasion Parliament met it could be swept away. It was found necessary that there should be some check; perhaps it was no check at all. It has been put in there, but he did not think it meant much.'

Despite these successes with influential sections of British society, the omens were not good. It was clear, even at this stage, that the campaign was not progressing well. W.T. Stead, publisher of the *Review of Reviews*, had known Dr Abdurahman since his trip to the Cape in 1904. He wrote to Schreiner explaining that he had held a 'long talk' with Louis Botha and some other Afrikaner delegates 'on the question of the natives'.[268] 'It is quite clear that they will accept no modification of the scheme in any form. The only new point that Botha made was that the Constitution really extends the rights of the natives inasmuch as it allows members elected by the Cape franchise, which includes blacks, to legislate for the whole South Africa, a privilege which blacks never before enjoyed'. Stead conceded that this was true, but warned that 'that very fact may increase the temptation on the part of the other Colonies to disenfranchise the natives in Cape Colony'.

The delegation had little option but to press on. Most of their support came from the British Labour Party. At this point it was a small opposition party, and hence fairly impotent. Although the Liberal Party was in government (and Liberal MPs were therefore required to support the official line), a number of radical Liberals were close to Labour at this time and happy to work with them. On 29 July a meeting was held in Committee Room 10 of the House of Commons. This was, as the official invitation put it, to allow MPs 'to hear from Mr. W.P. Schreiner, A. Abdurahman, W.B. Rubusana, and others, Members of the Delegation at present in London, on behalf of the native and coloured inhabitants of South Africa, upon the amendments for which they press in the Draft Act of Union shortly to be presented to Parliament'. The invitation was prepared by the Liberal MP Henry J. Wilson, and supported by six other MPs, including Ramsay MacDonald.

Wilson took the chair at the meeting, which was attended by about 40 Liberal and Labour MPs. *The Times* reported that the deputation heard them call for the 'elimination of the words requiring all members of the new Assembly to be of European descent, or at least only apply to representatives of the Transvaal and Orange River Colonies'. The deputation also called for the dropping of the clause allowing the 'native' franchise to be removed with a two-thirds majority. The assembled MPs agreed to move amendments to this effect when the details of the Bill would be discussed in parliament. On the face of it, the Schreiner delegation was making progress, but Dr Abdurahman knew they faced a huge task. 'Since our arrival here it has been a terribly up-hill fight,' he told the APO in a letter home.[269]

A ROYAL WELCOME

The doctor was right. While Schreiner and his colleagues had been given a polite hearing by the British government, the reception of the official delegation was altogether different. It is no exaggeration to say that the prime ministers of the Cape, Natal, Transvaal and the Orange River Colony were given a truly royal welcome. Some – like Generals Botha and Smuts – had been among Britain's most implacable foes until just seven years earlier. Now they were in the Imperial capital as friends and potential allies. The British government was determined to do all in its power to make them feel the warmth of the welcome. They dined with the royal family. When the Union constitution came before parliament, they were given generous access to the proceedings.

The London press could hardly contain its enthusiasm. 'If anyone five years ago had predicted that in the year 1909 General Botha and Dr. Jameson would have been sitting together on the steps of the Throne, while the Colonial Secretary presented to Parliament an Act of Union in the joint name of British and Boer, he would have been thought a mere visionary,' wrote the *Westminster Gazette*. 'The British Empire has its critics, but we may at least claim for it that only under its flag could this particular chapter of history have been enacted.'

The *Morning Post* observed that the audience for the debate in the House of Lords was more important than the speeches.[270] 'On the steps of the Throne among the members of his Majesty's Privy Council was to be seen the man who commanded the Boer forces during the South African War – General Botha … It is unusual for any but the wives and daughters of Peers to find places in the galleries to right and left of the canopy of the Throne. But the occasion was exceptional, and exceptional measures were taken to meet it … [The] wives or daughters of our distinguished South African visitors were comfortably seated in these places of vantage.' The other delegation – including Dr Abdurahman – could only look on from the sidelines.

There was a good reason for this. The British government not only wanted to end the hostility between themselves and the Afrikaners, but they wished to cement the future Union of South Africa into the Imperial system. This was a vital British goal since by 1909 it was clear that another European war was on the horizon. Without allies London knew it had little chance of success against the Germans militarily. The discussions over Imperial Defence were far more pressing for London. While the discussions between the British government and the official South African delegation over the Union constitution took less than two days (20 and 21 July), the second conference – concerning defence – lasted for no less than 22 days (29 July until 19 August).

Only one issue caused any real difficulty in concluding the Union discussions – whether the protectorates of Bechuanaland, Swaziland and Lesotho as well as Rhodesia would be included within South Africa. Here the British refused to budge, and Botha and his colleagues had to concede ground. The second conference, on Imperial Defence, brought together senior politicians from Australia, Canada, Newfoundland (still a separate territory), New Zealand and the four South African self-governing colonies.[271] The South Africans were keen to participate, but made it clear that they were only attending 'for completeness' since they were not yet a dominion, and could not bind a future South African government.[272]

With difficulty, London got grudging agreement. The South African delegates were prepared to play a significant part in British military planning, once Union was achieved. In the event, when the First World War was declared in 1914, the country supported the British war effort, fighting in South West Africa (Namibia), East Africa and on the European fronts. From London's point of view it was a tremendous benefit, but it came at a price. The white politicians demanded that they alone should settle their country's domestic issues. 'I understand the Dutch [Afrikaner] leaders have been impressing upon politicians in this country the wish of South Africa to be left alone to work out its own salvation,' reported *The Graphic*.[273] 'They have guaranteed they will play their part in the general scheme of Imperial Defence, more particularly since they have around them three European Powers whose policy may one day vitally affect them, but as regards all internal affairs they claim a free hand, and while they do not resent fair criticism, they will object to tactless and interested intervention on the part of the Home Government.'[274]

It was a clear warning: keep away from 'native' policy or lose our support in times of war. This was a threat the British government and bureaucrats in Whitehall could not afford to ignore. General Botha and his colleagues thus got their way. The price of this agreement would be paid by black South Africans: the British would not intervene on their behalf in future disputes.[275] All this was done behind closed doors; and the majority of South Africans would only see its consequences played out over the years to come.

Betty Molteno

The Schreiner delegation sensed that the debate was not going their way. It must have been a depressing few weeks, but just how difficult it was for them is not revealed in the newspapers. We have to turn to an extraordinary source to understand how they were feeling: the private letters of a South African woman. Betty Molteno was the daughter of the first prime minister of the Cape, Sir John Molteno. She was one of a handful of English-speaking women who had backed the Afrikaners during the Anglo-Boer War and was a strong supporter of the rights of all people, irrespective of race.[276] She had sufficient resources and loved to be where current developments were unfolding. Molteno travelled to London to be present in the capital when the Union constitution was being debated. As the daughter of a prime minister, she was as welcome in the salons of Botha and Smuts as she was in the company of Rubusana, Jabavu and Abdurahman.

Betty Molteno explained in a letter that she was in touch with the Schreiner delegates, including Dr Abdurahman. By the end of July, it was clear that the delegation was making little progress. They had the support of the Labour Party and a handful of Liberal MPs but they were not likely to win sufficient votes when the Union constitution finally came before the House of Commons. The impact of these setbacks on Schreiner and his colleagues is not difficult to imagine. They had travelled thousands of miles, at great expense to themselves and their communities, yet defeat stared them in the face. What did they feel about it? What did their families back home think of the reports they would have read with great care in the South African press?

Sadly, just one letter remains that provides us with evidence of the pressure they were under and of the concerns back home. It is from Nellie Abdurahman to her husband, dated 10 August.[277] It is a rare survival of the correspondence between them, and is therefore worth quoting at some length. 'My dearest husband,' she wrote from their home, Albert Lodge, Mount Street, in Cape Town's District Six.

When you receive this you will be on your way back to 'Home Sweet Home' and sunny South Africa. I was so pleased to get your letters today, although the news regarding your Mission to England was not so good as I hoped it would be. However I feel sure that the majority of the Coloured people are quite satisfied that you have done your utmost for them and time will do the rest.

I hope to see you looking well and fat when you arrive at the docks, have a good lazy time on board, put away all thought, books and worry for the rest of the voyage, so that you may be fit to start fresh when you get here.

The weather here is very bad at present; winds and rain for the last eight days, all the rooms in the house are leaking very badly, I can do nothing at present as the rain does not cease long enough to enable the man to repair the roofs, so that we are all praying for the rain to stop.

I have attended to all your orders, so that I trust when you return you will find all things to your satisfaction. One thing I have done which I hope you will agree with, that is I have transferred some of your fire assurances to the 'General', by doing so I have saved something on the premiums ...

We are all well so far, considering the cold, wet weather. Sometimes I feel rather tired, but the thought of your return keeps me up and I know that I shall be relieved of some of the work then. The paper [*APO*] is going along nicely, I have added a good many to the Individual Subscribers list since you left. I think I mentioned that Mr H. Tomas of C.T. took the agency but since then he has given it up. He came to me and said he could not sell them. However last issue I saw most of the people who took the paper and got rid of nearly all. I took Marcus round with me and told them that he would have the papers every second Saturday.

I must close as I am already late for the mail.

Remember us all to Mr F [Fredericks?] & Mr D [Dollie?].

With fondest love and kisses.

From your affectionate wife, Nellie.

This was a warm and loving letter, designed to boost her husband's flagging morale. It also says a good deal about what a resilient and capable woman Nellie was. Not only did she deal with the household in Dr Abdurahman's absence, but she clearly played an important role in ensuring the circulation of his newspaper, the *APO*.

By this time the long campaign was almost at an end. Sir Charles Dilke had presented a petition to the House of Commons, signed by Schreiner, Abdurahman, Jabavu and others.[278] The ever-observant Betty Molteno had been spending her days flitting between fashionable evenings attended by the official, white delegation and daytime meetings with the black deputation. On Saturday, 14 August, Molteno was waiting at her residence for Dr Abdurahman and Jabavu, who had said they would call on her at 11 am. Clearly in a good mood and with the sun streaming in through her window, she sat down to read the *Review of Reviews*: it was much to her liking.

William Stead had written a long article based on interviews with all shades of South African opinion.[279] Botha, Smuts, Merriman and Schreiner had been interviewed, as well as some black delegates, including Dr Abdurahman. Stead had put it to the whites that all they needed to do was get rid of three words, 'of European descent', and they would receive the backing of most of their critics. He had a good rapport with the Afrikaners (whose cause he had supported during the Anglo-Boer War) but he received a pained rejection. 'You know that I would be only too glad to accede to any request of yours if I could possibly see my way clear to doing so,' Abraham Fischer, prime minister of the Orange River Colony, told him. 'What you ask as to consenting to an alteration in the draft Union Act on a matter which the Convention thought of material importance, and resolved upon after maturest deliberation, is practically impossible. Acceding to your request would at this juncture mean wrecking union; this none of us are prepared to do, including, I hope, yourself.' All the white politicians took a similar stand, wringing their hands while saying they could do no other.

Stead summed up the position of the English-speaking liberals who supported this stand as being particularly odious – 'enforcing upon England the betrayal of her wards is the fly which causes the ointment of the apothecary to stink'. He then went on to quote the black deputation's reaction. 'We only demand justice,' Tengo Jabavu had told Stead. 'And the status quo which was promised us,' added Dr Abdurahman. Stead concluded the article by quoting General Botha, who had told him that 'natives are not fit to use it [the right to sit in parliament] and no self-respecting white man would sit beside a coloured man in Parliament'. Stead was outraged: 'I would certainly be better pleased to sit beside Dr Abdurahman or Tengo Jabavu in any Parliament than with certain white men whom I know in South Africa, or even in the British House of Commons.'

On that sunny Saturday, in the week before the Bill was to be debated in the House of Commons, Dr Abdurahman and Tengo Jabavu arrived to see Betty Molteno. She had been reading what Stead had to say in the *Review of Reviews*. Her letter home bubbled with excitement.[280] 'Jabavu large and smiling – a sea of human kindness and cheerful light – While Abdurahman looked a beautiful angel almost about to wing its way from dust and turmoil into sunnier skies – Didn't we talk and I read aloud Stead's article – dear Tengo – how good was his large, merry, jovial human laugh at Stead's many sallies – oh he did enjoy and appreciate the article – while Abdurahman was blue as [?] – I found myself stopping the reading to beg him to laugh too – saying he could not live much longer if he did not laugh more – and he replied "how can I laugh – my wife says I never laugh".'

PARLIAMENT DECIDES

As the final vote in parliament loomed before them, Liberal MPs, whose party was in government, peeled away from the Schreiner delegation. Only Labour remained standing with them. On 6 August the Labour leader, Keir Hardie, wrote to Schreiner inviting him to attend a meeting of Labour members as well as a few other sympathisers the following Tuesday, the 10th, at 7.30 pm.[281] Hardie suggested that two others, 'one coloured and one native', should also speak at the meeting. He concluded his letter: 'Excuse me for thus intervening, but if a fight is to be made you ought to make the best show possible.'

The meeting was reported by the *Daily Mail*.

'We are not here', declared Mr. Schreiner, 'for the purpose of urging this Parliament to extend to the Transvaal and the Orange River Colony the principles which have obtained for generations in Cape Colony, but to claim that the existing rights and privileges shall be maintained and that the territories under the protection of Great Britain shall not be handed over to the Union Government until the Government has given adequate and reasonable representation to all territories without bar to race or colour.'[282]

It was a last-ditch appeal, with little hope of success.

The final act before the debate got under way took place that Tuesday evening in the House of Commons. It was a dinner, presided over by Keir Hardie. He invited the Schreiner delegation to meet MPs from his party.[283] Of the Labour MPs who sat down with their South African visitors, two subsequently became cabinet ministers and two led the Labour Party. The South Africans were just as impressive: besides Dr Abdurahman, there were several Africans who would found the African National Congress in 1912.[284] These were the cream of black South African society, whose work would shape their country's future throughout the twentieth century.

A ROYAL PLEDGE

On Monday, 16 August, the Union constitution finally came before the House of Commons. Colonel John Seely, as Under-secretary of State for the Colonies, introduced the debate. He reminded the MPs that Britain had been considering a Union for a very long time – it had been proposed for over half a century.[285] He explained that it had been impossible to find a formula that gave a uniform franchise for all four colonies. 'In all the different Colonies which now form the Union, to put it in a phrase, a man who had not got the vote before will not get one under this Bill, and no man who has a vote now will lose it under this Bill.'[286] Thus coloured, African and Indian men in the Cape would continue to be allowed to vote, while in the rest of the Union they would not. Only men who were British subjects and had lived in South Africa for five years and were of European descent would be allowed to sit in either of the houses of parliament. This removed the theoretical right black men had had in the Cape since they were granted the vote fifty-five years earlier, although they could sit on the new provincial councils. But it was a compromise worth having, Seely contended. Without it the Union would not come into being.[287]

> The compromise effected is this, that while every native in Cape Colony retains his right to vote, the chance of being deprived of his vote is specifically made more remote than in the case of other classes of persons. On the other hand, the native is debarred from sitting in the Union Parliament because he was debarred from sitting in two of the Parliaments by our own action here. On that a compromise is arrived at, and I can only assure the House, speaking with all seriousness, that we know that if these words were struck out the Union would be smashed, with results most evil for the natives whom we wish to protect. I am told on all hands by those who have best reason to know that if we here were to break up and smash this great Act of Union for the sake of these words the result on the native races of South Africa in breaking down the rapidly growing sympathy between the two races must be disastrous in the extreme.

That, in essence, was the government's position and it refused to budge from it throughout the debates that took place over two long days. Seely did, however, have a final consolation for those who took up the 'cause of the native'. He argued that it was highly unlikely that the South African parliament would attempt to remove the black vote, since it had many more important things to do. But if it did, he had one further piece of information. Any attempt to amend the constitution would require a two-thirds majority of a joint sitting of both houses of parliament, but even if this was passed, there was one final safeguard: the King would protect this right. The Bill would be considered a reserved Bill and would not receive royal assent. 'I am quite confident that all these safeguards would not have been inserted at all unless South Africa meant to play fair by the natives,' Seely concluded. He had consulted with the government's chief legal officer, the Attorney General, and with Schreiner, and the matter was – in Seely's view – now merely 'academic'.[288]

In the view of the British government the non-racial vote was secure. But they were wrong. When these provisions were finally repealed by the South African parliament in 1936 in respect of African voters, the King did not act to prevent these rights from being abolished, although this lay many years in the future. But the impression was firmly left in the minds of many black South Africans that the King (or Queen) was their final protection – it was a promise that would not be forgotten.

On the last day of the debate Seely quoted from a letter he had received from Sir Henry de Villiers, chairman of the official South African delegation. Sir Henry wrote that he had listened to the debates and was therefore writing to him. This was the key point: 'The Delegation has no power, express or implied, to accept any Amendment of the nature referred to which would destroy a compromise that was arrived at after prolonged discussion.'[289] It was – to put it bluntly – a case of like it or lump it. South African whites had made up their minds on this subject, and the British government was unable or unwilling to make them change it.

All that was left was for Asquith, as prime minister, to express his regret that such illiberal measures were about to be given the force of law.[290] He concluded with an appeal to South Africa to amend the constitution to remove the racial restrictions preventing the majority of their countrymen from participating in government. 'I am sure our fellow subjects will not take it in bad part if we respectfully and very earnestly beg them at the same time that they, in the exercise of their undoubted and unfettered freedom, should find it possible sooner or later, and sooner rather than later, to modify the provisions.'

With that the Bill was passed. There had been only one vote on an amendment. Just 55 MPs out of the 670 sitting in parliament had voted for it: 26 Liberals, 26 Labour and three Irish MPs resisted the government. Writing in the *APO* newspaper, Dr Abdurahman declared: 'The only party which is not prepared to sacrifice principle is the Labour Party. It is the one party in whose hands the honour of Old England can be safely trusted.'[291] This exception was of limited comfort. The Union constitution was duly signed into law and the South Africans – black and white, official and unofficial delegates – packed their bags and headed home.

Before Dr Abdurahman left for home there was one final and significant encounter. Gandhi had spent his time in London confronting Smuts and the British about the rights of Indians, but he had been aware of the Schreiner delegation. Hearing of its lack of success, Gandhi wrote to his friend Abdurahman, just after the final debate in the House of Commons.[292] It was an important intervention at a moment of deep despair. The letter spelled out Gandhi's assessment of the deputation's strategy and (in the gentlest of terms) criticised Abdurahman and his colleagues for their approach to the British. They had relied upon British goodwill, he said, and an appeal to a sense of justice and fairness. In Gandhi's view this approach was bound to fail, unless it was underpinned by a vigorous campaign of civil disobedience. The letter was dated 23 August 1909.[293] 'Dear Dr Abdurrahman,' Gandhi wrote.

Please accept my sympathy as also congratulations in connection with your mission; my sympathy because you have got nothing substantially; my congratulations because no deputation deserves success as yours did, on account alike of the inherent justice of your cause and the solid work that you put forth. Mr. Schreiner has undoubtedly worked sincerely and like a giant.

That no amendment would be made in the Draft Bill was a foregone conclusion. One may derive whatever satisfaction is to be had from the fact of almost every member having regretted the insertion of a racial bar in an Imperial Statute-book; neither you nor I can live upon regrets. You are busy, so am I. Were I not busy, I should certainly have come down to you to offer what consolation I could, and yet I know that real consolation has to come from within. I can but recall to you the conversation we had on board. You are disappointed (if you are); you expected something from the Parliament or the British public, but why should you expect anything from them, if you expect nothing from yourself.

I promised to send you Thoreau's *Duty of Civil Disobedience*. I have not been able to procure it; I am writing for it to-day and hope to send it before you are off. All I can add is a prayer that you may have the strength for it and ability to continue the work in South Africa along internal reform, and, therefore, passive resistance, even though, in the beginning, you may be only a handful.

The letter ended with a suggestion of a meal together the following day. Its warm and friendly tone reflected Gandhi's care and consideration for Abdurahman's no doubt bruised feelings. The doctor and his colleagues had come so many miles, had expended so much energy and money, yet had so little to show for their efforts. In discussing the issue in his own paper, *Indian Opinion*, Gandhi was more forthright.[294] 'What should the Coloured people do now? The question should not arise. If they have courage in them, let them, with Rama's name on their lips, sound a call for satyagraha [passive resistance or civil disobedience]; otherwise, they are surely as good as dead. To have come over here and made big speeches would avail them but little. The days are past, so it seems, when something could be gained by making speeches.'

Gandhi was right. The time for making gains by giving well-crafted speeches was over. The question now was whether the unity that the political leaders had achieved between Africans, coloureds and whites during their time in London could be replicated and developed when they returned to South Africa. Might a non-racial party be launched to resist the rising tide of white racism and Afrikaner nationalism?

CHAPTER SEVEN

'The gladiators return':
From peace to war

STRIVING FOR UNITY

When the Schreiner deputation finally returned to Cape Town on 21 September 1909, it was abundantly clear that appeals to Britain were henceforth unlikely to succeed. London would not intervene to alter the racial clauses and restrictions being written into the South African constitution, despite all the protests from Dr Abdurahman and the rest of the delegation and the appeals of their British supporters.

W.P. Schreiner, physically and mentally drained by the lengthy campaign, decided to take his family to the Netherlands on a brief break, prior to the journey back to the Cape. Betty Molteno was keen to find how they were feeling following the parliamentary debates. She visited the Schreiners at their hotel – the Morley on Trafalgar Square – where they were busy packing. Other delegates had come to see them off, but were not too downhearted, despite the defeat.[295] Indeed, Dr Abdurahman, who had previously seemed so low to her, was – she wrote – 'plainly greatly cheered by the debates'. 'His face wore a quite different expression from what it did when I had that long conversation before Monday's debate.' Perhaps it was as much a feeling of relief at the prospect of returning to Cape Town and his family that uplifted the doctor.

For all the support the deputation had received in London, the situation that faced them on their return home was distinctly grim. An inkling of what was to come was provided by Louis Botha in an interview with a German paper, reproduced by the *Cape Times*.[296] 'On the native question in South Africa,' Botha told the Berlin *Lokal-Anzeiger*, 'the first decade was necessary for the consolidation of the Union. The whites ... have laid the foundations of, and must continue the erection of, that edifice to make it habitable. Afterwards they would negotiate to see how much room was left for the natives.'

A WARM WELCOME

It was a chilling statement, presaging what was to follow, but it did not dampen the enthusiasm of the welcome the deputation received from their own communities. They sailed into Cape Town harbour on board the RMS *Saxon*.[297] There to greet them at the docks was a welcoming committee from the APO. After breakfast, speeches were given on the promenade deck of the ship. The APO general secretary, N.R. Veldsman, speaking on behalf of his party, gave the formal address.[298]

> We desire to express to you all, more especially to you, Mr Schreiner, our heartfelt appreciation of your noble efforts, on behalf of the coloured races of South Africa. We are fully aware of the magnitude of the task you had undertaken ere you left these shores. We watched with the keenest interest the reports of your doings in Great Britain ... Though your mission has in some quarters been pronounced a failure, we feel that it has been a glorious success. The failure is but temporary. Truth and Justice must ere long prevail, and such success seems miraculous in face of the forces arrayed against you.

Veldsman's words set the tone for many of the speeches by coloured and African gatherings in the coming weeks and months: thanks to the deputation for what they had achieved and the hope that more would be delivered when Union came about.

Replying, Schreiner described the racial discrimination as a 'blot' on the new constitution, but the deputation had, he said, received support at the highest level in British society. 'We have done what we could, and we have received from the Prime Minister the assurance that he expected that the Union Parliament would take steps in the direction that we desired, and we [are] determined to stand on that.'[299] 'Hear, Hear!' the crowd responded. But, he said, appeals to Britain were a thing of the past. Now, declared the former Cape prime minister, it was 'in South Africa [that] our future work must be done'.

Dr Abdurahman, somewhat reluctantly, also made a short address, again thanking Schreiner for all he had done and calling on his supporters 'with level heads and cool temperaments' to continue their fight.[300] The dockside ceremony was followed by a grand reception in the Banqueting Hall of the City Hall, complete with a 'capital musical programme' arranged by the Ladies Committee. The arrival of the Schreiners was greeted with an ovation. When Dr Abdurahman, Lenders and Fredericks entered, the orchestra was, fortuitously, playing 'The Gladiators Return'.[301] The mood was upbeat and celebratory.

Others were more cautious. A Cape Town minister, the Rev. Ramsden Balmforth, who had done a great deal to persuade Schreiner to lead the deputation, wrote an assessment of the trip to London. It had not achieved its purpose, even if all sides in the House of Commons had implicitly condemned 'so unanimously' the racism now enshrined in the South African Constitution.[302] 'Our course is now clear,' he said. 'It is, never to rest until every civilised human being in the country, whatever his race, creed, or colour may be, is granted that freedom of opportunity which is the inalienable right of every man and woman wherever freedom is something more than a name.' It was a ringing declaration, probably written more in hope than in anticipation of rapid fulfilment.

The most well-judged assessment came in Jabavu's paper, *Imvo*.[303]

The blow has fallen, and the British Government and the House of Commons have passed the Union Constitution Act without the amendments we had hoped for … The Native and Coloured people must now realise that an entirely new chapter in South African history is opening, in which they have to depend on ourselves and their South African European friends for the securing and maintenance of their civil and political rights. They must become united politically and, refusing to cling to any of the present political parties, must work for the creation of a new political party in the State which will unite the religious and moral forces – European and Native – of South Africa upon lines of righteous legislation, justice and fair play, irrespective of race or colour.

Dr Abdurahman certainly had no illusions about the threat the coloured population faced. When the City Council met in February 1910 to discuss plans to spend £4,000 on the festivities to mark the Union, which would be attended by the Prince of Wales, Abdurahman used the opportunity to register his displeasure. He refused to vote for the expenditure. 'No coloured man can feel happy: no coloured man, I hope will sing "God save the King" on that day. I know I won't.'[304] How could any black man find anything to celebrate, he argued, when the right to stand for parliament had been denied them? 'No coloured man will see the Prince of Wales coming through the streets and feel happy, for he will know it is the consummation of robbing him of something he has had for fifty years … No Englishman or Irishman would have stood up here today and said it in the temperate way I have, and they had been robbed, disgracefully robbed, of something they would have shed their blood for,' he declared.[305]

The doctor's stand was deprecated by whites, but he refused to budge. An amendment, which he supported, reducing the municipality's expenditure on the Union festivities by £1,000, was rejected, but his stand was applauded by Gandhi.[306] 'In courageously expressing his sentiments, we think that Dr Abdurahman has cleared the atmosphere of cant and humbug and served Truth, the Crown, his people and himself at the same time … We congratulate Dr Abdurahman on his performance and hope he will have courage to follow out his programme when the time comes.' There was support from APO branches. Kimberley also protested against municipal expenditure to celebrate the Union and a telegram was sent to Abdurahman assuring him of the unanimous support of the coloured community in the city.[307]

'Our struggle', wrote Gandhi a few days later, 'is producing a profound effect on the Coloured people. Dr Abdurrahman has commented on it in his journal at great length and has held up the example of the Indian community to every Coloured person. Some of them have also passed a resolution in Johannesburg to defy the laws of the Government and take to satyagraha.'[308] But others in the community were less complimentary about the doctor's forthright stand. Peregrino, for one, labelled Dr Abdurahman a dangerous 'radical'.[309]

W.P. Schreiner, with his close links to Britain, was drawn into the controversy. Asked by the APO for his support in the stand they were taking, he replied cautiously. He said he appreciated the 'conflicting feelings' with which the celebrations would be marked and that it was not his duty to 'recommend any insincere manifestations of a joy that is not felt'.[310] At the same time, the Prince of Wales would be in South Africa as the King's representative and coloured people should carefully consider how to respond. 'Let each follow the natural guidance of his views, and do, within those limits [of law and propriety] what he sees to be right; neither pretending to be merry when he feels serious, nor assuming a sad demeanour when really he may have firm confidence in a bright future.' It was the advice of a lawyer, and carefully framed. Interestingly, when the detailed considerations of the pageant were being discussed, Dr Abdurahman did not stand aloof. He played a constructive role, suggesting that the 30 or 40 mules that were to be purchased by the City Council for the occasion should be bought without delay, before prices rose to reflect the increasing demand.[311]

On 4 April 1910 the APO met at the Oddfellows Hall in Port Elizabeth. Dr Abdurahman, aware that the coming months and years held many threats, did not mince his words.[312] 'Unrestricted citizenship which we enjoyed under the Cape Constitution ... has not been granted to us under the Union Act ... the door to political freedom has been slammed in the faces of our brethren of the other Colonies,' he told the gathering. 'No one who cherished the true ideals of British liberty can fail to regard the colour-restricted clauses of the Union Act with any feeling other than regret.' It was, he argued, up to the coloured population to prove that they were worthy of the vote.

It was a powerful statement, but addressed to the coloured people rather than the whole black population. 'The black races must be allowed to develop in their own way,' he argued. The APO was meeting in conference 'as an organisation of the coloured people only in South Africa'. This did not mean they were indifferent to the fate of other people of colour, Abdurahman pointed out. 'We have a deep interest in the native races of South Africa, and the Union Act of South Africa puts us in one fold: but it is my duty as the President of the APO, on the present occasion, to deal with the rights and duties of the coloured people of South Africa, as distinguished from the native races.'[313] It was a clear statement, as far as it went. Coloured people were organising themselves, even though there was a clear political affinity with Africans, as the doctor acknowledged. Some APO branches had in fact previously admitted Africans; the Kimberley branch was a case in point. But when the issue had been discussed in 1907, the APO passed a resolution supporting a 'better understanding' between all races, although several delegates expressed a concern that coloureds should not merge organisationally with Africans.[314]

The APO was clearly ambivalent about wider black unity, but then so too were other organisations. Gandhi was organising Indians; John Dube, Walter Rubusana and the rest of the African delegates to London were setting about uniting Africans. This did not imply a hostility to a wider black community, but other issues were more pressing than attempting to form a single, united opposition. Walter Rubusana, who had toured South Africa tirelessly after returning from Britain, made a point of attending the APO's April 1910 conference in Port Elizabeth.[315] The conference suspended its business to hear from Rubusana, who 'expressed his conviction that there should be more co-operation between the native and coloured people of the country'. A unanimous vote of thanks was passed for the speech and Dr Abdurahman followed, 'endorsing the view that the coloured and native people should amalgamate in political matters, and fight together for the welfare of all coloured people'.[316]

This point was underlined in the following edition of the *APO*.[317] Reporting on the conference, the paper said that the racial bar in the constitution had

done more for the coloured people than could have been achieved by any other means. It had produced a feeling of solidarity that will work wonders. The coloured races have been fused into one whole body, whose integration will defy the efforts of all ages and all the white races of this planet. The interests of all non-whites are identical. That lesson has been relentlessly driven home in the hearts and minds; and it will not be long ere the coloured races learn the increased power they have acquired by their fusion into one undivided and indivisible people.

These declarations were all very well, but no attempt was actually made to establish a popular, non-racial party. Dr Abdurahman was entirely sincere in his quest for a common purpose. He worked hard for the rights of Africans as well as coloureds. He had attended the Queenstown conference of 1907 that brought both groups together and rejected the draft South African Act as an attack on both coloureds and Africans. He had participated in the 1909 deputation to Britain. He had personally given a £100 contribution to Jabavu to meet his expenses in London.[318] But he also faced pressures from inside the coloured community to move in the opposite direction. There were voices calling for the APO to take a stronger stand on exclusively coloured issues. Dr Abdurahman was attacked by James Curry, John Tobin and F.Z.S. Peregrino for not taking these issues more seriously.[319]

It is perhaps less than surprising that this unity across the races was something of a mirage at this time. Black politics were still in their infancy, generally only involving the educated elite. There were also the problems of geography, distance and poor communications. Finally, there was the reality of the emerging white political agenda, which considered different racial groups as separate entities and treated them differently. The forces of division were simply too powerful to be overcome by the warm words and good intentions of individual leaders. An all-encompassing non-racial unity would lie in the future, but this did not imply that co-operation was not on the agenda in 1910.

FOUNDING THE ANC

In 1912 the much-anticipated unity of the various African organisations in the country finally took place. In Bloemfontein on 12 January a conference convened by Pixley Seme founded the South African National Native Congress (later to be renamed the African National Congress). It was a vitally important development for Dr Abdurahman, which he had encouraged and supported. As he wrote in the *APO*, the South Africa Act of 1909 had forced all black people 'to see that they were one, made one by their wholesale exclusion from political rights and privileges'.[320] The founding of the Native Congress would allow greater co-operation between coloureds and Africans.

Among the first acts taken by the Congress was to send a delegation to Cape Town to take up the issues that had been raised at its inaugral conference with the government. From Kimberley, Sol Plaatje, the Congress's general secretary, arrived in the city in March 1912, ahead of the president, John Dube, and other office-bearers to arrange meetings with government ministers and officials.[321] These took place, but alongside them was another meeting which was potentially as important. This was with the APO, and it was reported in Plaatje's own paper, *Tsala ea Batho*, under the headline 'A memorable meeting. The first step to union of non-Europeans'.[322] The meeting took place at the APO offices in Loop Street and were attended by, among others, Dube, Plaatje and Mapikela on the ANC side and Abdurahman and Fredericks on the APO side. A resolution was adopted:

> That in the opinion of this joint meeting of representatives of the APO and the South African Native National Congress, it is desirable that there should be closer co-operation between the Coloured and Native races of South Africa. It was further decided that the two bodies should keep in close touch with each other, and discuss matters affecting non-Europeans, and where necessary take united action.

Although there would be examples of the united action the resolution spoke of, this never became the kind of real solidarity that was envisaged. This was not because of an absence of goodwill between Abdurahman and Plaatje. Plaatje was an active member of the APO's Kimberley branch. The two men would enjoy what Brian Willan, Plaatje's biographer, described as 'a relationship of respect and friendship for years to come'.[323] There is a small but heart-warming example of this. On 26 July 1913, Plaatje's newspaper, *Tsala ea Batho*, carried this story under the heading 'Personalia': 'Among the list of successful candidates who passed the recent Music Examination (Cape) are Cissie and Waradea, the two daughters of Dr Abdurahman, the President of the African Political Organisation. We congratulate Dr. and Mrs Abdurahman on the attainments of their daughters.'[324]

Politics seldom follows a smooth progression. In the September 1913 municipal elections Dr Abdurahman was surprisingly defeated by Hyman Lieberman, a Jewish merchant who had previously been mayor of Cape Town. 'The defeat of Dr Abdurahman on Monday came as a great surprise,' declared the *APO* newspaper, 'not only to the Coloured but also to the European citizens of Cape Town.'[325] Africans also regarded this as a blow. *Imvo* described Abdurahman's defeat as 'a disappointment', saying that since his election in 1904 he had served as member and chairman of various committees and 'demonstrated that colour was no bar to the performance of useful work'.

The loss of the seat on the City Council must have been a bitter blow. Perhaps Dr Abdurahman had become complacent. He was used to challenges from the left rather than from a businessman who was a pillar of the Jewish community.[326] It seems that Abdurahman had been unaware that he was about to be so roundly defeated. In a speech just a few days before the election was held, he had told a meeting at St Patrick's Hall on Somerset Road about what he had achieved since coming onto the Council nine years earlier.[327] 'Enormous changes have taken place in Cape Town,' he said. The city had been converted from 'a town of ill-formed and unpaved streets into a modern city'. Lights had been installed so that ratepayers no longer 'blessed the Council when they tripped up on a dark night', he declared to laughter. There were washhouses for the poor to use, and regulations had been introduced covering everything from 'milk shops' and hairdressers to butchers. The speech appeared to go down well. Dr Gool moved a vote of thanks, saying that coloured people owed a great debt to Dr Abdurahman and that he was an 'honourable man and a credit to South Africa'. His defeat did not last long. He was back on the Cape Town City Council, winning re-election in 1915.

PROVINCIAL COUNCILLOR

Dr Abdurahman was not a man to be deterred by any setback. He was soon out campaigning again, this time as a candidate for the Cape Provincial Council. On 27 March 1914 he was elected for the

Woodstock division. With the backing of the Labour Party he defeated the Unionist candidate by over 500 votes.[328] The doctor became the first coloured person to serve as a provincial councillor. Abdurahman had attempted to be nominated as a Unionist Party candidate, and had stood as an independent when that failed.[329] In later elections he stood for the Provincial Council as an independent South African Party candidate.

Most of Abdurahman's time on the Provincial Council was devoted to the question of education. In his elections speeches he had repeatedly raised the issue, calling for state schools to be built in Cape Town, Kimberley and Port Elizabeth for coloured people who were too poor to pay for their children's education. 'They, the Coloured people, were not asking for equal rights with Europeans, although they were entitled to them,' the *Cape Times* reported him saying on 14 March 1914. 'They did, however, ask that a beginning should be made by placing facilities in the above-mentioned centres, leaving those who were able to pay, free to do so.' In the same speech he called for medical inspections of schools, the teaching of hygiene to children, and tests on children for eyesight and tuberculosis.

In 1919 Dr Abdurahman used a speech in the Provincial Council to support calls for the introduction of free primary education, but this was blocked when it was argued that the taxes would not support such a measure. Education continued to be his central concern. In 1920 he called for compulsory primary education for all coloured children and in 1938 he supported the provision of free school books for all pupils.

In all his work, the doctor kept in close touch with the coloured Teachers' League of South Africa, which he supported down the years, and with its leader and his close friend, Harold Cressy. Although Abdurahman worked on other issues during his time as provincial councillor (including championing amateur sport and the cause of coloured fishermen), these were not his primary concern. As Richard van der Ross concludes: 'Many of his surviving contemporaries consider his contribution to education as his most important public work, and it was in the Provincial Council that he was able to pursue these interests.'[330]

FIRST WORLD WAR

On 4 August 1914 Britain declared war with Germany and all attention became focused on the conflict. For the Louis Botha government the decision to support Britain appeared to be a foregone conclusion. Botha and Smuts had both participated in Imperial Defence conferences even before Union in 1910 and were now closely allied with Britain. Churchill wrote that in 1913 Botha had returned from a visit to Germany warning that the situation was ominous. 'I can feel that there is danger in the air,' he warned Churchill. 'And what is more, when the day comes I am going to be ready too. When they attack you, I am going to attack German South West Africa and clear them out once and for all.'[331]

On the day war was declared, Botha did just that. He offered to take over the duties of guarding South Africa, relieving the British garrison of the responsibility, so that they could be transferred elsewhere. On 7 August the British Colonial Secretary, Lord Harcourt, accepted Botha's offer and enquired whether South African forces would seize ports in the neighbouring German colony of South West Africa.[332]

The South African cabinet met the same day to consider the request. Acceding to London's wishes was not going to be easy. There was opposition from many Afrikaners, who questioned why they should take up arms on behalf of their old imperial enemy. It took the prime minister three days of persuasion to achieve a unanimous vote in cabinet in favour of going to war – and even then only by promising that the army would be composed solely of volunteers.

The consequences were immediate and dramatic. On hearing that parliament had ratified the government's decision to invade German South West Africa, a number of senior officers in the Defence Force resigned.[333] In a tragic accident one of these dissenters – the Boer War hero General De la Rey – was killed at a roadblock. When South African forces crossed into South West Africa, the initial battle at Sandfontein went catastrophically wrong. Botha's forces were surrounded by German troops and forced to surrender. Then General Manie Maritz, a fiercely anti-British officer who commanded an area just south of the border, led his troops into Namibia to join the Germans, much to the amazement of the German commander. Finally, in October 1914,

91

there was a full-scale rebellion in the Orange Free State and Transvaal with forces led by mutinous officers. The revolt was no small-scale affair. Some 13,000 South Africans took up arms against their own government. It required tough marches and sporadic fighting before the rebels conceded defeat.

Thus it was not until early 1915 that Botha could finally take up command of the South West Africa campaign and lead his troops into the territory. It took six months of hard fighting to force a German surrender. Coloured, Indian and black African men had been recruited as labourers to support the 45,000 white troops that Botha led against the Germans. But there was resistance among many whites to arming them. Dr Abdurahman skilfully turned the situation to his advantage. He argued that while some Afrikaners had been rebels and 'enemies within', the coloured population had been steadfastly loyal to King and country.

With internal troubles behind him and South West Africa under his control, Botha could concentrate on playing a full part in the wider war. Smuts was dispatched to lead the attack on German forces in Tanganyika (now Tanzania) and South African troops were also sent to join the war in the Middle East and Europe.

DILEMMAS FOR THE COLOURED PEOPLE

For the black community, the First World War offered the same opportunity as the Anglo-Boer War to show their loyalty to their country and the British Crown.[334] On hearing of the outbreak of conflict, the ANC halted its agitation against the iniquitous 1913 Land Act.[335] Sol Plaatje declared that Africans were keen to join up and 'proceed to the front'. The coloured community was just as enthusiastic. Dr Abdurahman was eager to help with the enlistment: 'By offering to bear our share of the responsibilities', he said, coloured men would prove themselves 'not less worthy than any other sons of the British Empire'.[336] This remained the case throughout the war, even though the Cape's large Muslim community would have to confront the Ottoman Empire, with which they had strong links.

On 11 August the APO sent a message to Botha offering to raise a Coloured Corps for 'active service in the Union or abroad'.[337] Dr

Abdurahman organised a 'great patriotic demonstration' of coloured people in Cape Town, calling on them to put aside their grievances and concentrate their energies on backing the war effort, since 'if the British Empire fell they would all go with it'. The meeting backed the war and the APO began raising funds and calling for coloured volunteers. By mid-September 1914 APO branches had ten thousand names on their lists for a Volunteer Corps.[338] A year later the government decided to raise a coloured infantry battalion – the Cape Corps. They were to see action in East Africa, Turkey, Egypt and Palestine.

At the same time, Dr Abdurahman was not under any illusion that their show of patriotism would sweep away the racism and segregationist policies at home. He did not even think that Britain was particularly virtuous. In August 1914 the *APO* reminded its readers that 'whatever British liberty means in abstract, few of us can honestly say that we love it much in practice'.[339] How true this was, but while the war raged, politics were put on hold.

Coloured people volunteered for reasons that were as diverse as any other section of the population. For some it was a simple question of patriotism. 'As a respectable British Subject,' wrote a northern Cape mission station farrier on joining the Cape Corps in 1915, 'it is my responsibility to help in the present war, which is forced upon all free men by the Kaiser. We have a duty to the country of our Majesty the King. I for one am willing to come forward on my life.'[340] A Cape Town court clerk who also signed up saw in the constitutional freedoms of the Cape Colony the inheritance of British liberties – rights that compared very favourably with the 'evil customs' of racial oppression practised in the Orange Free State and Transvaal. It was 'the duty of every aborigine under the English flag and blessed by English religion not to yield any of its rights and protection'.[341]

The government was less than enthusiastic about Dr Abdurahman's attempts at recruitment. For Botha this raised a tricky question. Coloureds had the vote in the Cape but were denied the right in the rest of the country. If they fought in the war, would they be rewarded with an extension of the franchise? Botha was asked in October 1915. No, he replied, assuring his white electorate.[342] Botha explained that the Coloured Corps was to be raised as an Imperial force, paid for by Britain at no cost to the Union. At the same time coloured people in the

Cape had to be mollified: some of them, after all, had the vote, making up 10 per cent of Botha's South African Party support in the Cape.[343]

Dr Abdurahman – frustrated that his repeated offers of assistance had been given such short shrift by the Botha government – wrote to the Governor General on 25 August 1915.[344] He outlined all the APO's offers to assist with recruiting coloured troops from the time of the outbreak of war. The doctor renewed the APO's offer. Three days later the South African government wrote to the Governor General proposing the formation of a Cape Corps. Whether this was because of the doctor's letter is a moot point. Botha's party had won the October general election and the views of white voters were no longer quite so pressing. In September 1915 a Cape Corps War Recruiting Committee was formed. Among those asked to serve on it was Dr Abdurahman.[345] He provided the committee with invaluable assistance, using the APO's network of branches to mobilise the coloured community to volunteer for active service.

A large number of black people had already served with the South African forces. Some 33,556 coloureds, Indians and Africans had seen action during Botha's campaign against the Germans in South West Africa, but they had served as non-combatants. Now they wanted to bear arms. In September 1915 Dr Abdurahman was informed that Botha had relented: they would serve under the Imperial War Council. However, at South Africa's insistence, they would be led by and answer to white South African officers.[346]

When recruitment began at the City Hall in Cape Town on 25 October 1915, the enthusiasm of the crowd that turned up threatened to overwhelm the staff. Barricades had to be brought in and police called.[347] The recruits were described as 'keen as mustard'. Almost 18,000 members of the Cape Corps were sent to East Africa where they served with distinction. Upon their return in 1917 the regiment was reorganised and a second battalion was established. They went on to fight in Palestine, suffering 152 casualties in one engagement. When General Allenby paraded in triumph through Jerusalem, he gave the coloured troops the place of honour behind his white horse.[348] 'No man can have the honour to command men of better fettle than the men of the Cape Corps of South Africa,' he declared.

A year later the war was over; the complex process of returning the troops home and demobilising them began. On 9 June 1918 Reuters reported from Durban: 'The Cape Corps, some 1,400 strong, arrived this morning from Egypt and marched through the town. They were heartily welcomed and proceeded to Congella for demobilisation.'[349] On 17 June the soldiers arrived back in Cape Town.[350] 'The first contingent of the Cape Corps who have been doing such splendid work in Palestine, arrived this morning and received an enthusiastic welcome. The men were received officially by the Governor-General, the Mayor and others, and after refreshments at the Drill Hall, the work of demobilisation commenced immediately.' Despite the many tributes, the contribution of the coloured troops was not rewarded by incorporating the Cape Corps into the Union Defence Force. The Corps was disbanded when the war ended. Only its band was retained.[351] All that remained in the long run was an annual memorial service, at which Dr Abdurahman always spoke.

With the war drawing to an end, Abdurahman resumed the political campaigning he had conducted before hostilities commenced. He led a deputation to the Cape administrator, calling for free education for coloured children.[352] Little had changed. Sir Frederic de Waal said he was 'anxious to remove the impression that the Provincial Council was hostile to giving coloured people the same opportunity as Europeans whenever it was possible to do so' but at present this was impossible. Instead, he told the deputation, an additional £75,000 had been given to mission schools and teachers in coloured schools would have three-fourths of their salaries paid by the government. The World War was over, South Africans of all races were pleased to welcome the coloured troops home, but the policies and priorities of the white government remained unaltered.

Chapter Eight

Nellie Abdurahman and the children

THE DOCTOR'S ELUSIVE PRIVATE LIFE

Dr Abdullah's personal life was as intriguing, complex and sometimes mystifying as other aspects of his story. He was a member of a small coloured elite that emerged in the late nineteenth century and lived a settled, middle-class life in Cape Town. He was also intensely private. While we know a good deal about the doctor's public persona, important elements of his personal life remain hidden. Consider his relationship with Nellie. They were married in 1894 in London according to Muslim rites. That much appears certain.[353] They had two daughters, both of whom were born in Cape Town. Waradea (known as Rosie) was born on 8 May 1896 and Zainunnissa (known as Cissie) was born on 6 November 1897.

Dr Abdurahman did not remain married to Nellie. After more than a quarter of a century of apparently harmonious family relations, he left her in the 1920s or perhaps the early 1930s and started a second family with Margaret (Maggie) Stansfield.[354] The date is unclear, and what sparked off this rupture also cannot be ascertained. None of those involved, including their children, spoke about his divorce and remarriage. It is possible that Nellie became infertile after Cissie's birth and that the doctor, who is said to have desperately wanted a son, left her for this reason.[355] Nellie continued to live at Albert Lodge to the end of her life, and remained on apparently good terms with her former husband, who visited her from time to time. Dr Abdurahman simply moved out, establishing a new life with Maggie.

As Eve Wong points out: 'if there is little known or discussed about Nellie, there is even less about Maggie'.[356] The daughter of an Englishman, Edward Stansfield of Bolton, she was born in Somerset West in the Cape. It is not clear if she was white or coloured. Exactly when Maggie and the doctor were married is also uncertain, but the couple did go on to have three children together: a daughter, Begum Jehanara Gadija, and two sons, Abdullah Dara Shikoh and Nizamodien Ebrahim Stansfield.[357] Their home at Oak Lodge (today Ivanhoe) on the corner of Kloof and Arthur streets was a quiet retreat, very different from the swirl of political and social activity that took place at Albert Lodge. Despite Dr Abdurahman's complex relations with these two women, he was nonetheless a successful parent, to judge by his offspring. Of Dr Abdurahman's five children, two became doctors, one a nurse and another a chemist. Cissie became one of the best-known and most successful politicians Cape Town has had.

No one can doubt that Nellie Abdurahman was a remarkable woman. Not only had she given up her country of origin and sailed off across the seas with a husband who was neither British-born nor white, but she had been warned by the doctor that they could face racial opprobrium once they reached Cape Town. She had been married under a religion she did not share – Islam – in a ceremony that was not recognised as an official marriage by the state. Nellie even took a Muslim name (Wahida), which she never used.[358] While she was respectful of the doctor's religion and formally adopted it to be married, she brought with her the culture and traditions of her native Scotland. The Abdurahman family enjoyed Christmas dinner and handed on this tradition to their daughters, with Cissie continuing the practice.[359]

Nellie was not very different from many middle-class women of her time who were left to run their households. She (and the doctor) also worried a good deal about the education their daughters would receive.

This was hardly surprising, since education was one of the passions of their lives. Cissie and Rosie benefitted from excellent schooling, whether at home or in a formal school. As Patricia van der Spuy argues: 'Unlike most Muslim girls in Cape Town, their childhood was shaped not by domesticity, but by parental determination to educate them well beyond basic literacy.'[360] At the same time, since Dr Abdurahman was frequently away from the house for business or politics, the two girls were probably more influenced by their mother than their father, and she would have been responsible for a good deal of their education.

In 1907, their daughters' application to be taught at Good Hope Seminary in Hope Street was rejected.[361] The Abdurahman family must have been devastated: after all, the doctor had been educated at 'white' schools, like SACS. Why should his daughters be deprived of the opportunity? Nellie demanded a response from the superintendent of education in the Cape, who promised to make inquiries. After some time, Nellie received a reply: 'Dr Muir has had the opportunity of a talk with the Chairman of the Board on the subject, and finds that his attitude is practically similar to that of the Managers of the Good Hope Seminary, and apparently his view is likely to be the view of the Board. Dr Muir regrets therefore that for the present he cannot give any helpful suggestion.'[362] For the time being, all that could be done was to have Rosie and Cissie educated by a governess at home,[363] but for both parents the situation underlined just how critical the issue of universal education really was. In due course their daughters went to Trafalgar High School, which opened its doors on 12 January 1912, in a building that Dr Abdurahman persuaded the City Council to donate.[364] Harold Cressy, whom the doctor had helped to get into the University of Cape Town, became its first headmaster. Cressy, together with the APO, pressured the Council to find more suitable accommodation for the school. After five years the Council agreed to provide a better site and the Cape School Board donated £3,000 for the erection of a new building.[365]

Being educated at home did neither Rosie nor Cissie long-lasting harm: both went on to obtain university degrees. Rosie qualified as a doctor, graduating in 1927 from the Glasgow University, just as her father had done.[366] Cissie went on to become a successful politician, after attending the University of Cape Town. She had a chequered history as a student at UCT, registering for courses in 1922, 1929 and 1930, and in 1933 obtaining an MA in Psychology.[367] This was not the end of her studies. She returned and finally studied law, taking an LLB in 1962, becoming the first woman of colour to be called to the Cape Bar.[368]

It is not difficult to see why the children were so successful. Albert Lodge was an ideal environment for them to grow up in, being at the heart of passionate, intellectual debate. It was one of the Cape's first salons in which debate was encouraged and ideas were discussed. Dr Abdurahman was famous for his hospitality. As one visitor recalled: 'His friends were always welcomed with open arms and were never allowed to leave without a long talk and tea, and departed with sound words of advice.'[369] Gandhi was among those who made frequent visits. So too did the author Olive Schreiner and her brother W.P. Schreiner. Politicians like J.X. Merriman and J.H. Hofmeyr as well as academics like the historian Eric Walker came to discuss the issues of the day with the Abdurahmans.[370] As Patricia van der Spuy concludes: 'from a young age, [Cissie] was party to a wide range of activities taking place within Albert Lodge, ranging from meetings of politically-orientated women, to gatherings of the intellectual and cultural elite of the city.'[371]

NELLIE AND THE WOMEN'S GUILD

So far, we have seen Nellie as a courageous woman, giving up her country and religion to join her husband, despite his warnings of the racism she might face. We have seen her as mother and hostess. Gradually another side of this remarkable woman emerged as she took on political roles that most women of her time avoided or were prevented from pursuing. Sometimes this was in her own right; sometimes as Dr Abdurahman's wife. It is worth noting that Ismail Meer recalls Abdurahman often visiting Durban to meet and debate with the Indian community. With him was, says Meer, 'his wife, who hailed from Scotland'.[372]

Nellie was an active member of the Women's Christian Temperance Union. Dr Abdurahman was himself a strong supporter of the temperance movement, believing that drink was the curse of many of his people. Gavin Lewis goes further, describing it as the doctor's 'obsession'. He went so far as to call for a total prohibition on the sale of drink to coloured people, if it was impossible to impose a ban for all South Africans.[373] This was, perhaps unfortunately, one of Abdurahman's least successful campaigns. Be that as it may, there can be little doubt that he would have been fully behind Nellie's association with the Temperance Union. At the same time, his views of the role that women should play both in the home and in wider society were typical of men of his generation. He laid out what he expected of women in a speech to an APO conference:

> A mother's influence is incalculable. The character of children is far more dependent on that of the mother than that of the father ... I must urge you women to cherish a high sense of duty. Avoid idleness, vice and slatternliness. Keep your homes and yourselves pure and clean. Make them such that what I may call homeliness may induce your husbands to regard their homes as their haven of rest and peace and comfort after their day's work ... Every one of you who have the upbringing of children should so live that you ... may see in your offspring your proudest jewels. If such aims guide your actions and control your conduct, the coloured people of South Africa will become strong and enduring, and worthy of a proud place in the annals of the world. A women's heart and life 'centred in the sphere of common duties' are an ornament to the nation, and if she instils into her children a love of work, and an overpowering sense of the dignity of labour, a love of duty, reverence for truth and virtue, and courage, she will have won the crown which never fades.[374]

In 1895 Julia Solly, who worked for the Temperance Union, founded a franchise section within the organisation.[375] In 1907 a fully fledged Women's Enfranchisement League was established in Cape Town, with forty white members.[376] Olive Schreiner, a good friend of the Abdurahman family, became its vice-president.[377] Its members were less radical than Olive, who was a rare example of a white woman who called for all South Africans to be entitled to vote. She soon fell out with the League, which was only prepared to call for votes to be extended to white women. Olive threatened to leave as early as 1908, furious that the organisation would not campaign for votes for black women.[378] In 1911 she carried out her threat and resigned.[379] Nellie, on the other hand, remained engaged. The franchise section of the Temperance Union, led by Julia Solly, may even have met at her home.[380] Nellie continued to fight for women to have the same rights to vote as men, and was among the speakers at a Women's Enfranchisement League meeting in 1930.[381]

The franchise was not the only issue to which Nellie devoted herself; she also served on the Cape Town and Wynberg Board of Aid.[382] Such philanthropic activities were perhaps what one might have expected from the wife of a politician, but soon Nellie was taking on a more directly political role. In 1909, seven years after the APO had been founded, the organisation initiated a women's wing, known as the Women's Guild. Until this point the APO had been a men's affair. After all, only men had the vote (and even then, only men of some wealth and property). Was this an initiative that Nellie had promoted, or was it a scheme dreamed up by Dr Abdurahman? We do not know. What we do know is that a meeting was held in their home, at which the Guild was launched. 'A number of ladies met at the residence of Mrs Abdurahman, for the purpose of forming an association, the aim of which would be to work towards uplifting and educating, to assist the men in their work, and to take a general interest in the welfare of the coloured people.'[383] Nellie was elected as chair of the organisation as well as its president.

The aims of the Guild combined a mixture of social and political objectives. On the one hand its members were required to campaign for political aims – education and the general 'uplifting' of coloured people. On the other hand, their activities centred on what were seen as traditional women's work – needlework and dressmaking. Importantly, it was also designed to reach out and include girls. The Guild was at least initially seen as an ancillary organisation, supporting the work of the APO's male members, while at the same time engaging in discussions of their own. This mixture of subservience and political activism was to be played out as the Guild developed.

The Guild was soon popular; within two years it had 70 branches.[384] Its activities were covered in the 'Women's Column' in the party newspaper, with Cissie's and Rosie's names being frequently mentioned. Fundraising was an important part of the Guild's work: the need was pressing. Soon after it was founded, Dr Abdurahman and the

102

APO secretary left on the delegation to Britain in connection with the constitution for the proposed Union of South Africa. The Guild held a 'Grand Concert' for the deputation. It raised £40 towards their costs and saw them off at the Alfred Docks. 'The climax came on Wednesday afternoon … Everybody of importance was there … Amongst the ladies … were, of course, Mrs Abdurahman and children.'[385] When the deputation returned, having failed to persuade British politicians to back their cause, Nellie and the Guild were there to welcome them home.

For coloured people, the question of education became critical after an important ruling in the Appeal Court in December 1911.[386] Racial segregation had been introduced into the Cape's school system in 1905, by providing compulsory public schooling for all white children up to Standard IV or the age of 14, while relegating all black children to inferior church schools.[387] This took place despite a fierce campaign against the Act by coloured leaders, supported by a handful of white liberals. The legislation blocked coloured advancement and was denounced by Dr Abdurahman.[388] As Crain Soudien puts it: 'Dr Abdullah Abdurahman was acutely aware of what was happening and complained bitterly. He led several deputations to the authorities and organised several large public meetings against the proposed legislation. In one particularly disputatious meeting between Abdurahman and Colonel Stanley Crewe, the Cape Colonial Secretary, Crewe was so incensed by Abdurahman that he refused to answer his questions.'[389]

The 1911 ruling – which effectively entrenched the 1905 Act – came about because Carel Moller of Keimoes in the Gordonia district of the Cape found his children excluded from the local school. He had paid their school fees, only to be faced with strong objections from white parents; 16 of the 37 white children were withdrawn from the school. Moller was European himself but his wife was coloured, and this was enough to arouse the parents. W.P. Schreiner, who appeared in court on behalf of the parents, argued that both parents were of European extraction, but this did not convince Chief Justice De Villiers, who ruled that 'the term [in the legislation is] European which means pure European'.[390]

That was the end of the matter, as far as the law was concerned. The ruling meant that coloured children in District Six would henceforth be provided with education by the School Board at a third-class school, for 'slightly tinged children', as an article in the *APO* described them.[391] Nellie refused to accept this. She reacted by holding a Guild meeting, with members attending en masse. They condemned the ruling unanimously, resolving to petition the School Board. The issue was passionately adopted by the Guild and by the wider APO. A year later the Trafalgar High School was established to cater for the needs of the children of the area.[392] It became an institution that educated the cream of the coloured community. Both Rosie and Cissie would be among its pupils.

In 1911 the Women's Guild planned to convene a conference and to hold a bazaar to raise the funds needed for a proposed exhibition of women's work.[393] W.P. Schreiner gave the opening address at the bazaar, which was held at the Masonic Lodge. He explained that while the APO, as a political body, 'was not supposed to be a friend of everybody', this was not true for the Guild: 'the Women's Guild aimed at raising the women and children – taking them in hand – and it aimed at the social and moral welfare of the Coloured people. Therefore it was an organisation which everybody should welcome (Applause).'[394]

Rosie and Cissie participated enthusiastically in the bazaar, as did Rawson Wooding, whose wife was on the executive of the Women's Guild. He was an enthusiastic musician who had founded the Western Province Amateur Musical Society in 1909, giving lessons in both piano and musical theory. As we have noted already, Wooding was from British Guiana, yet another Caribbean whose role in early Cape history has largely been ignored.[395] While the two Abdurahman girls were taught to play the piano, Nellie took singing lessons from Wooding. Rosie and Cissie performed regularly at his events and participated in the first full recital of the Musical Society in February 1913. It was something of a success for the family: the *APO* described Rosie as 'having rendered her solo with that brilliancy of touch and expression of feeling which only belong to a true artiste'.[396] It was not the only achievement by the children: both girls won prizes in an APO writing competition.

When it was first founded, the Guild held meetings on days other than those on which the APO met. But from 1911 the two came together, at least in the Cape Town branch.[397] This was partly to allow the men to assert their control over the women. There would be lectures, debates, cultural entertainment and food, with the women providing most of the last two items. But there was another reason for the decision, as the *APO* reported: 'it was decided that the debate meetings would be held on the third Tuesday – the Ladies' night – when men would, as it were, pay the ladies a visit, and get a cup of tea, and perhaps a cake into the bargain. This, it was thought, would entice the young men to the meetings.' Since Nellie would preside over these meetings, it gave her a measure of power and influence. She was even able to present lectures, including one about the role of the Montessori system of education in primary schools.

Only once – according to Van der Spuy – did the Guild actually hold a conference of its own. At the end of December 1911, the women met in Johannesburg, to coincide with the APO conference in the city. Nellie took the chair, explaining that 'the object of the gathering was to promote unity among the coloured women of South Africa, and to discuss and promote, if possible, the benevolent, social and intellectual welfare of the womenkind'.[398] The Guild drew up a constitution for itself, but sent it off to the men of the APO to approve – a sign that the organisation remained subservient to the wider party.

As the racist policies pursued by the government tightened their grip on the Union, women of the Guild were confronted with the harsh realities of life in the northern provinces. The pass laws were being imposed on both coloured and African women with increasing severity in the Orange Free State.[399] The APO and the newly formed ANC took up the question, issuing press statements and petitions and sending deputations to see the government.[400] From 1912 women became increasingly involved, establishing the Native and Coloured Women's Association and petitioning the government. Women in the APO were particularly active.[401] In March 1912, dissatisfied with the response from the relevant government minister, a group of women travelled to Cape Town to seek redress. The *APO* was less than sympathetic.[402] 'It is also regrettable that the coloured women of the Orange Free State did not consult the Executive of the APO Women's Guild. We feel sure that no deputation of Coloured men of the APO would have come to Cape Town without first acquainting the Executive with the object of its mission.'

From these instances we can conclude that the Women's Guild, with Nellie Abdurahman as president, had become a respected part of the APO. At the same time, when it came to really critical issues there is little sign that they were able to exert control over the responses of their male leaders. Nellie had put women on the political map; she had yet to show an ability to take charge.

CHAPTER NINE

Challenges from the Left

THE LEGACY OF WAR

Once the First World War was over, life gradually returned to normal. The troops were demobilised; the dead mourned; the widows, orphans and the wounded cared for; and the confrontational politics of South Africa resumed. For Dr Abdurahman this meant reinvigorating the APO, which had been allowed to go into abeyance for the duration of the war. It had held no conference since 1913. Its newspaper, the *APO*, began publishing again in August 1919.[403]

The hopes of the coloured community had been aroused by the war aims contained in American president Woodrow Wilson's Fourteen Points, which formed the basis for peace negotiations at the end of the First World War. The fifth principle dealt with Europe's colonies. It stated that after the war was over the United States believed there should be 'a free, open-minded, and absolutely impartial adjustment of all colonial claims, based upon a strict observance of the principle that in determining all such questions of sovereignty the interests of the populations concerned must have equal weight with the equitable claims of the government whose title is to be determined.'

Colonised peoples worldwide saw in this the hope that they would receive justice from the Allies, once Germany was defeated. When General Smuts praised the role of the Coloured Corps, the APO quickly responded that in 'the face of such proof of honour and patriotism and loyalty', the government had an obligation to 'recognise in future that we have proved our claim to an absolute equality in civil and political rights'.[404] They were soon to be disappointed.

As the war ended, Dr Abdurahman attempted to lobby on behalf of coloureds and black Africans in the former German territory of South West Africa. The APO wrote to the British Colonial Secretary, Viscount Milner, in January 1919, referring to the 'painful recollection' that hopes raised during the Anglo-Boer War had not been fulfilled and calling for full franchise rights for all British subjects, irrespective of colour, in South West Africa as well as all of South Africa.[405] Milner, predictably, replied that this was an issue to be settled by the government in Pretoria. Abdurahman continued to apply pressure, with his stand endorsed at the first APO post-war conference in April 1919. The party also appealed directly to the Peace Conference meeting in Versailles, but with little effect. Similar appeals were sent to the Union government, with similar results.

Their hopes dashed once again, Dr Abdurahman reflected the bitterness many of the troops must have felt when he addressed Cape Corps soldiers on 19 September 1919.[406] He pointed out that men of all colours and political beliefs had fought side by side in the war, only to return home to be faced with racism and discrimination. Many struggled to find work. 'Frequently they have the wherewithal to satisfy the barest animal wants and are being tormented by loud and disgusting proclamations that their avenues of employment will in future be curtailed ... I can see disaster looming on the horizon,' he said.

At the APO conference in 1923 he bemoaned once more the fate that had befallen his people. Coloureds had 'exhausted every constitutional method' open to them, but had made no advance. They had been 'tricked, fooled and betrayed on every occasion by the white man'. These were powerful statements.[407] They were an indication of the anger and impotence that he must have felt. He was attacked by the press for suggesting that in the long run the current situation would only provoke black unity and calls for the expulsion of all whites from Africa.

Among coloured and African people there was a growing weariness and sense of disillusionment with the tactics of Dr Abdurahman and others of his generation, including men like the ANC's John Dube and Walter Rubusana. They had shown that they could get a polite and sometimes sympathetic hearing from the white government, although even this was wearing thin. Abdurahman was able to influence events on the Cape Town City Council and at the provincial level, but his levers of influence, nationally and internationally, became far weaker in the 1920s than before Union. Britain was no longer willing to intervene in South African affairs and the authorities in Pretoria had little time for demands raised by black politicians, especially as they faced so many pressing concerns from the white electorate as the hard times of the 1920s bit.

The issues Dr Abdurahman confronted in the 1920s must have appeared all too familiar, but the context was not the same as it had been before 1914 and the outbreak of war. New forces were at work. White South Africans now exercised unfettered control over the destiny of the country. In particular the rise of Afrikaner nationalism, with its increasingly strident calls for a racial solution to the country's problems, presented a growing threat from the right.

But this was not the only challenge Abdurahman faced. On the left, especially among the growing working class that was emerging in the cities and industrial centres of South Africa, new movements and parties grew up to articulate their views and promote their causes. As early as 1909 a South African Labour Party had been founded, drawing on mostly English-born artisans and working men who had recently immigrated to the country. Dr Abdurahman had little time for the Labour Party, which he came to distrust. He saw it as exclusively representing white interests. In his view, Labour – like other white-led parties – was only interested in coloureds at election time, when their votes counted. Although Labour had amended its constitution to allow coloureds, who were, in its words, 'hardly distinguishable' from whites,[408] to join the party – as long as they gave 'practical guarantees that they agreed to the Party's policy of upholding and advancing white standards' – this was not a line that Abdurahman could support. The Labour Party had arisen from the white union movement, whose purpose was to protect white jobs and living standards. It was therefore 'the enemy of the coloured people and were keeping a steel fence round the trades', Abdurahman told a meeting in Stellenbosch in 1920.[409]

Far to the left of the Labour Party stood the Communist Party of South Africa. This had been founded in Cape Town in June 1921 by a number of left-wing socialist groups from Johannesburg and Cape Town.[410] Though they probably represented fewer than 500 members between them, and though their cause was far from universally popular – with the newspapers covering the atrocities of the Russian Revolution in great detail[411] – the emergence of the Communist Party in South Africa did mean that Dr Abdurahman had a new competitor for coloured support. The party – instead of embracing the APO as potential allies – repeatedly attacked it and put up candidates against Dr Abdurahman. The doctor was criticised as a 'strong emissary of capitalism' and his party dismissed as petty bourgeois in character.[412] As his ward was in District Six and was a coloured working-class stronghold, the communists saw it as ripe for the plucking. In reality Dr Abdurahman's seat was safe: despite repeated attempts, the Communist Party failed to dislodge him. Party historians Jack and Ray Simons were left noting ruefully that their party's political programme held little attraction for most coloured voters.[413]

Not all communists, though, dismissed Abdurahman as an agent of capitalism or the ruling class. The Communist Party activist Lionel Forman thought Abdurahman was genuinely radical. He had the highest regard for the doctor, whom he described as 'the first prominent non-European socialist'.[414] To substantiate his claim, Forman quoted from a speech Abdurahman gave in October 1911 during an APO meeting to discuss the topic 'Socialism and the Native Question', in which he said:

As a public man he could not help being socialist, for all men who read and thought and endeavoured to improve the position of the lower classes of society are inevitably driven to Socialism. The condition of the working man today seemed to him to be worse than that of a slave, for the Coloured workman was not only virtually the slave of a capitalist, but had in addition to look after himself, whereas the health and condition of the slave was always a matter of serious concern to the master. Yet the workmen had in their hands the best possible weapon for bettering their conditions, viz: co-operation. With co-operation the

Native and Coloured labourers of South Africa could bring the white capitalist to their knees within 48 hours.[415]

Indeed, Abdurahman long advocated the unionisation of all workers, irrespective of race. He argued that white workers were mistaken in seeing coloureds as their enemies. 'Workers of all creeds and colours must stand together; must put an end to all divisions,' he wrote. Sadly, he said, this solidary was not shared by all unionists, for this spirit was more 'deeply engraved in the hearts of the Coloured artisan than in that of the white'.[416] Racism was particularly present in the Transvaal union movement. Unlike in the Cape, where coloured workers were at least tolerated by most unions, Transvaal unions exclusively represented white working men.[417]

With the First World War at an end, the APO turned its attention to mobilising the coloured working class more widely and effectively. In the Cape there had been a long tradition of coloured artisans participating in the union movement, and in 1918 they still dominated several trades, including plastering, leather-working, furniture-making and carpentry.[418] But while skilled coloured artisans were represented by unions, the semi-skilled and unskilled were not.[419] In the poor areas into which workers crowded, like District Six, there was real squalor and destitution. It was the children who paid the price. In 1918 Dr Abdurahman pointed out that around a quarter of all coloured children born in the Cape Town municipality died before their first birthday.[420] He went repeatedly to see the authorities to press for better wages and conditions for workers. In June 1919 he led a delegation to Jan Smuts, who was by this time acting prime minister, and explained that the pay of coloured labourers, especially farm workers, was below the level of subsistence, and called for a government inquiry. Dealing with this and other issues, including the franchise in the Transvaal and the Free State, Abdurahman described the latter as the 'Slave State of South Africa'.[421]

Perhaps seeing its rivals on the left eroding its working-class support, the APO became increasingly hostile to left-wing movements like the Social Democratic Federation and the International Socialist League and the unions associated with them, such as the Cape Federation of Labour Unions.[422] It was against this background that

Dr Abdurahman decided to launch the APO's own union movement – the Federation of Labour Unions – on 16 August 1919.[423] He was not without support. Among the unions that joined was the South African Workmen's Cooperative Union, founded and led by C. Meyer. Many of its 8,000 members worked for the Cape Town City Council, on which Dr Abdurahman served. Abdurahman and Meyer toured branches of the union, urging them to join. The former declared that his goal was 'one large industrial Union', involving 'every Coloured man, skilled or unskilled'.[424]

The *APO* carried an optimistic report about the progress that had been made in unionisation: 'During the past fortnight the Doctor and Mr Meyer addressed three more branches with the same result [of joining the Federation]. Unions of Coloured workers, skilled or unskilled, are invited to write to Abdurahman for full particulars. The APO has a long list of able industrial organisers who are ready to assist workers in any trade to form Unions.'[425] It was hoped that this would become a major development. As the historian Gavin Lewis argues: 'while the 1919 conference's decision to move beyond the Coloured elites and harness urban Coloured workers to the APO's cause did indeed reflect a concern to preserve the organisation's supremacy in Coloured politics, this was not the only consideration. There is abundant evidence to show that the APO was also motivated by sincere and long-held convictions that trade unions would be in the best interests of Coloured workers themselves.'[426]

Dr Abdurahman's ambition to launch a single, large union for coloured workers foundered after a number of craft unions, in which many coloured artisans were already represented, refused to join the APO's Federation. Their members preferred to support the Cape Federation of Labour, to which they had been affiliated since 1914. Led by a Scot, Robert Stuart, the Cape Federation held strongly to the principle of multiracial unionism.[427] It was a real blow to the doctor's hopes, and the Federation initiative fizzled out.

Even after the APO Federation failed, Dr Abdurahman retained his belief that unionisation was the way forward for coloured working people. He wrote to John X. Merriman in 1920 expressing his doubts as to whether the black population would have sufficient patience to wait for the gradual education of white public opinion. The only means

The Cape Town Parade, circa 1890. The scene of much trade as well as many demonstrations and protests. Source: the author's collection

Dr Abdurahman as a young man, possibly taken at his qualification as a doctor. Source: William Hendrickse collection

THE SOUTH AFRICAN NATIVE AND COLOURED PEOPLE'S DELEGATES IN LONDON, 1909.

The names of the Delegates shown in this photograph are as follows: In the front row, from left to right—Mr. Matt. J. Fredericks, General Secretary of the African Political Organisation; Dr. A. Abdurahman, President of the African Political Organisation; the Hon. W. P. Schreiner, K.C., C.M.G., M.L.A., Ex-Prime Minister of the Cape Colony; the Rev. Dr. W. B. Rubusana, Ph.D., President of the South African Native Convention; and Mr. Tengo-Jabavu, Editor of "Imvo" and President of the King William's Town Native Association. In the back row, from right to left, are Mr. D. J. Lenders (Kimberley), Vice-President of the African Political Organisation; Mr. Daniel Dwanya, Agent-at-Law and Representative of the South African Native Convention; Mr. J. Gerrans, representing Bechuanaland Protectorate; and Mr. Thos. M. Mapikela, General Secretary of the Orange River Colony Native Congress.

Non-racial delegation to London, 1909, led by William Schreiner.
Source: National Library of South Africa

Nellie Abdurahman and her daughters, Rosie and Cissie, in fancy dress.
Source: William Hendrickse collection

Maggie Abdurahman, Dr Abdurahman's second wife. Source: William Hendrickse collection

Dramatic Cape Times *headline during the Rand Revolt, 11 March 1922, which led to considerable suffering for the Transvaal coloured community.* Source: Cape Times, *British Library*

The APO annual conference of 1926. Source: William Hendrickse collection

Sarojini Naidu, sent to South Africa by Gandhi to support the Indian cause, welcomed in Cape Town by Dr Abdurahman and Cissie, among others. 8 April 1924. Source: Smith Archive

Dr Abdurahman as an elderly man. In this period he typically wore a fez in public. Source: William Hendrickse collection

of checking the racism of whites, he argued, was industrial action. Workers needed to use the economic strength of the black population in a society increasingly reliant on their labour in order to overcome the impediments placed on their economic progress and political influence by white racism.[428]

THE INDUSTRIAL AND COMMERCIAL WORKERS UNION

While Dr Abdurahman attempted, rather unsuccessfully, to reach out to the coloured working class, others were considerably more effective. Beginning in the Cape Town docks, Clements Kadalie managed to establish the Industrial and Commercial Workers Union (ICU) in January 1919. Kadalie, born in British Nyasaland (Malawi), soon achieved spectacular union growth. Abdurahman was an early supporter of the ICU, sitting on a platform with Kadalie at a meeting called to protest against the high cost of living on 21 November 1919.[429] Kadalie spoke first, attacking attempts by General Hertzog of the National Party to create divisions between African and coloured workers. How will they make progress if they are divided? he asked, to applause. The doctor, supporting Kadalie, said he had never believed in such divisions. He urged workers to organise themselves. 'It was the unskilled labourer who was the backbone of the country, not the farmer, who is the biggest parasite the world has ever known,' a sentiment greeted with applause.

The ICU came to real prominence with a strike in the Cape Town docks on 17 December 1919. 'Between twelve and thirteen hundred natives and coloured labourers employed at the Cape Town Docks suddenly struck work yesterday morning,' reported the *Cape Times*.[430] Called jointly by the ICU and the syndicalist Industrial Workers of Africa (IWA), it was a protest against low wages. The strike continued the following day with about a thousand workers holding a mass meeting on the Parade. On 23 December it was reported that the government's patience with the strikers was exhausted, and urged them to return to work. A day later police and troops were deployed. On Christmas Day the *Cape Times* carried a story about strikers being evicted from Ndabeni location. Finally, on 27 December, it was reported that 'a fair number' of labourers had returned to work and on the 28th the strike committee called the action off.[431]

The resolution of the strike was partly the work of Dr Abdurahman. He chaired a meeting in the City Hall which heard from a 'native deputation consisting of the I.W.A.' (a purely African labour organisation) and the South African Native National Congress (soon to become the ANC) together with Kadalie and other members of the ICU representing the strikers.[432] After 'a very lengthy discussion', which began at 7.30 on the Saturday evening, an agreement was thrashed out. Z.R. Mahabane, president of the Congress, agreed to call the strike off on condition that a conference was held 'at the earliest possible date' to discuss the pay of coloured and African labourers with the City Council, the Harbour Administration, the Chamber of Commerce and a number of unions. The strikers were only reluctantly persuaded to go back to work after the promise of a conference was conveyed to them.

Speaking in Claremont Town Hall on 12 January 1920, Dr Abdurahman attacked the white unions, saying they had 'let down' the African and coloured workers who participated in the strike. He said the authorities did not care 'a button' for black wages.[433] Kadalie, who also spoke at the meeting, complained that white workers had 'deserted' them. He then continued with an ill-concealed dig at Dr Abdurahman, declaring: 'he had not received support from the leaders of coloured people either.' This public criticism must have stung. Dr Abdurahman responded: 'the last speaker had forgotten to say that before the natives at the docks had gone on strike they had not consulted the leaders or the spokesmen of the coloured people. As long as there were Europeans leading the strike,[434] they would not, as coloured people, associate with it or throw in their lot with it, when they had not been invited to do so.' Dr Abdurahman went on to call for the unity of the 'coloured races' and for their organisation, for without this they would remain on the 'lowest rung of the ladder'.

After declaring that the 'coloured races' and Europeans were interdependent, Abdurahman then laid out his own strategy. 'He did not say they must discard political action altogether, but he thought they would get what they desired sooner by means of industrial organisation. He said they must not follow the Europeans in all things; they must not do what Europeans had done [while striking] in Johannesburg or Durban. They must not violate constitutional authority. They wanted to use the roads and the methods which would enable them to obtain what they wanted without clashes. Gandhi had shown the way.'

Despite their differences, the APO went out of its way to work with and support the ICU.[435] The two organisations held a joint meeting to organise black women in 1920. About fifty women attended an event in Cape Town, but the initiative petered out.[436] Later that year a member of the APO executive spoke at an ICU meeting, encouraging women factory workers to join the union.[437] Dr Abdurahman also backed Kadalie when he demanded recognition from the Railways and Harbours Administration in March 1920. In October 1920 Kadalie attracted the suspicions of the police, who regarded him as a dangerous agitator. The commissioner of police suggested that his residence status should be investigated with a view to his deportation, on the grounds that he was 'engaged with certain European agitators spreading pernicious doctrines amongst the coloured persons of the Cape Province'.[438] The minister of the interior served Kadalie with a notice declaring him a prohibited immigrant. Abdurahman came to Kadalie's aid and supported an appeal against the minister's notice, which was lodged with the Immigration Board.[439] Although it was unsuccessful, it may have helped turn the tide of opinion in Kadalie's favour and the deportation was dropped.

During the 1924 general election the APO and the ICU found themselves backing rival white parties. Abdurahman continued his support for the South African Party of Smuts, while Kadalie took the extraordinary decision to back Hertzog and his hard-line National Party in alliance with the Labour Party.[440] Hertzog financed the *Worker's Herald*, the paper Kadalie had launched a year earlier. During the election campaign Abdurahman found himself again attacked by Kadalie, who accused him of being out of touch with coloured interests.

Faced with increasingly racist legislation which extended segregation between black and white and protected white labour at the expense of all other groups, the ICU turned to the APO for support. The ICU leadership participated in an APO meeting in Cape Town in 1926 opposing laws preventing Africans from taking skilled jobs on the mines.[441] Dr Abdurahman, addressing the APO conference in the same year, criticised government attempts to restrict Kadalie's movements while praising the union's use of 'constitutional and legitimate tactics'.

The ICU also decided to participate in the first Non-European Conference convened by Dr Abdurahman in Kimberley in 1927.[442] But to the doctor's annoyance, the ICU sent only an unofficial delegation, wishing to preserve its status as a purely industrial rather than a political organisation.

The ICU went on to turn its attention to the rural population of South Africa and won a huge following in the countryside. At its peak in 1927–8 the ICU claimed more than 150,000 members.[443] The majority of them were African, but there were a few thousand coloured members and even some whites. In the end Kadalie's ICU, despite being an important initiative, failed as an organisation. Beset by divisions and poor management, it split and then went into decline. Kadalie resigned in January 1929 and the ICU ceased to exist in the early 1930s.

CHAPTER TEN

Revolt on the Rand

DROUGHT, DISEASE AND DEPRESSION

The emergence of the left after the First World War had been difficult for Dr Abdurahman, but as the years progressed a far more serious threat took shape from the right. At the same time the 1920s proved to be one of the harshest decades for South Africans, imposing suffering on almost every section of the population. Drought, animal disease and pests hit farmers across the country. African farmers, already struggling with the painful consequences of the 1913 Land Act, were particularly badly affected, but so too were whites. Many former Boer fighters had been ruined by the earlier conflict: their farms razed to the ground, and their women and children sent to concentration camps, where many died. During the early twentieth century black and white poured into the cities in search of employment.[444] In the fight for jobs, race became the predominant issue. This increasingly bitter conflict – in which coloured people and supporters of the APO played little role – was to usher in a far-right alliance that was to threaten the APO's position and unleash new rivals within the coloured community.

In 1922 there was an armed insurrection on the Witwatersrand led by striking white mine workers. What had brought them out onto the streets was a decision by the Chamber of Mines, in a bid to reduce costs, to eliminate the colour bar in respect of semi-skilled work on the gold mines. Determined to maintain the colour bar, which reserved for them the best-paid skilled and semi-skilled jobs, the white miners, mostly Afrikaners, went on the offensive. They struck, supported by the Labour Party, the trade unions and the Communist Party. Drawing on their experience during the Boer War, they formed commandos and took to the streets in armed formations. Some five hundred men with weapons paraded in the suburb of Fordsburg; even more occupied the streets of Johannesburg.

On 22 March the *Cape Times* splashed a single headline across its main page: 'Civil War on the Rand.'[445] It was not far from the truth; the revolt was the closest thing South Africa has seen to a revolution. What had begun as a mining dispute began moving towards a full-blown insurrection. The Smuts government brought in army units from across the Union and some fifteen thousand troops were mobilised.[446] The miners were attacked with artillery and tanks and even bombed from the air. Hundreds of white miners were killed and thousands were detained before the revolt was broken.[447] Three of the leaders of the revolt were hanged in Pretoria Central Prison. They went to their deaths singing the socialist anthem, the 'Red Flag'.[448] While the white miners were being crushed, the black miners did what the whites had done to them in the past: they continued to go to work, allowing the mines to continue operating. Little wonder that there was no love lost between black and white miners. There were even reports of African miners stoning strikers and of whites responding with violence.[449]

The small coloured population of the Transvaal found themselves caught between these groups. Coloured workers in the Transvaal had been under attack from organised labour for many years. From the 1890s, when white workers began organising on the Witwatersrand, the unions were determined not to include African, Indian or coloured workers in their ranks. White unions were at the forefront of attempts to introduce segregation and a 'White South Africa' policy.[450]

Despite these efforts coloured workers gradually supplanted skilled and semi-skilled whites in the painting and paper-hanging trades, among others. As the competition increased, the white unions stepped up their attempts to restrict the employment of coloured workers. They met with some success. In 1911 the Johannesburg municipality decided to give building approval for plans only if white skilled labour was employed.[451] Some pragmatic union leaders did attempt to introduce in the Transvaal the Cape policy of 'equal pay for equal work', which meant the incorporation of skilled coloured workers into the union movement, but this was strongly resisted by most organised labour.

Matters came to a head in February 1919 when white building workers on the Rand and Pretoria went out on strike for a reduction in the length of the working week.[452] The action lasted for three months – among the longest strikes in South Africa's history. Coloured artisans came out on strike as well, although it is not clear whether this was voluntary or enforced. Their families were soon reduced to near starvation, since they were without any trade union funding or support.

Dr Abdurahman attempted to come to their aid. He called a meeting in Cape Town to 'protest against the actions of the white Trade Unions of the Rand'.[453] He described the white union policy as 'terrorism' since it refused to admit coloured workers to membership, yet forced them to cease working and then left them destitute. 'If any disgraceful act had ever been done in this country by white men, this surely was the worst. It was worse than the Germans would have done.' Abdurahman continued: 'This suffering of the coloured people was only part of the persecution going on for some time in Johannesburg' by white trade unionists, 'whose underlying spirit was to keep the coloured man out of the unions'. It was a stinging rebuke. This bitterness towards the Transvaal's white unions formed the backdrop to the APO's response to the Rand Revolt of 1922.

For Dr Abdurahman, the alliance between the white miners, the Labour Party and the Communist Party represented a real threat to the coloured people. His fears were soon borne out, as they were caught up in the interracial clashes during the Rand Revolt. These were fuelled by rumours that '5,000 coloured men are coming from Cape Town and Kimberley to replace white workers in the mines'.[454] A letter was read out at a meeting of white strikers held in the Johannesburg City Hall in February 1922, allegedly written by the president of the Chamber of Mines to Dr Abdurahman. The letter purported to say that thousands of coloured people could be recruited in Cape Town to take over mining jobs, 'for which purpose the colour bar must be removed'.[455] The letter was a forgery, but it only stoked the conflict.

The *APO* reported on an 'orgy of mob lawlessness which has culminated … in the killing and wounding of twenty-five Native and Coloured workers by gangs of hooligan strikers'.[456] Dr Abdurahman stepped up his protests. Interviewed by the *Cape Argus*, he warned that 'Non-European people' were not being fairly dealt with and said that there would be renewed agitation against the colour bar. 'If the movement is not successful, they will cease to look to Parliament for redress for their grievances, but will organise industrially,' he told the paper.[457]

On 10 March the *Cape Times*'s main story led with the headlines 'Johannesburg under the Red Flag: The shooting down of Natives continues'.[458] At the same time Dr Abdurahman received a telegram from the Non-European Auxiliary Section in Ventersdorp, Johannesburg, calling on him to raise in parliament the matter of the 'indiscriminate shooting of Coloured people in Johannesburg'.[459] Abdurahman immediately wrote to Smuts, the prime minister, calling for the imposition of martial law to prevent a repetition of the outrages. Smuts agreed and martial law was declared, although it is not clear whether he was responding to Abdurahman's appeal or other pressures. Smuts also replied in a letter, saying he hoped that 'all sections of the community' would work together to end the lawlessness.

THE POLITICAL FALLOUT

The Rand Revolt was finally put down, at a terrible cost in terms of lives lost. It did, however, produce a unity of sorts between working-class whites, irrespective of whether they were English or Afrikaans speakers. White miners had put aside the differences of the Anglo-Boer War and fought side by side against the mine owners. This relationship was transformed into an electoral alliance that was sealed in April 1923.[460] The Labour Party leader, Colonel Frederick Cresswell, and the National Party leader, General J.B.M. Hertzog, signed a pact to fight the following year's election on a common platform.[461]

The pact between Labour and Hertzog was a severe blow to Dr Abdurahman, since it brought forth new competitors for coloured support. He was already on the back foot and the APO was in decline. His brand of radical political rhetoric, combined with support for the

Smuts government and the South African Party, had failed to deliver significant benefits for the coloured people. His protests and pressure had managed to win some improvements in the education of their children. He had also been able to take up specific issues in the area of Cape Town that he represented, District Six, but on wider political questions there had been little, if any, progress. The coloured people still held the vote in the Cape, but had not made headway anywhere else in the country, and the movement was clearly running out of steam. As Gavin Lewis argues: 'In the 1920s ... the APO under Abdurahman found it had lost the initiative in organised Coloured politics.'[462] By 1923 this decline was evident for all to see. Funds from branches fell and the party was forced to shut down its publications. Its paper – the *APO* – closed, as did the *Educational Journal*, which it ran.[463] These were dark days for the party.

The 1923 conference of the APO was attended by just 44 branches, down from 60 or 70 a few years earlier. At the conference Dr Abdurahman made a powerful condemnation of the colour bar, alluding to the previous year's Rand Revolt.[464] 'The colour bar has cleft South Africa into two irreconcilable camps. One lords it over the other; and the one deems itself secure and happy, the other becoming daily more resentful and revengeful. This state of affairs cannot continue indefinitely; but it has to continue but little longer, when a rude awakening will startle the community.' And he continued: 'We hear much about the wickedness of capitalists, and to combat which there must be solidarity of the workers; but alas! The greatest exploiters of Coloured labour on the Rand are the white workers, and their solidarity has resulted in our being kept down in unskilled work: a position which we should not tolerate much longer.' This call to arms and to labour solidarity came in the wake of the APO's unsuccessful attempts to organise coloured workers. In reality it cut little ice.

HERTZOG'S COLOURED POLICY

The APO's declining fortunes were the spur for others to seek to win their constituency away from them. In the electoral politics of South Africa the coloured vote was still valuable and could be a decisive factor in elections in several constituencies. For the National Party, coloured voters came to represent an attractive prize.

The National Party had been formed in 1913 by General Hertzog after he led a walkout from the Louis Botha cabinet over the question of Afrikaner reconciliation with the English. By that stage Abdurahman had gradually moved the APO from a position of neutrality towards white parties to one in which they backed Botha and Smuts and their South African Party at elections.[465] It was not that the doctor was oblivious to their faults: he called the South African Party the 'dop' and 'strop' party (the wine tot and lash party), accusing them of being interested only in cheap coloured labour for the farms and mines.[466] With the emergence of the National Party, Abdurahman recognised it as a major threat facing his people and acted accordingly. This meant he remained silent on some important issues of this period, including the Bulhoek Massacre of 24 May 1921, when police opened fire on a group of religious African 'Israelites' who refused to leave the commonage near Queenstown where they were illegally squatting. Around 200 people were killed, more than 100 were wounded and 141 were arrested.[467] Criticised for his silence, Abdurahman replied that an attack on the Smuts government would only have been to the advantage of the hard-line Afrikaner nationalists.[468]

Abdurahman reserved particular venom for Hertzog and the National Party, whose programme called for the total segregation of black people. He feared that the traditional racial attitudes and policies of the Transvaal and the Free State would undermine the moderate liberalism of the Cape. But the APO's backing for the South African Party was not universally approved, either within his own party or within the wider coloured community. Indeed, there were conservative elements among coloured people who were prepared to ally themselves with the Afrikaners of the National Party. Abdurahman's own instincts were always in the opposite direction: to seek ties with Africans and Indians wherever possible. His radicalism in this respect, and the APO's determination to create links with other black parties, rankled with conservative coloureds. They saw themselves as a cut above the African population. It was to men like these that Afrikaner nationalists turned in the wake of the First World War, to strengthen their own political position. It was this strand of coloured opinion to which Hertzog appealed.

Hermann Giliomee, in analysing Hertzog's approach, concludes that for nearly two decades after its establishment, the National Party was 'remarkably ambiguous' about the coloured people:

> It was in this period predominantly a party for lower-income Afrikaners. Initially the leadership toyed with the idea of building a racially inclusive party based on the common threat white and coloured workers faced from ultra-cheap black migrant labour ... Hertzog saw coloureds as born and educated in the midst of white civilization, particularly among the Dutch-speaking Afrikaners with whom they shared a language and interests. Coloureds belonged with whites politically and economically. Socially, however, they had to accept segregation. As he phrased it: 'The place of the educated Coloured is under his own people ... He must serve his own people.'[469]

This was a policy that was not without appeal to coloured voters. In 1915 a National Party candidate in Paarl – Bruckner de Villiers – promised that if he was elected he would oppose any measure detrimental to coloured interests. Some APO branches supported him, until Dr Abdurahman reminded them that Hertzog was from the Free State, where coloured people still had to carry passes.[470] 'Mr de Villiers is a good candidate, but if you support him, you support the National Party,' the doctor explained, 'and if you support the National Party, you might as well vote for the Germans, who will deal with you as shown in this picture'[471] – here he appended a gruesome photograph of German executions of Herero people in German South West Africa in the early part of the century. The argument was somewhat convoluted, but it did the trick. De Villiers lost Paarl by 813 votes, and the votes of the coloured population proved decisive here.

The outcome of the election was a blow for the National Party, but they were not deterred. In early 1919 they renewed their appeal to coloured people. D.F. Malan, Cape leader of the party and editor of *Die Burger*, invited a number of coloured politicians, including N.R. Veldsman, to a meeting at which the Nationalists laid out their stall. Malan promised them 'equality for every Cape Coloured man if the Nationalists come to power', in return for their political support.[472] There were other inducements, including jobs in National Party-run businesses and promises of government posts if the party came to power. A new newspaper, *The Clarion*, was launched as the voice of coloured supporters of the National Party. The paper set about attacking the South African Party, claiming it was dominated by foreign capitalists and imperialists and aimed to increase immigration so that they could oust coloured and white Afrikaner workers 'with a flood of English scum'.[473] Dr Abdurahman retaliated, accusing the paper of being no more than a mouthpiece for the National Party and written and edited by whites. He was right: *The Clarion* was printed at *Die Burger*'s offices and was controlled by Cape Nationalists.

Hertzog continued his offensive. At the 1919 National Party conference in the Free State he spelled out his policy towards the coloured people.[474] Total segregation was to be imposed on Africans, but coloureds should be given economic and political equality with whites. Only social equality would be denied them, although he recognised that they shared with Afrikaners a common history, language and loyalty to South Africa. The coloureds, Hertzog argued, should have a status distinct from both whites and Africans, as they had had in the old days of the republican Orange Free State.[475]

Encouraged by what Hertzog offered, Veldsman and a group of other conservatives decided on 27 October 1919 to form a new party, the United Afrikaner League.[476] Backed by *The Clarion*, they supported a 'moderate' political position. This included accepting that they would fight for coloured rights without attempting to extend the Cape franchise to all black people in South Africa since these were demands they knew 'will not be conceded'.[477] The paper suggested that coloured voters should support Labour candidates in constituencies 'where the Africander is not contesting'. *The Clarion* turned up the pressure, attacking Dr Abdurahman's Muslim faith and attempting to smear his reputation by suggesting that he had Jewish support. The doctor was, in their view, an alien both in his religion and his origins. In an appeal to anti-Semites and racists, it declared it was wrong 'that Jerusalem should shake hands with Calcutta in Cape Town'.[478]

Dr Abdurahman and the *APO* hit back. They attacked Hertzog as 'the narrowest, most virulent, and most offensive of all the enemies of the Black races'. The Labour Party was also criticised for having led people astray in the 1922 Revolt. The APO urged 'Coloured fools who have placed great faith in white trade unionists' to take note of what had happened. As it turned out, the United Afrikaner League failed to deliver votes for the National Party in the 1921 election and *The Clarion* soon ceased publication. In place of the League the National Party established another party in 1924, the Afrikaanse Nasionale Bond.[479] Against this backdrop, and shortly after Smuts called the 1924 general election, Hertzog formally announced what he described as a 'New Deal for Coloureds'.

This 'New Deal' was again predicated upon imposing segregation on the African population, while promising that coloureds would be treated rather differently. Yet even this promise was vitiated. Although coloureds shared with many Afrikaners a common culture and values, they were to be regarded as distinct from the white community.[480] At the same time, they would receive some benefits. Under Hertzog's plan, coloureds would be protected from having their wages undercut by competition from African labourers by means of an extended version of the 'civilised labour' policy. They were even promised equal treatment with whites in some respects, including the ability to raise loans from the Land Bank for coloured farm settlements. Some coloured people found this a tempting offer.

Dr Abdurahman did his best to counter the National Party's appeal, touring the countryside to call for support for Smuts and the South African Party, but it was an uphill task.[481] In the end he was unable to turn back the tide. He was jeered and heckled when he addressed meetings in the Cape Peninsula during the 1924 election. Hertzog was victorious and the National–Labour Pact government was brought into existence. Veldsman wrote a letter to Hertzog congratulating him as the new prime minister, claiming that coloured votes had played an important role in the victory.[482] For Dr Abdurahman it must have been a bitter defeat indeed. It represented the failure of his strategy of backing Smuts which the APO had followed for years. For their part, Africans saw their potential allies among coloured people peel away, won over by Hertzog's promises. As Ben Nyombolo, general secretary of the Industrial and Commercial Workers Union of Africa, remarked sadly: 'While the native is not easily bluffed, the coloured man seems to be the victim of the propaganda of the Pact.'[483]

Chapter Eleven

Fighting for the Indian community

Gandhi and Abdurahman

In 1925 Dr Abdurahman led a delegation to the Viceroy of India to ask him to intervene in South African affairs by calling for an end to the repressive legislation that the government in Pretoria was planning to impose on the Indian population. It was an unlikely venture. The Viceroy, Earl Reading, was Britain's representative in India, one of the most powerful men on earth. He ruled over some 320 million people in a territory stretching from Afghanistan to China, including what is today Pakistan. What chance was there that he would receive a delegation led by a Cape Town City councillor? And why was Dr Abdurahman leading a delegation from the South African Indian Congress?

Abdurahman had a strong relationship with Indians in Cape Town and beyond. As we have seen, there was a widespread perception that he was the grandson of slaves from Bengal. His own daughter Cissie Gool reportedly told an American visitor that her father was 'part Indian, part Malay'.[484] While it is not possible to confirm this, what is certain is that Dr Abdurahman knew, and worked closely with, many Indians in Cape Town as well as the wider Indian community across the country. He was keen to co-operate with Indians whenever the opportunity

127

arose. His warm relationship with Gandhi illustrates the point. As we have seen, Gandhi first met Dr Abdurahman in person in June 1909, on board ship bound for London, when the latter was involved in the deputation to persuade the British parliament not to allow the racial restrictions in the draft South African Union constitution.[485] Gandhi maintained contact with Dr Abdurahman throughout the work of the 1909 deputation, finally attempting to reassure the doctor of the fine work he and his colleagues had done, even though they had been unsuccessful. By this time the two men had a strong bond and regarded each other with real respect.

From then onwards, whenever Gandhi visited Cape Town he would, as a matter of course, visit his friend's home.[486] The link between the two was further cemented when Dr Abdurahman's daughter Cissie married Dr Abdul Hamid Gool in 1916.[487] Gandhi was a particular friend of the Gools, staying at the family home at 7 Buitensingel Street when he visited Cape Town in 1911. Gandhi continued to use their home as his Cape Town base until he left South Africa three years later.[488] Dr Gool was a stalwart of the Indian community in the Cape. He had qualified as a doctor in Britain in 1910 and on his return to Cape Town he became honorary joint secretary of the Cape British Indian Union, and in 1911 its president.

Through his relationships with Gandhi and Dr Gool, Dr Abdurahman had excellent links with the Indian community, both in the Cape and beyond. These were to be important in the events that unfolded next.

Gandhi's deal betrayed

The story of South Africa's Indian community dates back almost to the start of white settlement. During the period of Dutch East India Company rule, thousands of slaves were brought to the Cape from the Indian subcontinent. The next wave of Indian immigration came in the 1860s when indentured Indian labourers came to Natal to work on the sugar plantations. Later, 'free' or 'passenger' Indians arrived, mainly to work as traders and retailers, and settled in Natal and the Transvaal. Over time, white governments began to impose restrictions on them, making life increasingly intolerable for the vulnerable and largely impoverished Indian population. It was into this situation that Gandhi stepped when he arrived in Durban to settle a dispute between two Indian traders on 24 May 1893.[489] After resolving the case, Gandhi made South Africa his home for the next seventeen years and gradually established himself as the leader of the Indian community. In a series of remarkable campaigns he fought government attempts to further restrict Indian rights in Natal and the Transvaal. His basic appeal was a simple one: South African Indians were part of the British Empire and as such had all the rights of British citizens. Why was the Imperial parliament not enforcing these rights and protecting all British citizens across the Empire? It was an entirely legitimate question, but it came up against entrenched interests, particularly of the whites who had settled in the colonies.

Gandhi fought many campaigns on behalf of South Africa's Indians, sometimes appealing to London, sometimes confronting the South African authorities, and frequently calling on Indians in India to back him. In 1912, faced with fresh restrictions on Indian immigration introduced by Smuts, Gandhi invited the leading member of the Indian National Congress, Gopal Krishna Gokhale, to visit South Africa.[490] The Botha government decided to receive Gokhale with courtesy and on 22 October 1912 he arrived in Cape Town to a tremendous reception. On the platform was Dr Abdurahman, who made a speech welcoming Gokhale to the city.[491] Gandhi was there too, as were his local hosts, the Gools, who transported Gokhale to their home in a procession of fifty carriages.

Gokhale's visit was meant to end the troubles of South African Indians; but it did not. Matters came to a head in 1913–14 when Gandhi managed to mobilise Indian labourers on Natal's coal mines and sugar plantations to take on the authorities. It was a do-or-die confrontation which Gandhi narrowly won.[492] Dr Abdurahman drew inspiration from the extraordinary courage and determination the Indians had shown and from Gandhi's policy of non-violent resistance to oppression. In his presidential address to the APO's 1913 conference, he said: 'If a handful of Indians in a matter of conscience can so firmly resist what they consider injustice, what could the Coloured races not do if they were to adopt this practice of Passive Resistance?'[493]

With Gandhi's fight for Indian rights finally concluded, he left

South Africa for India on 17 July 1914. He believed he had secured a pledge from Smuts and the South African government that his community's rights would be respected. This became known as the Smuts–Gandhi deal. It gave Indians some of the assurances they had been looking for. Gandhi left to join the fight for Indian independence. He was seen off from Cape Town by a crowd of well-wishers, including Dr Abdurahman, who delivered a speech praising him for what he had achieved.[494]

Sarojini Naidu: 'Wild revolutionary'

As the years passed, the Smuts–Gandhi deal came under increasing strain. Competition between Indian and European traders and the growth in the Indian population led whites to renew their familiar complaints about unfair business competition and their belief that they were being 'swamped'.[495] In 1924 the minister of the interior, Patrick Duncan, introduced the Class Areas Bill in parliament, which proposed compulsory residential and trading segregation for Indians throughout South Africa. While Duncan's Bill was being considered, Gandhi issued a statement pointing out that Smuts had promised him that no anti-Indian legislation would be enacted in future. Gandhi added that his 'compromise' with Smuts had been reached with the full knowledge and approval of the Indian and Imperial governments and that the proposed Bill would violate their agreement.[496] Meanwhile, P.K. Naidoo, secretary of the Transvaal British Indian Association, who had worked closely with Gandhi during his time in South Africa, wrote to the Indian National Congress requesting that they send Sarojini Naidu to South Africa to assist the Indian campaign to try to halt the Bill.[497] Sarojini Naidu, poet, feminist and a senior Indian nationalist, was an excellent choice. On being informed that Smuts was a powerful opponent, she replied: 'undoubtedly General Smuts is a strong man, but he will be confronted by a woman who is not afraid because she has the support of a united India behind her'.[498]

Naidu travelled to Africa in 1924 to review the position of Indians in Kenya and then went on to South Africa. Arriving there in March 1924, she went from public meeting to public meeting, calling on Indians to 'fight the unjust position. Don't accept a position of inferiority.' Naidu said she hoped that it would not be 'necessary to remind the people of the lessons of passive resistance'.[499] At the Cape Town City Hall on the evening of 18 March, she was received by five MPs, the mayor and Dr Abdurahman. It was the doctor who introduced her to the audience.[500] In what was described as 'an eloquent speech', she said that she did not want a 'settlement, but justice … The brotherhood of those who suffered was immutable.'[501]

The *Cape Times* did not take kindly to what she had to say. The paper attacked Naidu's speech, accusing her of 'wild oratory' and 'emotional, ill-balanced harangues' as well as 'revolutionary and unlicensed talk', and describing her visit as a 'mission of stirring up mischief'.[502] Cissie Gool, Dr Abdurahman's daughter, was so incensed when she read what the paper had reported that she leapt to Naidu's defence. 'You are absolutely wrong when you say that her "motives underlying all her speeches are to raise prejudice and to damage relations of white and black in South Africa".' She declared that Naidu had 'passed through the country from East Africa to Cape Town setting the country aflame with truth, touching the hearts of all with her inspiring message of truth'. This had given 'courage to the oppressed' and been a 'warning to Europeans'. Privately, Cissie Gool insisted that Naidu come and stay with her and her husband during her time in Cape Town, and the two women spent a good deal of time in each other's company.

On 1 April Naidu attended the second reading of the Class Areas Bill in parliament in the company of Dr Abdurahman. Her presence, according to *Indian Opinion*, seemed to make a difference. Naidu was also present at the South African Indian Congress conference held in Durban between 21 and 25 April 1924. The conference delegates adopted Naidu's suggestion of a round table conference between the Indian and South African governments and representatives of their movement to resolve the 'Indian question', and began pressing for it to be held. Naidu left to return to India on 22 May, but not before declaring that she felt a strong affection for Africa and its people. 'My body goes back to India but that part of me that belongs to you remains with you, your inalienable gift and possession.'[503] She was true to her word, continuing to do what she could for South Africans. Dr Abdurahman, encouraged by Naidu's visit and always keen to foster unity between communities, established a consultative committee consisting of the APO, the Cape Indian Council and the Industrial and Commercial Workers Union.[504]

Discussions with the Smuts administration about Indian grievances ended when he lost the election in June 1924. The change of government saw the Nationalists and Labour taking control. The new minister of the interior, Dr D.F. Malan, later the first National Party prime minister, introduced the Areas Reservation and Immigration and Registration (further Amendment) Bill, which was even more repressive than the one Duncan had initiated.[505] Not only did it propose a system of segregation, severely restricting Indian trading and occupational rights, but it described Indians as aliens and was designed to reduce the Indian population to an 'irreducible minimum' largely through repatriation.[506] Indians were furious, regarding it as a betrayal of previous government assurances. Fellow Indians across the globe shared their concerns: 'It created consternation and anger throughout the whole Indian world and for the first time the treatment of Indians in South Africa became a decisive factor in Indian nationalism and British–Indian relations.'[507]

Appeals and deputations to Dr Malan proved ineffective. The minister told the South African Indian Congress that he was not prepared to deviate from the principles of the Bill.[508] In August 1925 a mass meeting of Indians in Durban discussed the possibility of appealing to Britain.[509] 'This Bill', said the chairman, Shaik Hamid, 'is a challenge to the entire Asiatic world. To 350,000,000 Indians; to 40,000,000 Japanese; and to 450,000,000 Chinese. Is Asia prepared to take up the challenge? I tell you that Europe and Asia will be set ablaze by this Bill, introduced in South Africa, but bearing seeds of conflict that will be waged in Europe and in Asia.'

In late 1925, at the end of their tether, the South African Indian Congress decided to send a delegation to India to appeal to the Viceroy. They did so despite a telegram from the Viceroy asking them to 'defer or cancel' their proposed visit because the Indian government was sending its own deputation to South Africa to ascertain the facts. The South African Indian Congress refused to back down and turned to Dr Abdurahman to lead the delegation.[510] In a telegram dated 2 September 1925, Moulvi Abdul Karim, the president of the Natal Indian Association, informed the Viceroy that a mass meeting had been held on 31 August which 'strongly protested' against the 'Asiatic

Bill'.[511] Their case would be put to the South African government, but if this was unsuccessful, 'a deputation will leave for India and England to pray for support'.

The Viceroy, Lord Reading, chose not to resist their suggestion. He replied on 9 September, saying, 'If you decide to send a deputation to India the Government of India will be pleased to receive it.'[512] On 23 November Karim telegraphed the Viceroy, confirming that the delegation was indeed coming, and that the Natal Indian Association 'has the honour to appoint Dr Abdur Rahman M.P.C., to state the Association's case before the Indian Government independently of the case stated by him as spokesman for the South African Indian Congress deputation'.[513] Others who joined Dr Abdurahman were Sorabjee Rustomjee, Advocate J.W. Godfrey, Amod Bayat, V.S.C. Pather and A.A. Mirza.[514] Gandhi enthusiastically welcomed the announcement, describing the situation of South African Indians as 'the question of the hour'.[515]

On 12 November 1925, Dr Abdurahman wrote to E.S. Covaadia of Johannesburg. 'My Dear Friend,' he began, explaining that he had been asked to head the deputation. 'I feel that I cannot stand back and must accept the call on behalf of the Indian community. The deputation needs some strengthening and I am sure that my inclusion in it having the wholehearted support of the Conference will be of some service to all of you. The sacrifice on my part, I need hardly say, is very great but I will have to throw up everything and go.'[516] In an article published shortly thereafter, Abdurahman explained his reasons for accepting the role more fully:

> My reason for going is because I think everyone should help to solve the many difficult problems we – Indians, natives and coloured – have in South Africa. Being a South African myself, I am naturally anxious that the Indian problem should be settled in such a way that we can appeal to India and the whole of Asia, as well as to Great Britain, when any difference of opinion arises. South Africa should not ignore the opinion of the East. Our main object is to see if India cannot still use her powers, through England, to bring about a round-table conference in South Africa. That is what we desire most of all.[517]

The next day, a simple report was printed in the papers: 'Going East,' read the headline: 'Dr. Abdurahman, who left for Durban yesterday on his way to India, was given an enthusiastic farewell at the railway station by members of the Indian community. Large wreaths of flowers were hung around his neck, and for ten minutes before the train left he was busy shaking hands with grave, bearded men in fezzes, and replying to congratulations.'[518]

The Abdurahman delegation in India

Sarojini Naidu, in consultation with Gandhi, arranged an extensive tour for the delegates.[519]

The highlights of the visit were their reception by the Viceroy and their appeal to the fortieth session of the Indian National Congress, but there were many other events they attended. These included rallies backing their cause in Bombay, Madras, Delhi, Lahore and Calcutta. The deputation was not only welcomed, but they made an excellent impression. 'Dr Rahman who is a tall, slim, and graceful personality,' wrote the correspondent for the Indian *Sunday Times*, 'and Mr Sorabji who is extremely suave, ingratiating, and polite, were taken to "Lorangs"[520] where they are staying during their visit to Lahore.'[521] The delegation received support from a range of movements, including the Indian National Liberal Federation, the All-India Khilafat Conference, the All-India Non-Brahmin Congress and the All-India Muslim League.[522]

An article in the *Sunday Times*, entitled 'A clear duty', gives a flavour of the reception the delegates received.

It is with pleasure that we take this opportunity of welcoming to the Punjab, Dr Abdul Rehman and Mr Sorabjee members of the South African Deputation who come into our midst on a mission close to the heart of every Indian. Wherever Dr Rehman and his colleagues have been, and by this time they have practically covered the length and breadth of the country, they have met with unanimous warmth and welcome from the people of India. On the question of South Africa a singular unity of opinion has been demonstrated: much as the country is divided on other issues the issue of the position and status of Indian nationals in the dominions is one upon which all parties are agreed.

As in other parts of the country the South African deputation will, we are sure, receive demonstrations equally sincere and affectionate from Punjab. Dr Rehman and Mr Sorabjee come to Lahore after their triumphs in Bombay, Madras and Delhi.[523]

Headlines in other papers reflected similar sentiments: 'The last ditch: Indians shall not yield. Motherland's honour at stake. Delhi's protest against S. African tyranny.'[524] The *Sunday Times*, reflecting on what Dr Abdurahman had said to a Bombay newspaper, got to the heart of the issue: 'If the Empire has any reality it must be based on practical, not fictitious equality and upon common rights of citizenship. As early as half a century ago Lord Salisbury laid down the principle that "Indian settlers will be in all respects free men, with the privileges no whit inferior to those of any other of His Majesty's subjects resident in the colonies".'[525]

In December 1925 the Indian National Congress was holding its annual congress in Cawnpore (Kanpur), presided over by Sarojini Naidu. Attending this event, with its vast number of delegates, must have stayed in the minds of the South Africans for the rest of their days. The conference was held in a 'huge tent, large enough to house a four-ring circus, and made of cloth woven on hand-looms … Flags hung everywhere, thousands of them, red, green and white. The red stripe was for Hindus, the green for Moslems and the white for Christians, Parsis and others. Fifteen thousand Indians waited there in Cawnpore, in that tent, for the opening of the fortieth Indian National Congress – fifteen thousand radical patriots prepared to renew their campaign for national rights under the leadership of a woman.'[526]

Naidu used the occasion to make a passionate appeal on behalf of the South Africans:

In the whole chronicle of civilized legislation there has never been so cruel and relentless an outrage against humanity as is deliberately embodied in the anti-Asiatic Bill, which is calculated to exterminate the Indian community from South Africa. Shall we not send across the seas a loving and ready response to their heart-rending cry for succour, and, through their ambassadors whom we welcome today, offer to our harassed and afflicted brothers in South Africa the assurance that India stands behind their courageous struggle to vindicate their inherent civic and human rights against the onslaught of such terrific injustice and oppression?[527]

Gandhi proposed a resolution declaring the Bill a breach of the agreement he had reached with Smuts and he promised wholehearted support for Indian resistance in South Africa.[528] He said that the Bill was the result of 'the jealous fears of white traders, who, afraid of an Asiatic combination that might damage their trade, had devised this means of disposing of the Indians who had completed their terms of indenture and are no longer needed'.[529] Then Dr Abdurahman spoke, endorsing what Gandhi had said. An observer remarked: 'He was bitterness personified. "If you had some battle-ships today," he shouted, as he banged the lone chair, "if you had your army, a little handful of so-called whites who were vomited forth on the shores of Africa from the slums of Europe would not have dared do what they are doing today."'[530] It was perhaps the most vitriolic condemnation of the suffering whites had inflicted on Indians and other people of colour that the doctor ever delivered. It certainly did the trick: Gandhi's resolution passed without opposition. The session also demanded a round table conference to deal with the South African Indian question and called on the British government in London to withhold its assent to the Malan Bill.

By this time the delegation's cause had won over the Indian people. The mood was clearly in their favour and the British recognised the strength of their case even before the Abdurahman delegation arrived in the subcontinent. In February 1925 the Viceroy wrote to the Secretary of State for India, Lord Birkenhead, after receiving an Indian deputation about the plight of South African Indians. In a frank private letter the Viceroy described the problem as 'one of the most embarrassing and difficult problems before us … It is easier for us to keep calm than for the Indians who resent deeply the stigma of inferiority impressed upon the Indian peoples.'[531]

The Viceroy received Dr Abdurahman and his colleagues on 19 December 1925.[532] They were fortunate that Lord Reading was their interlocutor. He was a former Liberal member of parliament with a legal background. He was sympathetic to Indian concerns and happy to receive Gandhi, Nehru and other nationalist leaders. He had done what he could to mend fences, visiting Amritsar – the scene of the April 1919 massacres, one of the worst incidents during Britain's long colonial rule of India – as a gesture of reconciliation.

When the delegation met Lord Reading, Abdurahman made it clear that if the relationship between India and the British Empire was submissive and the Empire allowed her 'sons to suffer', he hoped the relationship would be changed 'so that India can speak, as she ought to speak, like a free man and say we will not allow our sons to be humiliated any longer because we have got the power to say so'.[533] The delegation then submitted to the Viceroy a prepared statement in which they impressed on him the urgency of a round table conference with the South Africans and the need for an intervention by Britain. If that failed, they argued, the Viceroy should appeal to the League of Nations on their behalf.[534]

Lord Reading replied to Abdurahman's speech in detail, outlining the number of occasions on which the Indian government had intervened in South Africa on behalf of its Indian population since 1881. He pointed out that it had sent a deputation to South Africa, which had made representations to the government in November 1925, before the Viceroy had even known that Abdurahman and his colleagues were coming. Lord Reading accepted Abdurahman's stress on the need for a round table conference to try to address the issues. He pointed out that South Africa was a sovereign dominion and would make its own decisions, but at the same time he accepted that Britain had a responsibility towards Indians living in South Africa. 'We have reason to know that our right to make representations and be heard is not disputed by the Union Government,' the Viceroy said.[535]

The delegation made a considerable impression on Lord Reading and he was particularly impressed by Abdurahman. The same day, 19 December, he sent a telegram to London addressed to the Earl of Birkenhead.

Private & Personal. I received Dr Abdur Rahaman and the deputation of Indians from South Africa today. Dr Rahaman put forward powerful and well-argued statements of disabilities of humiliating description in social, political and economic life which have been imposed on Indians by legislation in Union and of apprehension not without ground that contemplated Asiatic legislation will render position of Indians wholly impossible ... Much stress was laid by Dr Rahaman on favourable treatment of white element in population composed in many cases of races not born in or loyal to British Empire at expense of Indians born in and loyal to British connection ... I found the position very difficult. I am deeply impressed by the humiliations to which Indians in South Africa are subjected, and by the gravity of the implications of the projected legislation which will be hurried through the second reading stage in the new year.[536]

The Viceroy followed this up with a series of further letters and telegrams to London. All had the same purpose – to stress just how important an issue the South African situation was in India, while explaining that he understood that the South African government had the right to act without interference. Lord Reading discussed whether or not to send a deputation to meet the South African government.[537] The Viceroy was particularly concerned that the situation might undermine the standing of Britain in the eyes of Indians. The telegram, sent on 8 January 1926, summed up Lord Reading's position.

Private & Personal. My Government are sending you an important telegram on the above subject and on the impending Anti-Asiatic Legislation. The situation is serious and there is urgent need for action. We ... have repeatedly condemned and repudiated the principle of the Bill, but the Union Government are forcing on the second reading stage. It has been stated openly by Dr Malan that the object of the Bill is to stigmatise Indians as an alien element in population of Union and to reduce their numbers in Union. The Union Government have refused Conference with the Government of India on the positions of Indians generally and principle of the Bill, though they offered to confer on concrete questions if the purpose of Conference was restricted to securing effective measures to obtain considerable reduction of Indian population. We could not accept a Conference with latter object ... The Bill will, if the principle is accepted, be used to drive Indians out of the Dominion. They have already been subjected in all directions to special disabilities. Our only hope, though I realise the difficulties of His Majesty's Government, is that His Majesty's Government may secure postponement of second reading while principle is discussed.

The Imperial aspect of the Bill is serious. Indians feel that Imperial connection is of no use in protecting them, as representations from the Government of India are ignored by Union Government and His Majesty's Government have, so far, not secured any alleviation of the hostile measure directed against them in Union. It is further said that, in this direction, present Government has not made any attempt. They feel that partnership of India in Empire merely means inclusion of Indians in Empire on inferior standing which offers no advantages or privileges. Gandhi has reminded them that over a similar question when it affected White people, we went to war with Transvaal. Deputation from South Africa now in India have repeatedly alleged that it is better to be born outside Empire, as aliens and in late war even enemy subjects are admitted to privileges and excused from disabilities in Union, while latter are heaped on Indians with a view to drive them from Dominion.

A few days later, Lord Reading explained to the Secretary of State that he intended to address the opening of India's Legislative Assembly on 20 January and proposed to explain that he had received Dr Abdurahman's deputation and that he, as Viceroy, was fully aware of the depth of feeling in India about these issues.[538]

Meanwhile, in Britain, concern about the plight of the South African Indians was being raised in parliament. Lord Olivier, a former Labour Secretary of State for India, spoke on 24 February 1926, describing Malan's Bill as 'oppressive and repressive legislation that is continually being exercised against Indians'. He said that the proposed law was 'entirely repugnant not only in its foundation principles to the idea of the British Empire but also to statutory rights and common law rights under which Indians have settled in South Africa'.[539] His speech was not well received by the British government. The Earl of Birkenhead wrote a private letter to the Viceroy, Lord Reading, on 26 February 1926 describing the proposal that the British should veto the Malan Bill as a 'very dangerous doctrine'.[540] It would involve one part of the Empire intervening in the affairs of another – not something London was prepared to countenance.

The Abdurahman deputation had made its mark. As Sarojini Naidu put it, they had pleaded their cause 'with earnestness and eloquence, and ... kindled a living flame of love, sorrow and indignation in the hearts of your kindred here'.[541] The trip had been long and difficult, and it had taken a toll on the doctor physically and politically. On 22 April 1926, once back in Cape Town, he wrote in affectionate terms to Sarojini from his office at 119 Loop Street:

> At last I have a few minutes to write to you. Of course I am safe and quite well, but, needless to say, as a result of the very violent speeches which I indulged in while in India a storm of criticism awaits me.
>
> In the Provincial Council the leader of the Nationalist Party opposed a motion that leave be granted to me for the session, his reason being that my utterances in India justified the Council's refusing me leave. However, the matter was postponed till the Monday when I turned up in time to save my seat.
>
> Now I must thank you for the very many kindnesses that you showed me personally while in India. The Indians here will never appreciate how much you personally contributed to whatever the deputation has been able to achieve in rousing public opinion.[542]

It is interesting that Dr Abdurahman acknowledged the strength of the speeches he made and that he knew what trouble it might cause him, including, possibly, losing his seat in the Provincial Council because of his absence. In the event this did not take place.

On returning to South Africa, he visited Durban to report back to the Indian community. Ismail Meer recalls that on 24 March 1926 the delegation was 'greeted triumphantly' at the cinema Rawat's Bio on Victoria Street.[543] Dr Abdurahman called for black unity, as he had done many times previously, declaring that anyone who accepted the proposed legislation was 'a fool and a traitor to his own country ... To my mind, there should be no division between black and white, and the sooner we make common cause in South Africa as a solid block, as non-Europeans ... the sooner we will get our grievances remedied.' He then reiterated the call he had made before for the 'large masses of workers' to use their industrial power, 'which only needed organisation, direction, guidance and proper care, and if that is given, the trouble in South Africa will be over ... We want a South Africa in which both black and white can live together in peace and harmony,' Abdurahman concluded amid loud applause.[544]

SOUTH AFRICA UNDER PRESSURE

The support of the people of the Indian subcontinent and the backing of the Viceroy were significant in swaying opinion in London, but there were other forces at work. Indian concerns about the South African situation had been rising for many years, and gradually Indian activists and diplomats ratcheted up the pressure on Pretoria and London. India's huge contribution to the First World War had given it the right to have its voice heard in Britain. As early as 1915 Sir Mian Muhammad Shafi,[545] Indian lawyer and politician, called for Indian representation at the Imperial Conferences at which the future of the British Empire was discussed.[546] London conceded the case and two Indians were present at the Imperial War Conference of 1917, including Sir Satyendra Sinha,[547] another distinguished lawyer and former president of the Indian National Congress. India now had a presence at a key seat of power.

On the last day of the 1917 conference Sir Satyendra moved a resolution calling for reciprocity between India and the dominions with regard to the question of immigration. It was intended to deal with the discrimination Indians faced across the Empire, but was particularly aimed at the situation in South Africa. Smuts replied that the Indian problem in South Africa was not a question of race, but 'a matter of white anxiety'. Referring to his pact with Gandhi, Smuts assured Sinha that once Indian immigration had ceased, there would be little for Indians to fear.[548] As we have seen, this was not the case. At the Imperial Conferences of 1921 and 1923 the Indians kept up the pressure. Always pointing to the loyal service India had given to the Empire, they argued that the South African Indian diaspora should be treated as equal citizens. Smuts found himself increasingly isolated and cornered by their relentless pressure.[549]

After Smuts lost the election in June 1924, Hertzog now had to deal with the problem. Even though his slogan was 'South Africa first', Hertzog declared that he wished to have good relations with Britain. Speaking at a National Party reception, he said that he insisted on putting his country's interests first, but wished that 'Great Britain should be, and so far as my Government are concerned, always will be our first and best friend'.[550] At the same time he was acutely aware that South African government legislation had to be signed by the King and that if there was sufficient pressure from India, the possibility might arise that he would not give royal assent.

Hertzog was determined to end this kind of situation, and for South Africa to have unquestioned control over the making and passing of its own laws.[551] If Hertzog was to achieve this, he had to proceed with care. The South African Indian Congress appreciated that race relations were the prime minister's weak point. Together with the Indian National Congress, the South African Congress repeatedly pressed the British to disallow Malan's Bill. Indians called for the Imperial parliament in London to request the King not to sign it into law.[552]

There then followed a series of developments which combined to persuade Hertzog and Malan to change their positions. In South Africa there was sustained pressure from the Indian community, which staged a series of strikes and protests. One of Gandhi's closest allies, the Rev. C.F. Andrews, travelled to South Africa to provide the Indian community with support. And – critically – the Viceroy dispatched a deputation to South Africa to engage with the government. Led by G.F. Paddison, a senior Indian civil servant, the deputation left India for South Africa on 25 November 1925. Paddison's secret instructions included the following: 'If this Bill becomes law, public opinion in India may press for some form of retaliatory action against South Africa. You should ascertain how far such an idea has found any expression among Indians in South Africa, and how far such measures would be likely to affect their position.'[553]

The Paddison deputation spent four months in South Africa, where it made a favourable impression on Indians and whites alike. It was finally instrumental in getting the Union government to agree to a round table conference. This was the outcome the South African Indian Congress had long desired, even though it was denied the right to participate. 'Our aim right from the commencement', said an official statement from the Congress, 'was to secure the holding of the Round Table Conference for a[n] honourable and lasting settlement of the Indian question.'[554]

Negotiations began in December in Cape Town and concluded on 12 January 1927. Hertzog opened the conference, although he did not participate in the discussions which followed. In his opening address he dwelt on the need for mutual agreement on a policy based on the reduction of the Indian population, and said that if this could be satisfactorily dealt with, his government might be prevailed upon to exclude 'the more objectionable' provisions of the Bill.[555] It took a month of hard bargaining to reach a conclusion, but finally the talks succeeded. On 13 January, the Governor General of South Africa sent a secret telegram to the Viceroy: 'Have much pleasure in reporting that the Conference between the Union Government and the delegation from the Government of India has concluded in a most satisfactory manner.'[556]

On 12 February 1927, the Malan Bill was withdrawn and on 21 February the Cape Town Agreement was signed.[557] This was very much a compromise and was described as such at the time. On the one hand, it provided for increased Indian repatriation from South Africa; on the other hand, the Union government promised to improve the social and educational conditions of the remaining Indians. Perhaps best of all, it saw off the notorious Bill and the segregation it had proposed. A member of the Indian deputation, V.S. Srinivasa Sastri, said that the agreement was 'the very soul of political progress, and as such contained elements of high statesmanship and vision'.[558] The agreement was hailed by South African Indians as their 'Magna Carta', guaranteeing their rights.[559] The press in India largely agreed. 'We venture to offer our hearty congratulations to the members of the Round Table and the Governments of the Union of South Africa and India on the success that has attended the conference,' declared *The Servant of India*, 'even if it does not give us all we feel we are entitled to on the basis of justice and righteousness.'[560]

It was a remarkable achievement to have extracted so much from one of the most right-wing of South African governments, which had been determined to send Indians packing, if at all possible. Many people had played their part, but Dr Abdurahman's role should not be underestimated. While his standing in South Africa (and among the coloured people) might have been waning at this time, he had carved out an international role that genuinely contributed to the well-being of the local Indian population. As the years went by, the Cape Town Agreement was undermined and its provisions largely disregarded, but at the time it was rightly welcomed as a genuine step forward – one to which Abdurahman had done much to contribute.

CHAPTER TWELVE

The Hertzog offensive

THE RISE OF THE FAR RIGHT

D r Abdurahman returned to South Africa from India in 1926 a considerably enhanced figure. He had shown his mettle in an international arena, impressing the Viceroy by his persuasive presentation and winning the support of Indians at meetings across the nation. He had also contributed to the victory that South African Indians won the following year when the hated anti-Asiatic Bill was withdrawn, following the Cape Town Agreement. He had succeeded in cementing coloured ties with the Indian community, just as his participation in the 1909 delegation to London had strengthened his standing in the eyes of most Africans.

The Cape Town Agreement was, perhaps, the final achievement of a strategy that relied on political pressure together with appeals to the 'better nature' of British governments to intervene in South Africa on behalf of black people. An appeal to London – directly or via the Governor – could pay off. Yet, when it was most critically needed, this tactic generally failed. The worst excesses of racist legislation might be blunted, but when it came to a vital issue like the franchise and the rights of the black population in the 1910 Union constitution, the

British government deferred to the white government. Although black South Africans would call on Britain to intervene on their behalf for years to come, they did so with less and less success.

By the 1920s and 1930s movements representing people of colour in South Africa found to their alarm that their limited rights were increasingly under threat. They were fighting an uphill battle. For Dr Abdurahman – as for all political leaders seeking to work for the black majority – the question was what could be done to resist the steady erosion of their rights. Whether it was the African National Congress, speaking for Africans, the Indian National Congress or the African Political Organisation of Dr Abdurahman, each found itself on the back foot. During this period none was able to develop a successful strategy to resist the rise of segregation. Nor were the far left any more capable of devising a means of opposing this rising tide of racism.

Hertzog and his 'New Deal' for coloured people

Although Dr Abdurahman's status had been enhanced nationally and internationally, his own party was in decline. It had fewer branches and less influence and it was hardly in a strong position to confront the threat from Hertzog and the Pact government, intent as they were on introducing a thoroughgoing policy of segregation. The prime minister was a particularly shrewd politician, aware of how to reach out to sections of the population that he needed to win over to achieve his objective: making South Africa 'safe' for the white electorate. He had already wooed some members of the coloured community to win power and, in the case of N.R. Veldsman, found a willing partner.[561] Veldsman wrote a letter to Hertzog, congratulating him on his electoral victory in 1924. In May 1925 Veldsman was rewarded with the post of Inspector of Coloured Labour on the Cape Town docks, which he accepted.

The alliance between Hertzog and the Labour Party which had led to the Pact government was unlikely; the relationship between Hertzog and Veldsman and his supporters among conservative coloureds was – at least on the face of it – even stranger. It only makes sense if one considers the tradition represented by men like John Tobin, who had argued ever since the foundation of the APO in 1902 that coloureds shared a common history with their fellow 'sons of the soil', the

Afrikaners, and that their real enemy was British imperialism.[562] But Tobin had taken this stand from a left-wing perspective and was in favour of working-class unity, irrespective of race. Veldsman and his supporters were not. They formed the Afrikaanse Nasionale Bond in 1925 to further their aims, but it was in reality little more than a front for the Nationalists. Dr Malan and his colleagues drew up the Bond's constitution, printed its literature, supplied its funds and attended its founding conference.[563] Malan committed the Bond to protecting white and coloured people with a 'civilised' standard of living from competition from the 'natives'.[564]

Some of the Bond's policies echoed those of the APO. They opposed discrimination against coloureds and supported the abolition of the *tot* system, improved housing, better education and equal opportunities for coloureds in state employment. Veldsman also backed the extension of the Cape franchise to include coloureds in the Transvaal and Orange Free State. On other issues they differed sharply with the APO. The Bond attacked Dr Abdurahman for his radical rhetoric, accusing him of attempting to 'hold a pistol' to the government's head. It was the question of segregation that really separated the Bond from the APO. While Dr Abdurahman was, and continued to be, emphatically opposed to segregation in any form, the Bond accepted the notion of a separate coloured identity and backed a form of racial segregation that placed them above the African population. 'We strive … to look after, first of all, our own,' they declared.[565]

The Afrikaanse Nasionale Bond had some appeal. With the backing of Nationalist-controlled newspapers and funding, they grew in size and boasted 6,000 members by the end of 1925.[566] By 1928 Dr Abdurahman estimated the Bond's membership at 10,000. The Bond was particularly strong in the Transvaal, where many coloureds filled positions as skilled labourers and craftsmen. The party all but eliminated APO support in that province. There was also a second string to Hertzog's coloured strategy: the Cape Malay Association, which was assured of an 'enhanced status under the National Party Government'.[567]

For a brief moment it appeared that the strategy of conservative coloured politicians might succeed where the APO's tougher stance had failed, but it did not last. The issue that almost burst the bubble was employment. The Hertzog government introduced a 'civilised labour policy' which saw the dismissal of Africans from state employment. True to his word, the policy contained no reference to colour, while the Colour Bar Act expressly included coloureds and Malays with whites.[568] Africans lost their jobs and were replaced by whites and coloureds. But it soon became apparent that the policy was not all that it seemed. Far fewer coloureds were being given jobs and, when they were employed, they were paid lower wages. When the APO complained in 1926 to the minister of railways and harbours, C.W. Malan, they were brusquely dismissed. Malan denied ever promising equal wages, since 'The coloured man is different from the white man in his standard of civilization,' he declared, 'and must be treated accordingly.'[569] Dr Abdurahman attacked the civilised labour policy, declaring that 'Coloured men will not long be content with casual ill-paid work'. He described the wages they were being paid as 'miserable'.[570] Indeed, coloured people found that in all aspects of government policy they continued to be discriminated against. Whether it was the pensions they were given or the sums spent on the education of their children, the Hertzog government short-changed them.

In the end, Hertzog's so-called New Deal for coloureds was exposed as a fraud. After the National Party won the 1929 general election, obtaining an overall majority in parliament for the first time – a victory to which coloured voters had contributed – it no longer needed coloured support. It soon became clear that the Nationalists had no intention of keeping their promises to their coloured allies. At the Cape National Party congress in 1932, delegates backed a resolution from Dr Malan that coloureds be placed on a separate voters' roll – rather like the Nationalist proposals for Africans.[571] With this, support for the Afrikaanse Nasionale Bond among coloured people evaporated. Without Nationalist financial and political backing, the party disintegrated.[572] The policies of appeasement had failed to win conservative coloureds the progress that they sought, but – as Gavin Lewis has pointed out – they were not the only African or coloured organisation that did not succeed in winning reforms from white parties.[573]

ATTACKING AFRICAN VOTERS

The Hertzog government's primary objective was to put an end to what the prime minister regarded as the curse of the African franchise. His onslaught was relentless. In a series of Bills that he brought before parliament, Hertzog attempted to tackle this question over the course of a decade, from 1926 until 1936. Their right to vote was protected by the constitution and amending this required a two-thirds majority in a joint sitting of both houses of parliament. It was a big hurdle indeed, and it was resisted by the African National Congress and by Dr Abdurahman, who did all in his power to prevent African men from being stripped of a right they had enjoyed for nearly a century.

The Hertzog deal was formally presented in June 1926 in the form of four linked segregation Bills. The first abolished the African franchise; the second set up an African advisory council, with no real power; the third provided additional land for African reserves; and the fourth redefined coloured voting rights. The Coloured Persons' Rights Bill[574] would allow coloureds living outside the Cape to gain the vote, as long as they were 'civilised'. They were required to be able to fill in a registration form and have a 'standard of life conformable to that of European civilisation'.[575] Such coloureds would then be added to a separate voters' roll and would, together, vote for one white MP to represent all coloureds in the Orange Free State, Natal and the Transvaal. The Bill would only come into force once the other Bills stripping Africans of their rights had been passed. The plan was complex and bureaucratic, as well as racist.

The Afrikaanse Nasionale Bond attempted to engage with Hertzog's plan. They sent a deputation to see him, expressing dissatisfaction with the Bill in its 'present form' but dissociating themselves from the criticism of the APO and others. Hertzog argued that the proposed law fulfilled his pledge to treat coloureds equally and was merely a transitional measure. After seven years the Cape franchise would be extended to the whole country. In June 1927 Bond members embraced the scheme, with one claiming it to be 'one of the most momentous in the history of the Cape coloured people'.[576]

Dr Abdurahman was unrelenting in his resistance to Hertzog's plans. He attacked the Bills as 'one of the biggest political frauds that any political party has ever attempted'. Nor was he prepared to see a wedge driven between coloureds and Africans, and he drew on their past solidarity. 'It is particularly so in the light of the things the Prime Minister and other Ministers had said about giving the coloured people equal rights with the whites. Natives and coloured people had stood shoulder to shoulder in the past to maintain their political rights in the Cape Province and to fight for the extension of these rights in the Transvaal and Free State; and they are not going to be bribed to leave the Natives in the Cape in the lurch.'[577] He hammered home the same point at the APO conference in 1929, pointing out that the APO had sent delegations to see the prime minister two years earlier and had made it clear that 'however anxious the coloured people were for the extension of political rights to the Northern Colonies, no Bill, no matter how high the political status it conferred on them, would be acceptable if coloured people had to be a party to depriving the Native of his vote'.[578] Abdurahman reiterated his opposition to these measures:

> To my mind the attempt to disfranchise Natives will be a dastardly outrage on his rights – rights which they have never abused, but which they have exercised in a manner which should be an example to many Europeans. Some of the most brilliant men who ever graced the Old Cape House of Assembly represented Native constituencies. It will be a calamity to South Africa to deprive the Native of his political rights without any justification.[579]

Dr Abdurahman launched a countrywide campaign against the Bill.[580] He toured APO branches in all four provinces to explain its dangers. The APO sent a further deputation to Hertzog, again stressing that they would not accept any Bill that stripped away African rights. For his stand, Abdurahman won the support of the ANC, the Industrial and Commercial Workers Union, and the Natal Coloured Welfare Association. The time had arrived to take the campaign beyond the coloured population and to seek wider support across the black community. Abdurahman now launched his most ambitious campaign. It was one that he had been working towards his entire political life: to unite all black political parties in an attempt to halt the rising tide of white racism.

In March 1927 Abdurahman met black leaders attending a Dutch Reformed Church-sponsored 'European–Bantu' conference in Cape Town and received strong support for his suggestion.[581] The delegates appointed Dr Abdurahman as convenor of a Non-European Conference, to be held in Kimberley later that year. He wrote to all black organisations, inviting them to attend, and received support from the ANC, the Industrial and Commercial Workers Union, the South African Indian Council, the Natal Indian Congress, the Bantu Union, the Cape Native Voters' Convention, the Garveyites, and the Griqua Union.[582] Together with Professor D.D.T. Jabavu, son of the pioneering black newspaper editor John Tengo Jabavu, who led the Cape Native Voters' Convention,[583] he managed to persuade a host of other groups, including black churches, welfare bodies and voters' associations, to send delegates.[584]

In June 1927 delegates made their way to Kimberley from across South Africa and South West Africa. It was a very considerable achievement for Abdurahman and the APO. The conference brought together one of the most representative gatherings of South Africans ever held – comparable to the Congress of the People held by the ANC in 1955. Altogether, 114 delegates participated from all sections of the black population, including 45 Africans, 39 coloureds and 14 Indians.[585]

At the conference Abdurahman laid out his philosophy: he was determined to unite all those who opposed the rising tide of white racism. There was great pressure from the government, he said, on individual members not to associate with 'extremists'. This was an attempt to divide; to keep various groups in what he termed 'watertight compartments'. It was simply a tactic to weaken the government's critics, as he explained in his opening address. 'To the Malay the government said: "We will make you different from the Asiatics," and to the Coloured man: "You will get the status of the white man." Some poor deluded fools already walked about the streets as if they were white and really better than all others.'[586] Dr Abdurahman called for this divide-and-rule strategy to be resisted.

The conference expressed the anger of the black population, but was careful to remain strictly conventional in the protests that they would support. Dr Abdurahman made it clear that while the Hertzog laws were deeply unjust, the delegates had to be careful. 'In the initial stages they could do more than protest emphatically against unjust steps. They must be constitutional. Afterwards their friends might be able to devise better steps.'[587] In their closing speeches Dr Abdurahman and Professor Jabavu spoke of the historical importance the conference would one day assume.[588] This was their public stance and a necessary show of confidence if their efforts were to be more than just a three-day event. Sol Plaatje was privately less than hopeful. He wrote to a friend on the eve of the conference to say that it was no more than a 'vain hope' that the gathering could do anything to avert the 'drastic laws, most barbarous in character', designed to 'destroy the soul of the Native people', and which they were powerless to resist.[589]

In 1931 the conference met in Bloemfontein and this time Dr Abdurahman went further, suggesting that a delegation be sent to London to appeal, once more, to the British government.[590] The proposal was accepted, but in the end the delegation was reduced to just a single person: Professor Jabavu.[591] Although he succeeded in raising the issues in Britain, he was unable to persuade the government to intervene in South African affairs. Perhaps more importantly, Dr Abdurahman was successful in proposing at the conference that a single organisation should be established to bring black people together. As he argued, 'the want of unity was the greatest stumbling block to the improvement of non-European conditions in the Union of South Africa'.[592]

The Non-European conferences of 1927, 1930, 1931 and 1934 were indeed remarkable displays of unity. Each heard passionate debates and passed resolutions opposing the Hertzog Bills, but their efforts had little obvious impact on the tide of legislation being pushed through parliament. As Tom Karis and Gwendolen Carter conclude: 'Despite disagreements and the inability to advance beyond discussions and resolutions, the conferences did highlight the extent to which different non-white groups held common positions of opposition to government policies, in particular to the Native Bills ...'[593]

Reneging on a Royal Promise

In the maelstrom of South African politics since the First World War, it would have been easy to forget the solemn pledge made in London in 1909 that any change to the South African constitution affecting the franchise would require royal assent. White South Africans might have forgotten this promise, but Africans had not. In 1927 senior African leaders gave evidence in the South African parliament when it considered the Hertzog Bills.[594] They were Professor D.D.T. Jabavu, Walter Rubusana, the Rev. Abner Mtimkulu of the Cape Native Voters' Convention, and Meshach Pelem of the Bantu Union. They reminded South African MPs that during the 1909 debate in London 'King Edward VII took the extraordinary step of preserving the right of the Cape Native franchise against future dispossession in his "Letters of Instruction" to all future Governors-General'.

It was, in their view, a powerful argument. As late as 1932 Professor Jabavu referred to this pledge,[595] assuring his readers that they were secure. '[It] is fortunate that under the Union Act the final decision on any change in the Cape Native franchise rests with the British public and the Imperial Parliament, according to the Letters of Instruction to the Governor-General of South Africa signed by the late King Edward VII. We repose our faith on this final reference to England and this is where we hope to appeal to help us some day in the future whensoever any change is sought which may be detrimental to the interests of the Cape Native voters.' Professor Jabavu's faith could hardly have been more misplaced. When the Hertzog Bill was finally passed in 1936, the issue was not even mentioned to the King.[596] So why did the assurances, given on behalf of the Crown, prove to be so insubstantial?

The reason was that the status of South Africa as a British dominion had changed, and Hertzog had had much to do with this. In 1917, during the First World War, the Imperial War Conference endorsed a resolution devised partly by Smuts, which allowed for the 'full recognition of the Dominions as autonomous nations of an Imperial Commonwealth'.[597] This concession was accepted by London at a time when Britain was at its most vulnerable and dependent on its colonial subjects for men and materiel to fight the German war machine. At the 1926 Imperial Conference Hertzog, representing South Africa as its prime minister, insisted that the matter be taken further, and that South Africa's complete freedom of action should be guaranteed. In 1926 Arthur Balfour[598] drafted this definition of the dominions: 'They are autonomous Communities within the British Empire, equal in status, in no way subordinate one to another in any aspect of their domestic or external affairs, though united by a common allegiance to the Crown, and freely associated as members of the British Commonwealth of Nations.'[599] This position was formalised in the Statute of Westminster of 1931, which enabled the dominions to alter their constitutions without reference to London.[600]

The outcome for the majority of South Africans was simple enough. The British government would no longer give advice to the King on how he should act as the ultimate arbiter of the rights of his citizens in South Africa, even if the country remained part of the British Empire. This role would henceforth be undertaken by the South African government alone.[601] Once the Statute of Westminster of 1931 became law, there was no legal way in which the King could act on the advice of a British government in respect of South African affairs.[602] Hertzog's dream of fully controlling the destiny of the country had become law.

A LIBERAL INITIATIVE

The coloured population of the Cape was hard hit by the depression of the 1930s, losing jobs both because of the economic contraction and because they were replaced by whites. Dr Abdurahman protested against this, but his appeals to government went unheeded. A group of white liberals, including Anglican clergy and university academics, attempted to intervene, working through the recently established South African Institute of Race Relations.[603] They suggested the establishment of Joint Councils that would bring whites and blacks together to conduct joint investigations and resolve issues through negotiations and compromise. As Gavin Lewis points out, by dropping plans for mass action and protest, black elites were offered a chance to influence white thinking in general and government decision-making in particular.[604] In the Cape this attracted coloured people disillusioned with the APO's radical rhetoric. By 1936 Coloured–European Councils had been established in Cape Town, Durban, Johannesburg, East London and Pietermaritzburg.[605] They were mirrored by forty similar councils that brought whites together with Africans and Indians.

Dr Abdurahman and the APO had little time for this initiative, which was also rejected by the ANC. Both organisations saw these plans as undermining their political activities. As Abdurahman put it, the coloured people 'have their own Coloured men to speak for them'.

He turned down an invitation to join a Coloured–European Council conference on the welfare of coloureds in 1934, declaring it would do 'incalculable harm' to the interests of his community. Despite the APO's opposition, the conference was a considerable success, with 300 white and coloured delegates hearing calls for better housing, higher wages and improved employment for coloured people. Its most important outcome was a request for a government commission of inquiry into the conditions of coloured people, which was conveyed to the authorities together with a detailed plan provided by the Institute of Race Relations.[606]

Jan Hofmeyr, the leading liberal in the Fusion government, accepted the suggestion of a commission. In response to a request from the APO for a coloured representative, Dr Abdurahman was appointed as one of the commissioners in July 1934.[607] He was the only person of colour to serve on that body. The commissioners' mandate restricted them to investigating the socio-economic conditions of the coloured people. What they found was shocking: high levels of malnutrition, squalid and filthy housing, and the associated problems of poverty – ill health, alcoholism, tuberculosis and juvenile delinquency. Education in coloured schools received funding that was 'utterly inadequate', and the schools themselves were 'overcrowded and understaffed'.

In their recommendations the commissioners proposed an ambitious range of measures to tackle these problems. The commission split over the question of segregation. Some of the commissioners argued that a 'coloured person' could be defined by his or her physical features, including colour of skin, hair and facial features. Dr Abdurahman and his allies on the commission rejected this outright, pointing out that this had no scientific basis.[608] Plans for a coloured university were rejected by him, as were suggestions of segregated housing. Nor would he accept the concept of differential wages under the 'civilised labour' policy. As a result, Abdurahman and his allies put forward minority reports on a range of issues. Critically, he rejected attempts to change the franchise, since he was determined to defend the Cape vote.

The commission report noted: 'Dr Abdurahman recommends that the political rights which the Coloured people in the Cape Province had enjoyed equally with Europeans since 1854 and which they were deprived of by Sections 23 and 44(c) of the South Africa Act 1909 be restored.'[609] In conclusion, Dr Abdurahman insisted on an addendum to the report, in which he and his allies outlined a range of their concerns, from employment to education.[610] Their attack on segregation was powerful even if it was stated in moderate terms:

> We desire to state that we do not associate ourselves with this policy of segregation ... It has been represented from all quarters by the Coloured people that, although social equality is not asked for, equality of opportunity in the industrial, commercial, professional and political life of the country is sought, and that barriers, not created by the free and natural interplay of social and economic factors but, on the contrary, erected by legislation and other such machinery, should be thrown down. We advocate such a policy as being in the best interests of the European and Coloured sections of the population, as well as in the interests of the country as a whole.[611]

In the end the commission and its report achieved 'precisely nothing'.[612] This assessment, although accurate in the main, was perhaps a little harsh. One recommendation was that greater attention should be given to the physical education of coloured youth. This was picked up by the Teachers' League of South Africa, which Abdurahman supported. Physical education was something the League had campaigned on for years, but the commission gave an impetus to their work as a means of tackling the needs of young people. It encouraged the establishment of inter-schools competitions in the 1940s, which became an important part of education.[613]

At the same time, it is certainly true that the government had no interest in implementing its major recommendations and only accepted those of the most conservative of the commissioners. Dr Abdurahman, recovering from a heart attack, took part in a Coloured National Convention in 1938. He led criticism of the commission, stating in his opening address that it had been 'one long tale of woe without any redeeming features'.[614] Backed by a range of Cape liberals, including Bishop Sidney Lavis, he argued that only the restoration of the pre-1910 Cape franchise would be acceptable. But the cards were stacked against them and there was little they could do to reverse the prevailing tide of segregation.

CHAPTER THIRTEEN

The final clashes

UNDER ASSAULT FROM ALL SIDES

The problems Dr Abdurahman had to confront only multiplied as the 1930s progressed. The major threat to the community he represented in District Six, and beyond, came from the right. Hertzog's campaign to remove the African vote finally succeeded in 1936. All the work and time that had been invested in the Non-European Conferences had come to naught.[615] The strategy that Dr Abdurahman had pursued since the early 1900s of backing the South African Party, latterly under the leadership of Smuts – as the least oppressive white party with which coloured people could ally themselves – had run into the sand. In 1934 Smuts entered into an alliance with Hertzog's National Party, out of which emerged the United Party, with Hertzog at its head. Attempts to find allies among the trade unions had also not succeeded and the APO faced the hostility of the Communist Party, which criticised it at every turn. Dr Abdurahman's attempts to reach out to the rest of the black community, which he had pursued since the delegation to London in 1909, had also been unproductive. The ANC was in disarray.[616] Moreover, though his work with the Indian Congress had been useful, it had not really strengthened his hand. Despite his best efforts, black unity appeared as much of a mirage as it had ever been.

The international situation was increasingly threatening, with the rise of fascism and a Second World War looming on the horizon. This was not just a threat from abroad. Local groups had come into being that looked to Nazi Germany for inspiration. A fascist movement, the South African Christian National Socialist Movement (better known as the Greyshirts), was formed in 1933.[617] They were not a major force but they drove Afrikaner politics still further to the right. Other right-wing movements that emerged at the time included the Ossewa Brandwag, under the leadership of Oswald Pirow, a member of the Hertzog government. In October 1935 the Italian invasion of Ethiopia underlined the rising power of the fascist regimes in Europe, as well as the impotence of the democracies. The arrival of fascism on the African continent was deeply disturbing for South Africa's black politicians, who struggled to find an adequate response.

At home the Great Depression hit South Africa badly, and there was a sharp rise in poverty and joblessness, which affected coloured people deeply. By 1937 coloured workers were said to be earning half of what they had earned ten years previously.[618] The Western Cape saw large-scale protests led by the Coloured Unemployment League, which by 1932 had approximately thirty thousand coloured members.[619]

As insecurity and unemployment rose, the politics of Cape Town began to change. For decades the coloured community had looked to Dr Abdurahman for leadership, many taking his opinions as their natural point of departure. This was something even the Communist Party recognised. As S.P. Bunting conceded in 1923: 'Dr Abdurahman, say the malicious, can sway his followers *en masse* to vote for whichever political party succeeds in getting on the right side of him. Yet after all there must be solid reasons why he retains their confidence year after year: he must express their temper pretty correctly.'[620] Richard van der Ross recalled his father and friends talking politics in the pre-war years: 'I listened and I heard the way in which they spoke … My father and his colleagues used to speak with great respect, indeed one could say they spoke with awe of the Doctor. "Die doktor, die doktor!" "What did the Doctor say?" or "We can't do this because the Doctor won't approve." The Doctor was Dr Abdurahman – the only coloured leader who got that title.'[621]

But by the 1930s a younger generation had grown up who had a rather different perspective and who were no longer inclined to defer to leaders like Abdurahman. Their frustration at the inability of their elders to shape events led them to search for new ideas and new organisations. One of the most prominent of this new generation was Abdurahman's own daughter Cissie Gool, who had grown up in an intensely political environment. Perhaps her first speech was delivered at a meeting organised by the APO in May 1930 to protest against Hertzog's segregationist programme. The highlight of the evening was Cissie Gool's powerful speech:

> I am afraid that I am slowly going Red and this is the last time I shall address you from a political platform ... In the face of so much political oppression it is hard to keep one's temper, although often it is better to be patient and reap the benefit in the end. The fact is that we are not politically thirsty enough to rise to a man and a woman and demand our rights ... But you are the workers – in your hands lies the power! But look for your white friends. We must have white friends.[622]

Cissie captivated her audience. Far from being the last time she spoke in public, the speech marked the beginning of a long and distinguished political career. She was an appealing personality: her contemporaries recall her as being 'very reserved and proud' but also friendly, while her 'wit and sharp tongue are what people remember best'.[623]

Cissie was a member of the Anti-Fascist League, founded in Cape Town in 1930 by her husband, Dr Abdul Gool, and others.[624] She became a regular speaker at Anti-Fascist League events, stressing the need for a united front of black people. It was here that she met and interacted with communists like James La Guma, Sam Kahn and Johnny Gomas.[625]

Cissie and Abdul Gool's home also became an informal focus for discussion, debate and friendship, much as her parents' home had been. Bernhard Herzberg, who had fled from Nazi Germany, befriended Abdul Gool at a concert at the City Hall in 1934. Abdul had been sitting alone in the segregated area set aside for coloureds, where Herzberg joined him. They walked home together, and Gool invited Herzberg and his companion to his house the following Saturday. According to

Herzberg: 'Every Saturday, Dr Gool and his wife Cissie held open house. It was the only dwelling in this racially divided city where folks from all walks of life, and kind of origin, met, in defiance of ingrained custom. We met ... Frederick Bodmer [a UCT professor]. Next to him sat Sam Kahn, a leading Stalinist Communist [whom Cissie was later to marry] ... Cissie presided over this gathering with her husband. She was sitting next to her father ... busy berating him, calling him Uncle Tom, for his lack of radical opposition to the prevailing political and social system in South Africa. I spotted an African intellectual [I.B.] Tabata, a prominent member of the Trotskyist Spartacus Club, in earnest conversation with Dr Eddie Roux.'[626]

Divisions and disputes

By the mid-1930s young coloured radicals had divided into two main factions. One backed the more established Communist Party, the other the emerging Trotskyist movements.[627] Cissie Gool was part of the communist faction,[628] while the Trotskyist group was led by Cissie's brother-in-law, Dr Goolam H. Gool. Their ideological rift with the communists, and their differences with each other, were complex and intense, but it was the practical outcome of these debates that is relevant for this narrative. The Trotskyists adhered to a policy of non-collaboration with all governmental or quasi-governmental organisations and institutions. This marked a definitive rupture with the traditional approach of the APO and Dr Abdurahman, as well as with other black movements, including the ANC.

As the activist and teacher Richard Dudley has explained: 'Goolam Gool's group believed strongly in noncollaboration ... They also believed that it was wrong to participate in the political party system, pointing out the collaboration of the African People's Organisation, because the parties were all servants of capitalism. Finally, they strongly condemned "colouredism" and what some called "Abdurahmanism" as they argued for full equality for all people.'[629] Their aim was a radical party that appealed to the working class, irrespective of race. The division between the two groups was deep and sometimes fractious. Communists like John Gomas had a deep loathing for the Trotskyists, who reminded him of a 'poisonous swamp'.[630]

The differences separating Cissie Gool from the Trotskyists can be seen most clearly in the formation of the National Liberation League (NLL), founded in Cape Town in December 1935. Cissie, as well as her sister Rosie and their mother, Nellie, played a leading role in its establishment. According to the novelist Peter Alexander, 'Her [Cissie's] organisation, the National Liberation League, was thrustful and young ... Coloureds from all walks of life flocked to it ... And her father's group, the African People's Organisation, once the most famous Coloured body in the Cape, was little more than a name. It had never been popular with the mass of the ordinary Coloured people. But they had followed its lead at election times because there had been no other lead. Now, all were for the Liberation League.'[631]

While its 'methods of struggle' called for public meetings, boycotts and strikes, the League also considered more conventional political activity legitimate. This included the 'election of approved candidates to the governmental and other public institutions of the country'.[632] The League also drew on the APO's tradition of deputations, petitions, resolutions and propaganda. If there was a difference with the tactics of the APO, it was that the League put greater emphasis on demonstrations, boycotts, strikes and passive resistance.

Gavin Lewis regards the formation of the League as marking what he calls 'a fundamental departure from the established traditions of Coloured political organisations since 1900. It rejected the basic premises of Cape liberal theory. It opposed the earlier leaders, from Peregrino to Abdurahman ... And it placed a greater stress on black unity and a non-racial working-class alliance using mass direct action to defeat segregation.'[633] Is this an accurate assessment? In many ways the League represented much the same strata of coloured society as its predecessors. Most of the participants were – like their parents – members of the upper echelons of coloured society, but with one important difference. 'Unlike their parents, many of them had a university education. They had close ties through attendance at the same schools, and through marriage and family links. Almost all of them worked in the professions, especially as school teachers, giving them high status within their communities.'[634] The novel approach the young radicals adopted did not always go down well with their elders. Divisions emerged across the generations and inside families. For the older generation, the resulting conflicts were distinctly unsettling. 'The young radicals shout ... as if they are on the verge of nervous breakdowns,' complained one member of the Teachers' League.[635]

Cissie was elected president of the League at its inaugural conference on 6 March 1936.[636] She was already close to the communists, although not yet a full member of the party. This must have been something of a triumph for the Communist Party, an indication of its re-emergence at the centre of Cape politics after being in the doldrums for many years. For the party it was a way of winning back black people's support, many of whom had shunned the party after its purges and the intervention of the Comintern.[637] Work in the trade unions had paved the way for the party's rehabilitation; now an opportunity presented itself for reintegration into the political life of the community.

The League, containing as it did so many different political strands, was hardly a stable organisation. It was also at least partly a family affair. As has been pointed out, the political twists and turns of the League were played out among members of Dr Abdurahman's extended family. Leading members of the National Liberation League included 'both his daughters, his first wife, Nellie, his son-in-law Dr A.H. Gool; Gool's [second] wife Hawa Ahmed; Gool's brother, Dr Goolam Gool; and the sisters Minnie and Jane Gool, the latter married to I.B. Tabata.'[638] The debates and controversies ran straight through the Abdurahman family.

Led by Cissie – who was more interested in political engagement than the 'purist' politics of non-collaboration advocated by the Trotskyists – the League sent deputations to the Cape Town municipal authorities to try to get relief for the unemployed.[639] The League also opened a bureau on the corner of Tennant and Hanover streets, offering practical help and advice. It was 'set up to deal with exploitation and victimisation of non-Europeans', as *The Sun* newspaper put it.[640] It was just the kind of activity the APO might have engaged in. The League also discussed with the APO the possibility of organising a united movement to represent the black population. Moreover, Cissie Gool organised protests against the Greyshirts, while the League began its own publication, *The Liberator*.[641]

Despite these achievements, the Trotskyist members of the NLL were uncomfortable about the direction Cissie had taken the movement in. At the League's second conference, in March 1937, they criticised her pragmatic politics, and had her replaced as leader by her brother-in-law, Dr Goolam Gool.[642] The conference went on to pass resolutions calling for the establishment of a united working-class front against imperialism in solidarity with the struggles of colonial peoples worldwide. Cissie was formally suspended from the League, and only readmitted in November 1937 after giving a written guarantee to 'uphold the discipline of the League and carry on constructive work'.[643] Initially she was not reinstated as the movement's president, but by April 1938 her position had been reversed. Fed up with Gool's ineffective, purist tactics, the NLL gave Cissie the leadership of the movement once more.[644]

Cissie had clearly emerged as a serious political figure in her own right. As a pragmatic politician unencumbered by the purist demands for 'non-collaboration', she saw her next step as seeking a seat on the City Council. She stood for election in September 1938. Posters went up all across Ward 7, proclaiming her to be 'the Jeanne d'Arc of the Coloured People'.[645] She had to miss her first election rally because of ill health, but this did not prevent her from being enthusiastically endorsed. 'Mrs Gool, by reason of her courageous fight for the rights of the oppressed Non-Europeans and all sections of the people, is a worthy representative who will take up the grievances of the ratepayers of Ward 7,' declared a resolution passed by the meeting.[646] She was also given enthusiastic support by her father, even though he had backed her opponent in previous elections. At her next meeting Cissie told the crowd at Cosmopolitan Hall that 'there is only one thought in my mind and that is to serve humanity, irrespective of race, creed or colour … I want justice and fair play for my people. They contribute thousands of pounds to the Council's coffers and get nothing in return.'[647] Her father joined her on the platform, declaring: 'No-one is more able or capable or enthusiastic to enter the Council than Mrs Gool.' Clearly the Abdurahman family might have its differences, but blood was thicker than water. The doctor would stand by his daughter.[648] The result was a triumph for Cissie, who was elected with a majority of 370 votes.

On the Council, Cissie Gool wasted no time in deploring the treatment which had been meted out to her ward residents in the past. Her ward was, as she put it, the 'Cinderella' of the city, having been neglected for years. She put most of the blame on the Streets and Drainage Committee, which her father had chaired for years.[649] For nearly two years Cissie and her father were colleagues on the City Council. Often, they supported or seconded motions put forward by each other.[650]

CONFRONTING HERTZOG

While these developments were taking place, the threat from the Hertzog government was growing. On 6 April 1936 Hertzog finally managed to achieve his ambition of abolishing the Cape African franchise – to loud cheers from the white members of parliament – but his legislative programme did not end there. In 1937 a further raft of Bills was proposed, ending marriage across the colour line, prohibiting the employment of whites by blacks, and restricting Indian ownership of property.[651] An APO deputation went to Hertzog and appealed for him not to go ahead. He assured them that the legislation would not be enacted and that he would bury them by referring the laws to a select committee. The APO had won a battle, but – as Gavin Lewis points out – it was losing the war.[652]

The League, under Cissie Gool's influence, took a very different approach. While Dr Abdurahman organised a National Convention of coloured organisations in 1938, the League set about organising a rival conference, but one that was open to all black people.[653] The League called on all black organisations to attend a 'Non-European United Front' conference. This was held on 18 April, with delegates from 45 organisations, including the ANC, the Communist Party, and the Trades and Labour Council. They voted to establish the Non-European United Front on the basis of 'the cooperation of the native, Indian and coloured voters in the struggle against the colour bar in South Africa'.[654] The delegates promised to use political and industrial action if any of their members was threatened and called on white workers to support them. Cissie Gool was elected president, an indication of her growing political stature.

With the decade drawing to a close, the threats to coloured people only increased. For many years the Afrikaner nationalists under D.F. Malan had been demanding residential as well as political segregation for blacks in general, but particularly for Africans, and now it seemed that segregation might be extended to coloureds as well. In July 1938 a draft ordinance was published allowing local authorities in the Cape to 'define and set aside any area within its jurisdiction for the occupation for residential purposes by Europeans and non-Europeans only'.[655] There was anger and outrage in the coloured community. Both the APO and the National Liberation League decided to campaign against the measure, though in different ways. Dr Abdurahman promised 'the greatest fight ever'.[656] He launched a blistering attack in the City Council and in May 1938 succeeded in getting a vote in Council resolving to oppose the draft ordinance. He described racial segregation as 'highly undesirable' and called on the Council's representatives on the Cape Municipal Association to oppose the measure.[657] In June Dr Abdurahman and Councillor S. Dollie called together a range of organisations, including the Coloured Ex-Servicemen's Association, the Cape Malay Association and Indian groups like the Cape Indian Congress.[658] They too strongly opposed the measures. Only the National Liberation League refused to support their stand, with James La Guma writing to say they were 'unable to accept your kind invitation'. His absence was duly noted and deplored.

In August Abdurahman chaired a mass protest in Cape Town, which was also addressed by Cissie Gool. There were similar protests in fifteen Cape towns against the measures. The League and the Non-European United Front, led by Cissie Gool, took a different stand. They supported a nation-wide campaign mobilising all black people, on the grounds that 'any law which discriminates against Native or Coloured or Indian weakens the position of them all'.[659] Their campaign bore some fruit. The segregation ordinance was temporarily blocked when the United Party members of the Provincial Council made it clear that they would not support the proposals.[660]

The campaign against segregation exposed the divisions between father and daughter. Their political differences had been clear for some time, but in May 1939 Cissie Gool went further, calling for the coloured community to turn away from the APO and her father and back her instead. She told a meeting in Paarl: 'Follow me, trust me, I'll be your mouthpiece; I'll stop segregation, and don't leave your destiny in the hands of the President of the APO.'[661] Somewhat caustically, *The Sun*'s correspondent pointed out that 'she studiously avoided taking the Nationalists to task – the originators of this virulent racial campaign … Instead of casting vague aspersions on Dr Abdurahman, I think Mrs Gool would serve her people better if she joined with other sane and sensible persons in expressing appreciation to Dr Abdurahman for the great services they have during the present crisis rendered to the Coloured community in their representations to General Hertzog not to give way to Dr Malan's violent racism.' The same edition of the paper quoted Dr Abdurahman replying to a heckler at a meeting in Kimberley, by suggesting that the League was 'hanging on the skirts of Mrs Gool. Take her away and the League would die.'[662]

While coloured politicians wrangled about leadership, Hertzog pushed his government programme forward. The United Party, attempting to satisfy both white and black opinion, introduced a compromise that satisfied neither. A revised scheme proposed that if 75 per cent of property owners in a district voted to restrict ownership in their area, then segregation would be written into the title deeds of the properties. The coloured community, seeing this as the thin end of the wedge, were furious. On 26 March 1939 a day of prayer was held in Wynberg, which drew a crowd of almost three thousand. The next day was designated a day of protest by the APO and the United Front. Their supporters took action in fourteen towns and villages across the Cape.[663] Some five thousand came out in Kimberley, while between ten and fifteen thousand joined a protest in Cape Town, which Cissie Gool addressed, calling for the 'complete emancipation of all Non-Europeans'.[664] As Gavin Lewis remarks, mass opposition on this scale had not been seen in Cape Town since 1909.[665]

THE SECOND WORLD WAR

All the while the Second World War was looming. On 1 September Germany invaded Poland, and three days later Britain and France declared war on the aggressors. When Hertzog lost a vote in cabinet against participation in the war, Smuts took over as prime minister and South Africa entered the war on Britain's side. Abdurahman immediately understood the dangers that a victory for Hitler would pose for all people of colour, and gave his backing to the British war effort.[666] He knew he had the support of the coloured population. On 5 September 1939 he faced another election, but it was hardly a contest. The front page of *The Standard* carried the headline 'First days of the war'. Right next to it was another: 'Dr A. swamps La Guma: 1083 votes to 263.'[667] Abdurahman had seen off yet another challenge from the left.

Coloured ex-servicemen were keen to serve in the war effort. They signed resolutions 'commending' Smuts for his stand and 'pledging loyalty to the British Empire'.[668] Determined as he was to back the fight against fascism, Abdurahman had learned from bitter experience not to expect too much from the sacrifice coloured people were about to make. He warned that there was little hope that their loyalty would be rewarded, and that they should be prepared to continue their fight against 'narrow South African nationalism' after the war.[669]

The APO expressed concerns about the treatment of coloured volunteers, who would receive lower wages and family allowances than their white compatriots. They urged the government to give them fair treatment and to allow coloured troops to play a full part, including serving as armed combatants. The Cape Coloured Corps started recruiting in June 1940, with offices in Johannesburg, Cape Town, Port Elizabeth and Kimberley.[670] It was not until February 1944 that Smuts allowed coloured troops to carry weapons.[671]

Cissie Gool, on the other hand, took her lead from the Communist Party on deciding how to respond to the war. Since the Soviet Union was not involved (because it had signed a non-aggression pact with Nazi Germany) the party refused to support the Allied cause. In June 1939 the party's central committee denounced the conflict as an 'imperialist war' being fought for 'raw materials'.[672] In June the communists declared that 'the fight against Fascism must start in our own country,' and that African, coloured and Indian South Africans could not be expected to volunteer while being denied equal treatment and the right to bear arms.[673] The Cape Town City Council passed a motion of loyalty to the government following the declaration of war, but Cissie Gool voted against it. 'In the first place I had no mandate from the citizens whom I represent in the City Council to support such a resolution,' she later explained.[674] 'The Non-Europeans cannot be expected to fight in defence of a system of colour bars, segregation and starvation wages.

By extending democracy to the Non-Europeans the Government can give something real and worthwhile for Non-Europeans to defend.' It was only when Germany attacked the Soviet Union in June 1941 that the communists reversed their position: henceforth the war effort had to be supported in defence of the socialist homeland.[675]

When the war was over, the Cape Corps returned home. Although their welcome was warm, and their courage was saluted, the coloured community saw as few benefits as they had after the First World War. Abdurahman's warnings about how little the coloured community could expect in return for their loyal service proved to be entirely correct. In 1956 the government (by this time in the hands of the Nationalists) forbade coloured and black Africans from attending the annual Remembrance Day services.[676] It was a cruel snub to people who had sent their young men to die for their country's freedom.

CHAPTER FOURTEEN

The doctor's death and legacy

A FINAL JOURNEY

On 20 February 1940 Dr Abdurahman died at his home at 173 Kloof Street. The outpouring of grief was truly extraordinary. Cape Town has seldom witnessed anything like it before or since. The funeral procession was so long that when its head entered the cemetery in Mowbray, two hours after leaving his home, the end was still in Woodstock.[677] As the funeral cortège processed through the streets, much of the city ground to a halt.

The *Cape Standard* produced a special supplement, complete with a flag at half-mast, entitled simply 'Dr A. Abdurahman: A leader of men.'

> Although the cortège left Kloof Street at 5 pm, thousands of people lined the streets from early in the afternoon … Hundreds of children of Coloured schools assembled in Darling Street to pay their last respects to a man who had done so much in the past years for Coloured education in particular. In traditional Malay fashion the coffin was borne on the shoulders of the men from the home of the Doctor in Kloof Street to the Malay cemetery in Mowbray. A short service was

169

held in the Long Street mosque, while the crowds increased in size until vehicular traffic found difficulty in getting to and fro.[678]

Twenty white members of the fire brigade, in dress uniform complete with brass helmets, joined the procession at the City Hall, where flags flew at half-mast. The mayor, Councillor Snyman, stood dressed in his ceremonial robes, complete with his mayoral chain of office. A photograph shows him with two members of the city's Muslim community: Councillor Sarleh Dollie and Khan Gool, a trustee of the Schotsche Kloof Institution, which Dr Abdurahman had helped found.[679] Wearing fezzes, they stood by the mayor, heads bowed as the coffin passed by. The procession, which included the Moslem Boys Brigade, was led by a car carrying the family. Cissie Gool, Mrs Nellie Abdurahman and Mrs Bey, Abdullah's elder sister, were in the first car. Then came a lorry laden with flowers and guarded by the fire brigade. The line of cars stretched back over a mile.[680] Crowds lined the pavements all along Sir Lowry's Road. At the cemetery itself the mayor, in his scarlet robes of office, walked to the grave preceded by an official in braided uniform and bicorne hat, bearing the city's mace.

Tributes to the doctor poured in from across the country. Smuts, as prime minister, sent a message of condolence, describing the 'indelible mark' he had made, and saying that he deeply regretted the doctor's passing given 'the great services he had rendered to society'.[681] Even Hertzog paid his respects.[682]

From the coloured community and the APO there came a deluge of messages. The Paarl branch paid what were described as the 'finest tributes possible' to the doctor: 'What Kruger was to the Dutchman, Rhodes to the English, was Dr Abdurahman to the Coloured people,' declared the Paarl chairman, J.P. Benjamin.[683] Richard van der Ross, then general secretary of the Teachers' League, summed up the feelings of his members. 'It is a bitter loss indeed; and the teaching fraternity today is overwhelmed with a sense of sorrow too deep for me to describe ... In the great struggle for educational betterment of the Coloured people Dr Abdurahman easily towered above all others ... The Doctor helped many a teacher in distress. He found time to attend every Teachers' Conference held in the Mother City. He was a model to teachers in the meticulous care he displayed in the preparation of his many speeches and lectures delivered to them on all manner of instructive topics. He was greeted at each gathering with warm-hearted feelings of affection and respect.'

Indian traders closed their vegetable stalls on the Parade to mark the loss they felt. A mass meeting was held by the Natal Indian Congress to record their 'abiding gratitude' for what he had done for their community.[684] Perhaps the most poignant tribute came from the chairman of the African Traders' Union, Leo Masholo.[685] 'I believe firmly that I express the feelings of the whole Peninsular community of native peoples when I say how deeply we feel the death of the late Dr A. Abdurahman, MPC and city councillor for many years. Gone is the only man of colour upon whom the natives looked as a real father, a true guide and a sincere member of the human family. South Africa yes, Black South Africa, has lost a pillar of justice and fairplay, common sense and hope in the person of the late Doctor.' Even James La Guma, an old political rival, expressed his somewhat grudging respect, describing the doctor as 'one of the greatest non-Europeans in South Africa … while not agreeing with his political views and his methods of approach on the non-Europeans in the Union'.[686]

THE DOCTOR'S LEGACY

Dr Abdurahman was very much a public figure, who had lived in and enjoyed the political spotlight. The conventional image of him is of a tall man with a gaunt, serious face, wearing a fez – the politician, orator and leader. Yet he was by no means the unsmiling figure he frequently appeared to be on such occasions, spending all his time at work or in politics. His home on the edge of District Six was a meeting place for numerous friends and guests, who were welcomed with tea and talk. He built a very successful medical practice: in 1934 he had an income of £5,000 a year – a very substantial sum.[687] This allowed him to afford a house for his second family in Kloof Nek, a middle-class area of the city. He also owned a holiday cottage and a yacht.[688] He was an early car enthusiast, often spending his time mending his vehicle when it broke down. As 'The Wanderer' columnist wrote in the *Argus*, the doctor used his car to indulge his passion as a fisherman. 'He knew every fishing rock on the False Bay coast, and it was his love of that neighbourhood that made him the chief protagonist in the City Council of the Cape of Good Hope Game Reserve.'[689]

Even though most of what has been written about Dr Abdurahman has considered his APO activities, he was best remembered locally for his many improvements to the daily lives of coloured people made during his time on the City Council. During his long career, he served on most of its committees, including Finance, Public Works, Markets and Gardens, Electric Lights, Waterworks and Fire Brigade, and the Public Works. At one time he served on no fewer than fourteen committees simultaneously.[690] Dr Abdurahman was a powerful and commanding figure. 'For service in the City Council he should have been mayor of Cape Town,' his daughter Begum told her son. 'He virtually ruled the City Council.'[691] Cissie Gool told an American visitor, Ralph Bunche, that 'He fought chiefly for more municipal jobs for coloureds, more clinics, etc ... One of his main achievements was to get about seventy-five per cent of the street improvements' labor for coloureds.'[692]

The working class loved Dr Abdurahman. When he was ill in 1937, Ralph Bunche wrote: 'The colored workmen putting down the pavement on Exner Avenue [in Vredehoek] all speak to me genially and never fail to ask how Dr. Abdurahman is getting along ... The city has roped off the streets all around his [Kloof Street] estate, guards are stationed nearby to caution "hooters", etc.'[693] Nor was he someone whose only concern was fighting for the franchise, or the problems of drainage or lighting in District Six, important as these issues were. Everything from cricket on the Parade to New Year festivities captured his attention. In 1920 he and Stephen Reagon managed to book Green Point Track as a venue for the New Year Carnival, a traditional venue, at which the celebrations had been held in 1908 and 1909, but which had become too expensive for the organisers.[694]

Members of the black community saw in the doctor someone to turn to. John Raynard, who worked for him, described his work: 'Day after day, month after month, and year after year, Coloured people, Natives, Indians and Cape Malays from Cape Town to the Zambezi wended their way to his office at 119 Loop Street, with their grievances and complaints. Deputation after deputation was sent from up country to seek his assistance. No one having a genuine complaint was ever turned away. His office was a real legal bureau.'[695]

Dr Abdurahman's lifework – the APO – did not long outlast him. Perhaps he had been too dominant a figure for anyone else to lead it effectively. Stephen Reagon, the doctor's friend and deputy, took over the organisation. Despite having been a vigorous organiser and able administrator of the APO's ancillary organisations, the APO Building Society and the APO Burial Society,[696] he proved incapable of filling the doctor's shoes. Reagon failed to hold another APO conference or to respond to calls from the ANC and Cape Indian Council to revive the Non-European Conferences.[697] He did lead several deputations to government, protesting about conditions in the Transvaal, but to no effect. In 1942 Reagon also died and his place was taken by Dr Francis Herman Gow, of the African Methodist Episcopal Church.[698] Gow toured the provinces, attempting to revive the APO, and managed to hold a party conference in 1943, but its time had passed. Despite this, some organisations that the party had founded survived its demise. The APO Building Society and the APO Burial Society, which Abdurahman had helped initiate, continued to contribute to the community for years after his death.

The APO became sucked into the controversy over Hertzog's reforms, which among other things established the Coloured Affairs Department (CAD), analogous to the toothless Department of Native Affairs. A bitter dispute about the CAD erupted within the coloured community and enveloped the Teachers' League. The movement split, with the majority rejecting involvement in Hertzog's project, and forming the Anti-CAD movement instead.[699] In April 1944 Anti-CAD supporters captured the APO executive, but then turned to the All-African Convention, led by Goolam Gool and I.B. Tabata, in an attempt to unite black opinion. This development 'proved fatal' to the APO.[700] The party limped along until 1951 by which time it was effectively moribund. Only 18 delegates attended its conference held in the same year, following which it 'faded into obscurity'.[701]

The end of the APO was perhaps inevitable. It had been overtaken by other organisations, including the National Liberation League, led by Cissie Gool. It was Cissie who took up her father's baton, even though she did so from a rather different political perspective. She became the most well-known coloured politician of her generation. Like the doctor, she was re-elected to the City Council continuously for nearly twenty-five years, with one notable expulsion in 1952 when she was jailed for refusing to pay a fine imposed after a protest.[702]

Cissie Gool remained on the City Council until her death in July 1963. When this took place, a memorial meeting was held in the Council's Banqueting Hall, at which tributes were paid to her. 'She was a fearless personality who was a great inspiration to all who knew her. She gave her time and energy continuously for her people and always worked in their interests ... She will be missed by thousands of people who knew her for her unselfish and kindly ways.'[703] The words echoed those said of her father at his death nearly a quarter of a century earlier. Both father and daughter were held in esteem and affection by many who knew them.

Significant as Dr Abdurahman's political achievements were, his primary legacy was in education. It was a passionate interest that he pursued throughout his career. Abdurahman took the lead in establishing Trafalgar High School in 1911, the first institution in the country to offer secondary education to coloured students. He was also behind the founding in 1926 of Livingstone High School, only the second such school in Cape Town.[704] He also addressed the needs of Muslims in particular, establishing primary schools to provide secular education for their children. The Rahmaniyeh Institute, founded in 1913, was the first of fifteen similar schools established by the 1940s. It still exists as a primary school, in Zonnebloem, with eighteen teachers and over five hundred pupils.[705] With the support of his son-in-law, Dr Abdul Hamid Gool, Dr Abdurahman formed the Schotsche Kloof Institution in 1924.[706] As he put it in a letter to the town clerk, 'the property was purchased for the Moslem community of Cape Town for the purpose of establishing a school, which in the process of time, it is hoped, will be developed into a large industrial school'.[707] By the end of his life, Abdurahman could look back on tens of thousands of coloured pupils who had been taught at schools he had done so much to found.[708] In addition, he helped establish the Teachers' League of South Africa, the first association for coloured teachers. The League played an important role in pressing for the reform of the education system, as well as being a focus for political activity within the coloured community.

AN ASSESSMENT

There is no evading the fact that Dr Abdurahman did not succeed in his major objectives. He was not able to protect the liberal order that he regarded as his birthright. Along with the rest of those who went on W.P. Schreiner's 1909 delegation to London, he failed to secure a non-racial vote for all South Africans. Nor could he prevent the torrent of racist legislation that was enacted by successive governments after the Union of South Africa came into being in 1910. All his life he fostered repeated attempts to found a broad-based black alliance, uniting all the country's people of colour. Yet he was unable to build a permanent, non-racial movement.

At a personal level Dr Abdurahman was a past master at establishing and maintaining relationships. One only need think of his ties with Gandhi, Sol Plaatje and Walter Rubusana, among others, to see how well this network served him and how he maintained friendships down the years. His strategy of working closely with liberal white politicians proved helpful to his cause. But the political plight of the majority of South Africans was worse at the end of his life than it had been when he first entered politics.

Dr Abdurahman admitted as much, as the clouds of another world war were gathering, when he rose to address his final APO conference in 1939:

> The age of chivalry, tolerance and kindliness has passed away, and an age of fear, of unreasoning suspicion and of blind prejudice which is the deformed offspring of the union of these two has usurped its place. True learning is in the course of liquidation; fresh, constructive, far-sighted and dispassionate thinking is at an awful discount, and mere lip-service is being paid to the great principle of love already distorted by racial bias, that its original purity and simplicity can no longer be found or even recognised.[709]

Yet, despite these setbacks, it would be a mistake to view Dr Abdurahman as little more than an interesting local Cape Town politician, without a lasting legacy. He was a major figure, working across South Africa and the British Empire in an attempt to secure the rights of his own people and of the wider black community. His work in India was particularly significant, impressing the Viceroy as well as the most senior political leaders in the Indian Congress party. All the political movements and parties that came after the APO and attempted to win coloured support bore the imprint of Dr Abdurahman's years in office, for good or ill.

The doctor's failures need to be seen in the context of his time. In Afrikaner nationalism he faced a movement that grew inexorably as the years progressed. The wind was in the sails of men like Botha, Smuts, Hertzog and Malan, whose policies shifted the politics of the country further and further to the right. Dr Abdurahman warned what this would mean for the country. 'Their political morality is so low, their racial prejudice so intense, that even the complicated fabric of civilisation in this country is bound to suffer if they remain in power for any length of time to control the destinies of South Africa.'[710] His response was essentially defensive: trying every tactic, from trade union organisation and calls for black unity, to delegations and petitions. Abdurahman was certainly not beyond issuing threats, explaining to whites that they would in the long run lose out if they pursued racist policies – that 'one day the name of liberty lit up in Egypt would sweep down over Africa, causing a great white scuttle from our shores'.[711] But he drew the line at political violence, something that all black and non-racial parties did in this era. As John Raynard put it: 'the Doctor knew that the time had not yet arrived for the non-European to resort to "direct action", and that any premature movement in this direction would irreparably injure their cause'.[712] Abdurahman's strategy was to arm his people with the skills they needed to resist, and this required – in his view – a good education.

It is also worth noting that in this era *all* parties and movements that sought to represent black South Africans failed to halt the onslaught of white racism. The parties of the far left that took over the APO's mantle in the coloured community were no more successful than Dr Abdurahman had been. From the 1930s they attempted to build alliances with other black and anti-fascist movements, but with limited success. As Mohamed Adhikari has said: 'However much the radicals may have prided themselves on their principled stance on non-racism and their egalitarian values, they had to come to their own accommodation with their marginality, the tenacity of racial identities within their society and the structurally ambiguous position of the coloured bourgeoisie.'[713]

By the time of Dr Abdurahman's death in 1940 neither the ANC nor the Indian congresses had managed to make any headway against the white authorities. Nor had they established a united movement that brought together all sections of the black community. The Communist Party was equally ineffective. If anything, its unquestioning support for the Soviet Union tarnished the image of socialism for many ordinary South Africans.

One other criticism that has sometimes been raised is that although Dr Abdurahman searched for black unity (particularly after 1909) he was really a coloured politician whose primary concern was for his own community. This is certainly accurate. Yet once again the same charge can be levelled against the other parties. The ANC at this time was an exclusively African party (something that only changed after the ANC was banned in the 1960s); the Indian congresses only organised Indians. Only the Communist Party and the small Trotskyists groups held out a welcome to all races.

Perhaps we should see Dr Abdurahman as a giant of his era, whose life and work were curtailed by the circumstances in which he lived. In the most difficult of times he held a beacon aloft for the coloured people. As Richard van der Ross said: 'Abdurahman taught the Coloured people, among other things, that it was possible to stand on a public platform and criticize the White man, his laws, and his ways. For this the Coloured people loved him and lionized him, as they, the ordinary folk, could not on their own speak publicly in such terms, of the White people on whom they were dependent for their living. But Abdurahman was independent, and he could – and did – speak out. So he became their mouthpiece, their *alter ego*, and their hero.'[714]

Abdullah Abdurahman has thrown a long shadow down the years.

Notes

INTRODUCTION

1   Wellington is 70 km north of Cape Town. It remains a country town, with a population of approximately 62,000, with nearby farms producing wine, table grapes and deciduous fruit.

2   https://www.rhodesia.me.uk/rhodes-death-and-funeral/, accessed 26 September 2019

3   *The Cape Argus*, 20 February 1940

4   See the select bibliography at the end of this book

5   https://www.sahistory.org.za/people/john-gomas

6   Jack and Ray Simons, *Class and Colour in South Africa: 1850–1950*, IDAF, London, 1983, p. 490

7   Patricia van der Spuy, *Not Only 'the Younger Daughter of Dr Abdurahman': A Feminist Exploration of Early Influences on the Political Development of Cissie Gool*, PhD, University of Cape Town, 2002

8   Mohamed Adhikari, *They Shaped Our Century: The Most Influential South Africans of the Twentieth Century*, Human & Rousseau, Cape Town, 1999, p. 437

9   Gavin Lewis, *Between the Wire and the Wall: A History of South African 'Coloured' Politics*, David Philip, Cape Town, 1987, p. 199

10 Ibid.

11 UCT Special Collections, BCZA83/30-34, Abdurahman Family Papers; BCZA85/21-23 Abdurahman Papers

12 *Report of the Commission of Inquiry Regarding the Coloured Population of the Union*, UG45, Government Printer, Pretoria, 1937

13 Private correspondence with Ri'aad Dollie, 11 September 2019. Dr Abdurahman's mother, Khadija, was Mr Dollie's great-grandfather's sister.

CHAPTER 1

14   Henry Longland, *Progressive Cape Town: An Illustrated Historical and Commercial Review*, Argus Printing and Publishing, Cape Town, n.d., p. 26

15   Vivian Bickford-Smith, 'Protest, Organisation and Ethnicity among Cape Town Workers, 1891–1902', *Studies in the History of Cape Town*, edited by Elizabeth van Heyningen, vol. 7, UCT, Cape Town, 1994, p. 85

16   Ibid., pp. 27–8

17   Robin Hallett, 'Policemen, Pimps and Prostitutes: Public Morality and Police Corruption, Cape Town 1902–1904', *Studies in the History of Cape Town*, vol. 1, UCT, Cape Town, 1984, p. 4

18   Owen Charles Mathurin, *Henry Sylvester Williams and the Origins of the Pan-African Movement, 1869–1911*, Greenwood Press, Westport, 1976, pp. 113–29

19   Vivian Bickford-Smith, *Ethnic Pride and Racial Prejudice in Victorian Cape Town: Group Identity and Social Practice, 1875–1902*, Cambridge University Press, Cambridge, 1995, p. 11

20   Bickford-Smith, 'Protest, Organisation and Ethnicity among Cape Town Workers, 1891–1902', p. 99

21   Ibid., p. 100

22   Achmat Davids, 'Politics and the Muslims of Cape Town: A Historical Survey', *Studies in the History of Cape Town*, vol. 5, edited by Christopher Saunders, Howard Phillips, Elizabeth van Heyningen and Vivian Bickford-Smith, UCT, Cape Town, 1984, p. 176

23   Robert Shell, 'Rites and Rebellion: Islamic Conversion at the Cape: 1808–1915', *Studies in the History of Cape Town*, vol. 5, edited by Christopher Saunders, Howard Phillips, Elizabeth van Heyningen and Vivian Bickford-Smith, UCT, Cape Town, 1984

24   Rafael Marks and Marco Bezzoli, 'The Urbanisation of District Six, Cape Town', in David Anderson and Richard Rathbone (eds.), *Africa's Urban Past*, James Currey, Oxford, 2000, p. 266

25   Lucien van der Walt, 'Anarchism and Syndicalism in an African Port City: The Revolutionary Traditions of Cape Town's Multiracial Working Class, 1903–1931', *Labour History*, vol. 52, no. 2, p. 142

26   Elizabeth van Heyningen, 'Cape Town and the Plague of 1901', *Studies in the History of Cape Town*, vol. 4, UCT, Cape Town, 1981, p. 77

27   Ibid., p. 93

28   Robin Hallett, 'The Hooligan Riots: Cape Town: August 1906', *Studies in the History of Cape Town*, vol. 1, UCT, Cape Town, 1984, p. 42

29   Ibid., p. 45

30   Mohamed Adhikari, *Not White Enough, Not Black Enough: Racial Identity in the South African Coloured Community*, Ohio University Press, Athens, 2005, p. 68

31   Van der Spuy, *Not Only 'the Younger Daughter of Dr Abdurahman'*, p. 36

32   Van der Walt, Anarchism and Syndicalism in an African Port City', p. 143

CHAPTER 2

33   Bill Nasson, 'Abdurahman, Abdullah', *Oxford Dictionary of National Biography*, https://doi.org/10.1093/ref:odnb/73214, accessed 20 March 2020

34   Eve Wong, *The Doctor of District Six: Exploring the Private and Family History of Dr Abdullah Abdurahman, City Councillor for District Six of Cape Town (1904–1940)*, MA, University of Cape Town, 2016

35   I.C. Meer, *I Remember: Reminiscences of the Struggle for Liberation and the Role of Indian South Africans, 1924–1958*, edited by Enuga S. Reddy and Fatima Meer, p. 24, https://www.sahistory.org.za/archive/i-remember-reminiscences-struggle-liberation-and-role-indian-south-africans-1924-1958-i-c

36   Robert R. Edgar (ed.), *The Travel Notes of Ralph J. Bunche, 28 September 1937 – 1 January 1938*, Ohio University Press, Athens, 1992, p. 61

37   Nigel Worden, 'Indian Ocean Slaves in Cape Town, 1695–1807', *Journal of Southern African Studies*, vol. 42, no. 3, 2016, p. 397

38   Lady Duff-Gordon, *Letters from the Cape*, edited by John Purves, Humphrey Milford, London, 1921

39   Ibid., p. 36

40   Ibid., p. 160

41   See, for example, Jack and Ray Simons, *Class and Colour in South Africa (1850–1950)*, IDAF, London, 1983, p. 117

42   Neil Rennie, 'Ballantyne, Robert Michael (1825–1894)', *Oxford Dictionary of National Biography*, online

43   http://www.gutenberg.org/files/21701/21701-h/21701-h.htm. Ballantyne left England in early 1876, promising to write to his wife every few days of his experiences 'among the settlers and natives of the Cape of Good Hope'. He returned home in June 1876, publishing *The Settler and the Savage*, a 'fictional adventure story set in the period immediately after the Kaffir Wars, the sort of tale that had an appeal for boys of all ages'. The book was ignored by the public and was a failure. Eric Quayle, *Ballantyne the Brave: A Victorian Writer and His Family*, Rupert Hart-Davis, London, 1967, p. 272

44   Jack and Ray Simons, *Class and Colour in South Africa*, p. 117

45   Bill Nasson, 'Abdurahman, Abdullah'

46   R.E. van der Ross, *Say It Out Loud: The APO Presidential Addresses and Other Major Political Speeches 1906–1940 of Dr Abdullah Abdurahman*, Western Cape Institute for Historical Research, Cape Town, 1990, p. 3

47   Ibid.

48   Eve Wong, *The Doctor of District Six*, p. 30

49   Mogamed Ajam, The Raison D'Etre of the Muslim Mission Primary School in Cape Town and Environs from 1860 to 1980 with special reference to the role of Dr A. Abdurahman in the modernisation of Islam-Oriented Schools, University of Cape Town, PhD, 1986, p. 190

50   Seraj Hendricks, Tasawwuf (Sufims): Its role and impact on the culture of Cape Islam, MA dissertation, University of South Africa, 2005, p. 383. As Hendricks puts it: '…the parents of Dr Abdurahman, Abd Allah and Kadija, had escorted their son to Britain to pursue his medical studies.'

51   Jack and Ray Simons, Class and Colour in South Africa, op. cit. p. 117

52   England & Wales, Civil Registration Death Index, 1837–1915, St Pancras Register of Deaths, July – September 1902. Eve Wong, The Doctor of District Six, op. cit. p. 32. In the St Pancras Register she is recorded as Khudeja Abdurahman, aged 55.

53   Death Certificate of Hadjie Abdurahman, Cape Town 20 July 1920

54 Tom Wheeler, Turkey and South Africa: the development of relations, 1860 – 2005, South African Institute of International Affairs, Report No. 47, 2005, p. 2

55 Ibid., p. 3

56 Rakea Maker was the daughter of Hajji Haruon, who loved in Keerom Street, Cape Town. Halim Gencoglu, Abu Bakr Effendi, A Report on the activities and challenges of an Ottoman Muslim theologian in the Cape of Good Hope, MA, University of Cape Town, 2013, p.30

57 Halim Gencoglu, The first Muslim politician of South Africa, p. 96

58 Ibid.,

59 Halim Gencoglu, Abu Bakr Effendi, A Report on the activities and challenges of an Ottoman Muslim theologian in the Cape of Good Hope, op cit. p. 31, Eve Wong, The Doctor of District Six, Exploring the private and family history of Dr Abdullah Abdurahman, p. 15. Wong names her Gacilla Mohsena.

60 Halim Gencoglu, Abu Bakr Effendi, A Report on the activities and challenges of an Ottoman Muslim theologian in the Cape of Good Hope, op cit. p. 31

61 Serhat Orakci, A Historical analysis of the emerging links between the Ottoman Empire and South Africa between 1861 – 1923, op. cit. p. 60

62 Halim Gencoglu, Abu Bakr Effendi, A Report on the activities and challenges of an Ottoman Muslim theologian in the Cape of Good Hope, op cit. p. 31

63 Abdur Rahman Khan Mohd, My life and experiences, Krishnavas International Printers, Hyderabad, 1951, p. 36 "It was rented by Mrs Ataullah, the widow of a Turkish Consul at Singapore. She lived there with her two daughters (Miss Khairun Nisa and Miss Khadejah Hasanah) and a son, Abu Bakr Rushdi Bey. Several Indian students (mostly from Punjab) were living there at the time as paying guests. I called on Mrs Ataullah on 21 September (1911) and fixed up my residence at her house from the 30th." https://archive.org/details/mylifeandexperie029154mbp/page/n3/mode/2up

64 Halim Gencoglu, The first Muslim politician of South Africa, p. 98

65 Ibid.,

66 It was to this address that Gandhi wrote Dr Abdurahman a letter on 23 August. Gandhi Collected Works Vol. 09: September 1908 – November 1909

67 Ri'aad Dollie, Introduction, p. xxx

Chapter 3

68 Email from Glasgow University archive

69 Spotlight, 12 March 1948. Zelda Friedlander (1908–83) lived in Cape Town and was a researcher and writer of both fiction and non-fiction. She published books on Olive Schreiner and Jan Smuts. See UCT Special Collections, https://atom.lib.uct.ac.za/index.php/z-friedlander-papers

70 It is not clear for whom she was campaigning: there were five candidates for the position. See https://www.universitystory.gla.ac.uk/biography/?id=WH1108&type=P, accessed 28 March 2020

71 Graduate Record for the Glasgow University, 1892–1894, https://www.universitystory.gla.ac.uk/browse-graduates/?submit=y&gt=1&name=&gyear=1892-1894&country=South+Africa&gender=M&degree=, accessed 28 March 2020; B.M. Mayosi, 'The First Black Doctors and Their Influence in South Africa', South African Medical Journal, vol. 105, no. 8, August 2015,

http://www.scielo.org.za/pdf/samj/v105n8/12.pdf, accessed 27 March 2020

72   Mayosi, 'The First Black Doctors and Their Influence in South Africa', p. 635

73   Andre Odendaal, *The Founders: The Origins of the ANC and the Struggle for Democracy in South Africa*, Jacana Media, Johannesburg, 2012, p. 25

74   Ibid., p. 249. As Odendaal remarks (p. 250): 'The experiences of the Soga children are even more remarkable if one recalls that their illiterate grandfather was killed by colonial forces during the last Cape-Xhosa War in 1878 while they were being educated in Scotland.

75   Anne Digby, 'Pioneer Black Doctors in South Africa, 1883–1915', *South African Medical Journal*, vol. 97, no. 4, April 2007

76   See Van der Spuy, *Not Only 'the Younger Daughter of Dr Abdurahman'*, p. 30; Wong, *The Doctor of District Six*, pp. 39–41

77   *Cape Times*, 6 February 1895

78   *Cape Times*, 21 February 1895

79   *Cape Times*, 9 April 1896

80   *Cape Times*, 10 April 1896 and 17 June 1896

81   *Cape Times*, 26 August 1897, 11 November 1897, 22 November 1897

82   *Cape Times*, 30 January 1897

83   *Cape Times*, 7 February 1899

84   Van der Spuy, *Not Only 'the Younger Daughter of Dr Abdurahman'*, p. 30

85   J.H. Raynard, *Dr A. Abdurahman*, ed. by M. Adhikari, Friends of the National Library of South Africa, in association with the District Six Museum, Cape Town, 2002, p. 23

86   E. van Heyningen, *Public Health and Society in Cape Town, 1880–1910*, PhD, University of Cape Town, 1989, p. 325

87   Raynard, *Dr. Abdurahman*, p. 34

88   Lewis, *Between the Wire and the Wall*, p. 21

89   Ibid., p. 21

90   Ibid., p. 10

91   Bickford-Smith, *Ethnic Pride and Racial Prejudice*, p. 201

92   A.G. Cobley, 'Far from Home: The Significance of the Afro-Caribbean Community in South Africa to 1930', *Journal of Southern African Studies*, vol. 18, no. 2, 1992, p. 358

93   Marika Sherwood, *Origins of Pan-Africanism: Henry Sylvester Williams, Africa and the African Diaspora*, Routledge, London, 2011, pp. 98–9

94   His decision was explained in an article in the *Northampton Chronicle and Echo*. 'Henry Sylvester Williams, the inspiration behind the Association, recently called to the bar in mid-1902, decided to go to South Africa. The reason for this surprising move to a country where he knew there was deep racial animosity by whites towards Africans, is provided by comments he made at a speech in Northampton in March 1903. On a platform in the town hall … in speeches devoted to "The British Empire and its varied peoples", Williams highlighted South Africa as the "major question". In those colonies native peoples were forced to work, robbed of their customs, and mine labourers were forced to live in compounds. He continued that he was "in correspondence with natives in South Africa every week, and therefore knew what he was talking about. The natives had written to him asking for his support in the law courts of the Transvaal, whence he was very shortly proceeding."' *Northampton Chronicle and*

Echo, 24 March 1903, p. 3. I am indebted to David Killingray for this reference.

95   Cobley, 'Far from Home', pp. 361–2. 'Mr. H. Williams, barrister' sailed from London for Cape Town on the Australian bound *Wilcannia* (Blue Anchor Line) on 29 Sept 1903. The ship arrived at Cape Town sometime in mid-October. Cost of the voyage varied from nine guineas to £30; I suspect Williams took the cheaper fare (*London Standard*, 25 September 1903). TNA BT27/412/14/1. I am indebted to David Killingray for this reference.

96   R.T. Vinson, *The Americans are Coming! Dreams of African American Liberation in Segregationist South Africa*, Ohio University Press, Athens, 2012, p. 74

97   Sherwood, *Origins of Pan-Africanism*, p. 146. Joosub (Joseph) Mohammed Hamid Gool, born in Rander, in the district of Surat, in the Gujarat Province of India, was a well-to-do trader in spices from a warehouse at 25 Church Street, Cape Town. He was a trustee of the Hanafi Quwatul Islam Mosque in Loop Street. The Abdurahmans and Gools had strong family ties. Selim Yusuf Gool, *The Gools of Cape Town: A Family Memoir. A South African Muslim Family in Search of Radical Modernity* (Unpublished MS)

98   Sherwood, *Origins of Pan-Africanism*, p. 146

99   Ibid.

100   *Cape Times*, 26 August 1904

101   David Killingray and Martin Plaut, 'F.Z.S. Peregrino: A Significant but Duplicitous Figure in the Black Atlantic World', *South African Historical Journal*, vol. 68, no. 4, 2016, pp. 493–516

102   *Cleveland Gazette*, 28 July 1888, p. 1

103   Killingray and Plaut, 'F.Z.S. Peregrino'

104   Chris Saunders, 'F.Z.S. Peregrino and the South African Spectator', *Quarterly Bulletin of the South African Library*, 1977–78, pp. 82–7

105   Richard van der Ross, 'The Founding of the African People's Organisation in 1903 and the Role of Dr Abdurahman', *Munger Africana Library Notes*, vol. 28, February 1975, pp. 8–9

106   Richard van der Ross, *A Political and Social History of the Cape Coloured People, 1880–1970*, thesis submitted to the School of African Studies, University of Cape Town, 1973, UCT Special Collections, Appendix 3

107   Lewis, *Between the Wire and the Wall*, p. 27

108   *Cape Times*, 9 February 1904, p. 10

109   Mathurin, *Henry Sylvester Williams and the Origins of the Pan-African Movement*, p. 120

110   Ibid., p. 20

Chapter 4

111   Ajam, *The Raison d'Etre of the Muslim Mission Primary School in Cape Town and Environs*, p. 193

112   *Review of Reviews*, vol. 31, no. 183, March 1905, pp. 250–15

113   *Review of Reviews*, vol. 32, no. 188, August 1905, pp. 152–3

114   *Cape Argus*, 2 November 1904, quoted in Mathurin, *Henry Sylvester Williams and the Origins of the Pan-African Movement*, p. 124

115   Bickford-Smith, *Ethnic Pride and Racial Prejudice in Victorian Cape Town*, pp. 156, 213

116   *Cape Times*, 8 September 1904
117   *Cape Times*, 10 September 1904
118   D. Ticktin, *The Origins of the South African Labour Party, 1888–1910*, PhD, University of Cape Town, September 1973, p. 330
119   *Cape Times*, 12 September 1904
120   Bickford-Smith, *Ethnic Pride and Racial Prejudice in Victorian Cape Town*, p. 213
121   *Cape Times*, 13 September 1904
122   Cape Times, 13 September 1904
123   *Cape Times*, 11 November 1904, p. 7
124   *Cape Times*, 25 November 1904, p. 5
125   Vivian Bickford-Smith, *The Emergence of the South African Metropolis: Cities and Identities in the Twentieth Century*, Cambridge University Press, Cambridge, 2016, p. 112
126   *Cape Times*, 10 December 1904, p. 7
127   Rachel Bright, *Chinese Labour in South Africa, 1902–1910: Race, Violence and Global Spectacle*, Palgrave Macmillan, London, 2013, p. 30
128   Ibid., p. 51
129   Ibid., p. 51
130   Ibid., p. 131
131   *Cape Times*, 15 December 1905, p. 6
132   Gavin Lewis, *Between the Wire and the Wall*, p. 7
133   Richard van der Ross, *In Our skins: A Political History of the Coloured People*, Jonathan Ball, Jeppestown, 2015, p. 38
134   *South African Spectator*, 25 October 1906, p. 6
135   Van der Ross, 'The Founding of the African People's Organisation', p. 11. It is possible that there was a private pre-meeting before the public meeting described by Van der Ross.
136   Van der Ross, *Say It Out Loud*, p. 5
137   *South African News*, 1 October 1902, quoted in Van der Ross, 'The Founding of the African People's Organisation', n. 17
138   Lewis, *Between the Wire and the Wall*, p. 19
139   Killingray and Plaut, 'F.Z.S. Peregrino'
140   Lewis, *Between the Wire and the Wall*, p. 26
141   Ibid.
142   Lewis, *Between the Wire and the Wall*, p. 27

CHAPTER 5

143   Ibid., p. 30
144   Mohamed Adhikari, *Hope, Fear, Shame, Frustration: Continuity and Change in the Expression of Coloured identity in White Supremacist South Africa, 1910–1994*, PhD, University of Cape Town, 2002, p. 122 n. 2
145   Vivian Bickford-Smith, Nigel Worden and Elizabeth van Heyningen, *Cape Town in the Twentieth Century: An Illustrated Social History*, David Philip, Cape Town, 1999, p. 29; Adonis Carolus Booyse, *The Sovereignty of the African Districts of the African Methodist Episcopal Church: A Historical Assessment*, PhD, University of the Western Cape, 2010, pp. 63–4
146   Van der Ross, *Say It Out Loud*, p. 19

147   Orange River Colony, to use its official name at the time
148   *Globe*, 1 February 1906
149   Adhikari, *Not White Enough*, p. 74
150   Ibid., p. 70
151   *Cape Standard*, 27 February 1940, quoted in Patricia van der Spuy, 'The Politics of Race, Gender and Class in Cape Town, South Africa, c1910: Dr Abdurahman and the African Political Organisation', African Studies Association of Australia and the Pacific (AFSAAP)Annual Conference, 26–28 November 2004, University of Western Australia
152   Adhikari, *Hope, Fear, Shame, Frustration*, pp. 300ff
153   *Cape Times*, 26 August 1897, p. 4
154   Jacqueline Maingard, 'Cinemagoing in District Six, Cape Town, 1920s to 1960s: History, Politics, Memory', *Memory Studies*, vol. 10, no. 1, 2017, p. 25
155   Bickford-Smith, *Ethnic Pride and Racial Prejudice in Victorian Cape Town*, p. 202
156   Ibid.
157   See G.B. Pyrah, *Imperial Policy and South Africa: 1902–1910*, Oxford University Press, Oxford, 1955, esp. pp. 138–82
158   Lewis, *Between the Wire and the Wall*, p. 35
159   Ibid.
160   Van der Ross, *Say It Out Loud*, p. 20
161   Lewis, *Between the Wire and the Wall*, p. 36
162   Ibid., p. 36
163   Heather Hughes, 'The Coolies Will Elbow Us Out of the Country': African Reactions to Indian Immigration in the Colony of Natal, South Africa', *Labour History Review*, vol. 72, no. 4, August 2007, p. 163. Sol Plaatje took a similar position, tending to treat Indians as sojourners in South Africa who had taken land at the expense of Africans. Private communication from Brian Willan. Note that Dube's position changed during Gandhi's 1913–14 campaign and the two men were good friends, co-operating during these events. See Catherine Corder and Martin Plaut, 'Gandhi's Decisive South African 1913 Campaign: A Personal Perspective from the Letters of Betty Molteno,' *South African Historical Journal*, vol. 66, Issue 1, no. 2014
164   https://liberalhistory.org.uk/wp-content/uploads/2014/10/29-Winter-2000-01.pdf
165   W.K. Hancock, *Smuts, the Sanguine Years: 1870–1919*, Cambridge University Press, Cambridge, 1962, pp. 213–14
166   Ibid., p. 215
167   Ibid., p. 217
168   Leonard Thompson, *The Unification of South Africa, 1902–1910*, Oxford University Press, London, 1960, p. 32
169   Ibid., p. 35
170   Lewis, *Between the Wire and the Wall*, p. 37
171   *Cape Times*, 28 February 1906, p. 7
172   *Cape Daily Telegraph* (Port Elizabeth), 3 March 1906, p. 5
173   *Review of Reviews*, vol. 33, no. 195, March 1906, p. 230
174   Peter Fryer, *Staying Power: The History of Black People in Britain*, Pluto Press, London, 1984; David Olusoga, *Black and British: A Forgotten History*, Macmillan, London, 2016

175 *Morning Advertiser*, London, 7 Sept. 1895, quoted in Neil Parsons, '"No Longer Rare Birds": Zulu, Ndebele, Gaza, and Swazi Envoys to England, 1882–1894', in Gretchen Gerzina (ed.), *Black Victorians, Black Victoriana*, Rutgers University Press, New Brunswick, 2003, pp. 124–77

176 Ibid., p. 124

177 Harish P. Kaushik, *Indian National Congress in England*, Friends Publications, Delhi, 1991, p. 25

178 Some attempts had been made to form this kind of organisation. In 1905 the Sierra Leonean author A.B.C. Merriman-Labor established a West African Agency and Information Bureau, offering help on a wide range of issues, but his primary focus was – as his organisation's title suggested – West Africa, and was of little help for southern Africans. Danell Jones, *An African in Imperial London: The Indomitable Life of A.B.C. Merriman-Labor*, Hurst and Company, London, 2018, p. 72

179 James Heartfield, *The Aborigines' Protection Society: Humanist Imperialism in Australia, New Zealand, Fiji, Canada, South Africa and the Congo, 1836–1909*, Hurst and Company, London, 2011, pp. 233ff

180 'Time and again, the Aborigines' Protection Society called on Britain to defend native territory against Boer encroachment.' Ibid., p. 235

181 Ibid., p. 280

182 Jabavu letters to Fox Bourne, 28 March 1887 and 2 July 1887. Bodleian Library, MSS Brit. Empire S 18 C153, Aborigines' Protection Society Correspondence

183 Soga letter to Fox Bourne, 16 January 1906. Bodleian Library, MSS Brit. Empire S 18 C152, Aborigines' Protection Society Correspondence

184 Letter from Dr Abdurahman to Society, 13 July 1906. Bodleian, MSS Brit. Empire S 22 G198, Aborigines' Protection Society 1900–1906

185 *The Aborigines' Friend: Journal of the Aborigines Protection Society*, March 1906, p. 484

186 *The Aborigines' Friend*, August 1906, pp. 602–15

187 *The Aborigines' Friend*, August 1906, p. 605

188 Martin Plaut, 'Olive Schreiner and the Taaibosch Derailment: From "Pro-Boer" Activism to Networking with the Early British Labour Party', Bulletin of the National Library of South Africa, vol. 70, no. 1, June 2016

189 Ramsay MacDonald, *Labour and Empire*, with a new introduction by Peter Cain, Routledge/Thoemmes Press, London, 1998 [1907], p. 59

190 London School of Economics Archive: ILP 4/1906: 284, A. Abdurahman to Hardie (London), 30 July 1906

191 *London Daily News*, 12 July 1906, p. 8

192 https://hansard.parliament.uk/Lords/1906-06-14/debates/7aea72a2-0dd1-4b7e-b438-55ca859f57ff/TransvaalAndOrangeRiverColony(NewConstitution)

193 *Indian Opinion*, 11 August 1906, p. 20

194 https://api.parliament.uk/historic-hansard/lords/1906/jul/31/the-transvaal-constitution

195 *Indian Opinion*, 28 July 1906, p.e 15

196 *Indian Opinion*, 1 September 1906, p. 10

197 *The Journal* [Grahamstown], 23 August 1906, p. 5

Chapter 6

198 Thompson, *The Unification of South Africa*, p. 110
199 Hermann Giliomee, *The Afrikaners: Biography of a People*, Hurst and Company, London, 2003, p. 285
200 Ibid., pp. 63ff
201 Van der Ross, *Say It Out Loud*, p. 24
202 *Papers Relating to a Federation of the South African Colonies*, HM Stationery, Cd 3564, July 1907, p. 8
203 Odendaal, *The Founders*, p. 335
204 Ibid., p. 338
205 Ibid., p. 339
206 Lewis, *Between the Wire and the Wall*, p. 42
207 Ibid., p. 44
208 Chris Ash, *The If Man: Dr Leander Starr Jameson: The Inspiration of Kipling's Masterpiece*, Helion and Company, Solihull, 2012, p. 300
209 Ibid. The letter was dated October 1903. As Jameson's biographer points out, these positions are not as contradictory as they appear. Jameson is distinguishing between 'civilised' and 'uncivilised' Africans – a position which is of course completely unacceptable today, but was in line with much current thinking at the time, including that of some Africans themselves.
210 Giliomee, *The Afrikaners*, p. 296
211 Merriman was prime minister of the Cape, 3 February 1908 – 31 May 1910.
212 Lewis, *Between the Wire and the Wall*, p. 43
213 Phyllis Lewsen (ed.), *Selections from the Correspondence of John X Merriman, 1905–1924*, Van Riebeeck Society, Cape Town, 1969, pp. 16–17
214 Ibid., pp. 17–18
215 Lewis, *Between the Wire and the Wall*, p. 46
216 Lewsen, *Selections from the correspondence of John X Merriman, 1905–1924*, p. 18
217 Universal suffrage was only introduced in Britain in 1918.
218 Thompson, *The Unification of South Africa*, p. 121
219 Odendaal, *The Founders*, p. 340
220 Odendaal, *The Founders*, p. 342
221 Heather Hughes, *First President: A life of John L. Dube, Founding President of the ANC*, Jacana Media, Johannesburg, 2011, p. 147
222 https://www.sahistory.org.za/people/dr-walter-rubusana, accessed 25 August 2019
223 Odendaal, *The Founders*, p. 341
224 Odendaal, *The Founders*, p. 342
225 Not only for its stand on federation rather than union, but also because it called for restrictions on access to liquor – another of his policies
226 Raynard, *Dr A. Abdurahman*, p. 42
227 Barry Kennedy Ross, *A Study of Politics in the Cape Colony from January 1908 to May 1910*, MA thesis, University of Cape Town, 1950, p. 5
228 Odendaal, *The Founders*, p. 377
229 Olive Schreiner, BC16/Box4/Fold2/1909/21, University of Cape Town, Manuscripts & Archives; The Olive Schreiner Letters Online, https://www.oliveschreiner.org/vre?view=collections&colid=101&letterid=21
230 Olive Schreiner, BC16/Box4/Fold2/1909/20, University of Cape Town, Manuscripts & Archives; The Olive Schreiner Letters Online, http://www.

oliveschreiner.org/vre?view=collections&colid=101&letterid=20, accessed 12 December 2018

231 *Cape Times*, 6 March 1909

232 Lewis, *Between the Wire and the Wall*, p. 50

233 Odendaal, *The Founders*, p. 396

234 Ibid., p. 327

235 Ibid., p. 327

236 Ibid., p. 327, quoting *Cape Times*, 17 April 1909

237 *APO*, 19 June 1909

238 Peter Walshe, *The Rise of African Nationalism in South Africa: The African National Congress, 1912–1952*, C. Hurst, London, 1970, p. 16

239 South African Library, Cape Town, Schreiner Correspondence, MSC27 Box 8, 1446, Abdurahman to Schreiner, 11 May 1909

240 Lewis, *Between the Wire and the Wall*, p. 51

241 Ibid., p. 52

242 Saunders, 'F.Z.S. Peregrino and the South African Spectator', p. 87

243 Lewis, *Between the Wire and the Wall*, pp. 49–50

244 Ibid., p. 53

245 *Cape Times*, 22 June 1909

246 *APO*, 3 July 1909

247 *APO*, 17 July 1909

248 *Cape Times*, 16 September 1909. Hofmeyr said: 'that the representative bodies of coloured men from whom the address emanated did not intend to agitate in England against the bar or against any portion of the Bill, because they held, in common with the bulk of their white or European fellow-colonists, that any amendment of that document should come from the Union Parliament of the future, and, finally, because they anticipated no beneficial results from any agitation across the water.'

249 National Archive, Cape Town, Item P1020733 - P1020734

250 National Archive, Cape Town, Item P1020732

251 *The Times*, 8 July 1909

252 *The Times*, 12 July 1909

253 Martin Plaut, *Promise and Despair: The First Struggle for a Non-Racial South Africa*, Jacana Media, Johannesburg, 2016, p. 76

254 Gandhi to Schreiner, 17 August 1909, UCT Special Collections, Schreiner Correspondence, BC 112

255 *A Cambridge Alumni Database*, University of Cambridge, http://venn.lib. cam.ac.uk/cgi-bin/search-2018.pl?sur=&suro=w&fir=&firo=c&cit=&cito=c&c=all&z=all&tex=SCRR878WP&sye=&eye=&col=all&maxcount=50, accessed 19 September 2019

256 See Chapter 3. His sister turned it into a boarding house. The 1911 Census records her as a widower from the Ottoman capital, Constantinople; born in 1873; of 'private means' and living at the address with her three daughters, Kadidga, Nessa and Rushdi. The house was home to 13 people, mostly students from India. It was to this address that Gandhi wrote Dr Abdurahman a letter on 23 August. Gandhi, *Collected Works*, vol. 9: September 1908 – November 1909, https://www.gandhiheritageportal.org/cwmg_volume_thumbview/OQ==#page/400/mode/2up

257 In 1923 the capital of Turkey, the successor state of the Ottoman Empire, was moved to Ankara and the name Constantinople was officially changed to Istanbul.

258 British Library, Add MSS 43941 (155)

259 Dilke to Schreiner, 7 July 1909, UCT Special Collections, UCT BC 112 File 12 (7.28)

260 UCT Special Collections, Schreiner Correspondence, BC 112, File 11, c. July 1909

261 National Library of South Africa, Schreiner Correspondence, MSC27 Box 8 Letter 1502 1

262 *The Times*, 23 July 1909

263 Travers Buxton to Schreiner, 15 July 1909, UCT Special Collections, SC27 Box 8 Letter 1492 1; *The Times*, *The Scotsman*, 28 July 1909

264 *South Africa*, 31 July 1909, p. 275

265 *The Times*, 28 July 1909

266 *South Africa*, 31 July 1909, p. 275

267 *The Times*, 28 July 1909

268 Stead to Schreiner, 26 July 1909, UCT Special Collections, UCT BC 112 File 12 (19.5)

269 Letter dated 29 July 1909, *APO*, 11 September 1909

270 *Morning Post*, 28 July 1909

271 *Imperial Conference, Correspondence and Papers relating to a Conference with Representatives of the Self-Governing Dominions on the Naval and Military Defence of the Empire, 1909*, HMSO, London, 1909, Cd 4948, p. 17. The South Africans representing the colonies were Merriman (Cape), Greene (Natal), Smuts (Transvaal) and Fischer (Orange Free State). The urgent need for a unified South African military to face potential threats, including from German South West Africa, was discussed in detail by a member of the Natal Legislative Assembly, P.A. Silburn, in *The Colonies and Imperial Defence*, Longman, Green and Co., London, 1909.

272 *Imperial Conference, Correspondence and Papers relating to a Conference with Representatives of the Self-Governing Dominions on the Naval and Military Defence of the Empire, 1909*, p. 44

273 *The Graphic*, 21 August 1909

274 The three European powers and their colonies were Germany: South-West Africa and Tanganyika; Portugal: Mozambique and Angola; and Belgium: Congo.

275 This was by no means the only occasion on which the Dominions challenged British leadership of the Empire. See Martin Plaut and David Killingray, 'Race and Imperialism in the British Empire: A Lateral View', *South African Historical Journal*, March 2020

276 I am indebted to Catherine Corder who kindly shared her work on Betty Molteno with me. The Molteno letters are mostly to be found in the University of Cape Town archive.

277 UCT Special Collections, Schreiner Correspondence, BC 506, A1.2

278 UCT Special Collections, UCT BC 112 File 11 (7.24), Petition from Schreiner, Jabavu, etc.

279 *Review of Reviews*, August 1909

280   Letter from Betty Molteno, 14 August 1909, UCT, Manuscripts & Archives. Betty Molteno's writing is notoriously difficult to read. I am indebted to Catherine Corder for deciphering the letters and making them available.

281   Hardie to Schreiner, 6 August 1909, National Library of South Africa, Cape Town, MSC27 Box 8 Letter 1529 1

282   *Daily Mail*, 11 August 1909

283   National Library of South Africa, Cape Town, Schreiner Papers, MSC27 Box 8 Letter 1521A 1

284   South African History Online, for a partial list of the delegates to the South African Native National Congress (which was renamed the African National Congress in 1923), http://www.sahistory.org.za/topic/delegates-attendance-sannc-founding-conference-1912, accessed 1 October 2013

285   Hansard, 16 August 1909, http://hansard.millbanksystems.com/commons/1909/aug/16/south-africa-bill-lords

286   This was not entirely accurate. All men had previously had the vote in Natal as well, although it was so circumscribed with regulations that few African, Indian or coloured men had ever been able to exercise the right.

287   Hansard, 16 August 1909, http://hansard.millbanksystems.com/commons/1909/aug/16/south-africa-bill-lords

288   'I am glad to be able to announce that I have dealt with the matter, having consulted my hon. friend Mr. Schreiner, and the matter is now merely an academic one. For in order that there may be no possible mistake in the matter it is provided in the Royal Instructions that any such Bill shall be reserved, and therefore the matter becomes purely academic. If anyone takes the view that the Instructions are liable to alteration, I may say that that is not a likely case, because we in our party are not likely to advise His Majesty to alter the Instructions with a view to taking away other people's votes easily. I trust that I have met the points which have been raised.' Hansard, 19 August 1909, https://api.parliament.uk/historic-hansard/commons/1909/aug/19/clause-35-qualifications-of-voters

289   Hansard, 19 August 1909, http://hansard.millbanksystems.com/commons/1909/aug/19/clause-26-qualifications-of-senators

290   Hansard, 19 August 1909, http://hansard.millbanksystems.com/commons/1909/aug/19/schedule

291   *APO*, 28 August 1909

292   Gandhi, *Collected Works*, vol. 9: September 1908 – November 1909, https://www.gandhiheritageportal.org/cwmg_volume_thumbview/OQ==#page/400/mode/2up

293   It was sent to Dr Abdurahman's residence, at 36 Longbridge Road, Earl's Court.

294   *Indian Opinion*, 18 September 1909; Gandhi, *Collected Works*, https://www.gandhiheritageportal.org/cwmg_volume_thumbview/OQ==#page/400/mode/2up

295   UCT Special Collections, Molteno Murray Family Papers, BC 330

296   *Cape Times*, 21 September 1909

297   *Cape Times*, 22 September 1909; *APO*, 25 September 1909. Those who arrived were Schreiner, Abdurahman, Fredericks, Lenders, Rubusana, Dwanya and Mapikela. Others, like Jabavu and Gerrans, were expected back within a fortnight.

298   *Cape Times*, 22 September 1909

299   *Cape Times*, 22 September 1909

300   *APO*, 25 September 1909

301   *APO*, 9 October 1909

302   *APO*, 9 October 1909

303   *Imvo*, 31 August 1909, quoted in Odendaal, *The Founders*, p. 435

304   *APO*, 26 February 1910

305   *Rand Daily Mail*, 22 February 1910

306   *Indian Opinion*, 26 February 1910

307   *Cape Times*, 4 March 1910

308   *Indian Opinion*, 5 March 1910

309   Lewis, *Between the Wire and the Wall*, p. 55. Peregrino had a habit of attacking people he disapproved of, even some of his previous allies, denouncing them to the white authorities. Killingray and Plaut, 'F.Z.S. Peregrino', pp. 493–516

Chapter 7

310   *Indian Opinion*, 23 April 1910

311   *Cape Times*, 29 April 1910

312   Van der Ross, *Say It Out Loud*, p. 31

313   Ibid., p. 34

314   Lewis, *Between the Wire and the Wall*, p. 60

315   *APO*, 9 April 1910

316   *APO*, 9 April 1910

317   *APO*, 23 April 1910

318   Lewis, *Between the Wire and the Wall*, p. 59

319   Ibid., p. 81

320   Ibid., p. 78

321   Brian Willan, *Sol Plaatje: South African Nationalist, 1876–1932*, University of California Press, Berkeley, 1984, p. 237

322   *Tsala ea Batho*, 6 April 1912

323   Willan, *Sol Plaatje*, p. 239

324   *Tsala ea Batho*, 26 July 1913

325   *APO*, 6 September 1913

326   Hyman Liberman became Cape Town's first Jewish mayor in 1904. He was mayor twice more (1906 and 1907) and an institute, named after him, was built as a cultural centre in District Six in 1934. Bickford-Smith, Van Heyningen and Worden, *Cape Town in the Twentieth Century*, p. 84. See https://www.sahistory.org.za/dated-event/mayor-cape-town-hyman-lieberman-opens-great-synagogue-gardens-cape-town. Hyman Liberman became Cape Town's first Jewish mayor in 1905. See https://www.jewishvirtuallibrary.org/south-africa-virtual-jewish-history-tour, accessed 5 April 2020

327   *Cape Times*, 29 August 1913

328   *Financial Times*, 28 March 1914

329   Most of this section is drawn from Van der Ross, *A Political and Social History of the Cape Coloured People*, pp. 545–58, which deals with Dr Abdurahman's time as provincial councillor. The Unionist Party, led by Dr Jameson, existed from 1910 until 1921 when it merged with Smuts's South African Party, https://en.wikipedia.org/wiki/Unionist_Party_(South_Africa), accessed 2 September 2019.

330   Van der Ross, *A Political and Social History of the Cape Coloured People*, p. 557

331   Johannes Meintjes, *General Louis Botha: A Biography*, Cassell, London, 1970, p. 205

332   S.B. Spies, 'The Outbreak of the First World War and the Botha Government', *South African Historical Journal*, no. 1, 1969, pp. 47–8

333   Adam Cruise, *Louis Botha's War: The Campaign in German South-West Africa, 1914–1915*, Zebra Press, Century City, 2015

334   See Timothy C. Winegard, *Indigenous Peoples of the British Dominions and the First World War*, Cambridge University Press, Cambridge, 2012

335   Bill Nasson, *WWI and the People of South Africa*, Tafelberg, Cape Town, 2014, p. 42

336   Ibid., p. 46

337   Lewis, *Between the Wire and the Wall*, p. 85

338   Ibid.

339   Bill Nasson, *WWI and the People of South Africa*, p. 50

340   Bill Nasson, 'Why They Fought: Black Cape Colonists and Imperial Wars, 1899–1918', *International Journal of African Historical Studies*, vol. 37, no. 1, 2004, p. 64

341   Ibid., p. 66

342   Anne Samson, *Britain, South Africa and the East Africa Campaign, 1914–1918: The Union Comes of Age*, PhD, University of London, 2003, p. 156

343   Ibid., p. 161. The thesis has a discussion of the impact of the Dr Abdurahman letter on British and South African policy.

344   Ibid., p. 161

345   Kyle Harmse, *The Cape Corps: South Africa's Coloured Soldiers in the First World War*, MA thesis, University of Johannesburg, 2017, p. 35

346   Kenneth W. Grundy, *Soldiers without Politics: Blacks in the South African Armed Forces*, University of California Press, Berkeley, 1983, p. 53

347   Captain Ivor D. Difford, *The Story of the 1st Battalion Cape Corps, 1915–1919*, Hortors, Cape Town, 1921, p. 22

348   Ibid., p. 54

349   *Rhodesian Herald*, 13 June 1919

350   *Eastern Province Herald*, 17 June 1919

351   Grundy, *Soldiers without Politics*, p. 63

352   *Eastern Province Herald*, 20 May 1919

CHAPTER 8

353   Van der Spuy, *Not Only 'the Younger Daughter of Dr Abdurahman'*, p. 30; Wong, *The Doctor of District Six*, p. 41

354   The date of the separation is unclear. Van der Spuy suggests it took place 'some time after 1927 – perhaps as late at 1931'; Van der Spuy, *Not Only 'the Younger Daughter of Dr Abdurahman'*, p. 139. Wong cites sources suggesting the separation took place in 1923 and the marriage to Maggie took place in 1925, but Wong is not convinced by these dates. See Wong, *The Doctor of District Six*, p. 112

355   Van der Spuy, *Not only 'the younger daughter of Dr Abdurahman'*, p. 45

356   Wong, *The Doctor of District Six*, p. 113

357   https://www.geni.com/people/Begum-Gadija-Jahanara-Hendrickse/6000000048604047056

358   Van der Spuy, *Not Only 'the Younger Daughter of Dr Abdurahman'*, p. 28

359   Ibid., p. 29

360   Ibid., p. 51

361   Ibid., p. 64

362   Ibid., p. 64

363   Elizabeth Everett, *Zainunnissa (Cissie) Gool: 1897–1963*, BA (Hons) dissertation, University of Cape Town, 1978, p. 2

364   https://www.sahistory.org.za/archive/trafalgar-high-school-cape-town-marks-100-years

365   https://www.sahistory.org.za/people/harold-cressy

366   https://pdfs.semanticscholar.org/3971/6cc6ec886d93f8190ddf61262394d-3f0e468.pdf

367   Gairoonisa Paleker, *'She Was Certainly Not a Rosa Luxemburg': A Biography of Cissie Gool in Images and Words*, MA, University of Cape Town, 2002, p. 29; Van der Spuy, *Not Only 'the Younger Daughter of Dr Abdurahman'*, p. 184

368   https://www.sa-venues.com/attractionswc/cissie-gool-memorial.php

369   Van der Spuy, 'The Politics of Race, Gender and Class in Cape Town', p. 3

370   Van der Spuy, *Not Only 'the Younger Daughter of Dr Abdurahman'*, pp. 59–61

371   Ibid., p. 61

372   Meer, *I Remember*, p. 52

373   Lewis, *Between the Wire and the Wall*, pp. 39–40

374   Van der Ross, *Say It Out Loud*, pp. 34–5

375   Pamela Scully, 'White Maternity and Black Infancy: The Rhetoric of Race in the South African Women's Suffrage Movement, 1895–1930', in Ian Christopher Fletcher, Philippa Levine and Laura E. Nym Mayhall (eds.), *Women's Suffrage in the British Empire: Citizenship, Nation and Race*, Routledge, London, 2014, p. 73

376   Lou Haysom, 'Olive Schreiner and the Women's Vote', *Searchlight South Africa*, vol. 3, no. 3, October 1993, p. 30, https://disa.ukzn.ac.za/sites/default/files/pdf_files/sloct93.5.pdf

377   Deborah Rochelle Klein, *Negotiating Femininity, Ethnicity and History: Representations of Ruth First in South African Struggle Narratives*, PhD, University of Cape Town, 2006, p. 42

378   Olive Schreiner, BC16 Box 12 Fold1 Undated 44, University of Cape Town, Manuscripts & Archives, Cape Town; https://www.oliveschreiner.org/vre?view=collections&colid=114&letterid=44

379   H.C. Dampier, 'Going On with Our Little Movement in the Humdrum Way Which Alone Is Possible in a Land like This': Olive Schreiner and Suffrage Networks in Britain and South Africa, 1905–1913', *Women's History Review*, vol. 25, no. 4, 2016, p. 540

380   Patricia van der Spuy, *Not Only 'the Younger Daughter of Dr Abdurahman'*, pp. 40–1

381   Ray Alexander Simons, *All My Life and All My Strength*, STE Publishers, Johannesburg, 2004, p. 56

382   Patricia van der Spuy and Lindsay Clowes, '"A Living Testimony of the Heights to Which a Woman Can Rise": Sarojini Naidu, Cissie Gool and the Politics of Women's Leadership in South Africa in the 1920s', *South African Historical Journal*, vol. 64, no. 2, June 2012, p. 11

383   *APO*, 7 May 1910

384   Van der Spuy, *Not Only 'the Younger Daughter of Dr Abdurahman'*, p. 65

385   Ibid., p. 68

386 Crain Soudien, 'Institutionalising Racial Segregation in the South African School: The School Board Act, 1905', *Paedagogica Historica*, 2018, p. 12, https://doi.org/10.1080/00309230.2018.1521847

387 Adhikari, *Hope, Fear, Shame, Frustration*, p. 130

388 Ibid.,

389 Soudien, 'Institutionalising Racial Segregation in the South African School', p. 10

390 Ibid., p. 14

391 Van der Spuy, *Not Only 'the Younger Daughter of Dr Abdurahman'*, p. 73

392 https://www.sahistory.org.za/archive/trafalgar-high-school-cape-town-marks-100-years

393 Van der Spuy, *Not Only 'the Younger Daughter of Dr Abdurahman'*, p. 75

394 *APO*, 25 March 1911

395 Victoria Collis-Buthelezi, 'Caribbean Regionalism, South Africa, and Mapping New World Studies', *Small Axe*, no. 46, March 2015, https://criticaltheoryconsortium.org/wp-content/uploads/2018/07/VJCB-Caribbean-Regionalism.pdf

396 *APO*, 8 March 1913, quoted in Wong, *The Doctor of District Six*, p. 83

397 Van der Spuy, *Not Only 'the Younger Daughter of Dr Abdurahman'*, p. 78

398 *APO*, 3 February 1912, quoted in ibid., p. 79

399 Julia C. Wells, 'Why Women Rebel: A Comparative Study of South African Women's Resistance in Bloemfontein (1913) and Johannesburg (1958)', *Journal of South African Studies*, vol. 10, no. 1, October 1983, p. 56

400 Cherryl Walker, *Women and Resistance in South Africa*, Onyx Press, London, 1982, p. 29

401 Ibid., p. 30

402 Ibid.

CHAPTER 9

403 Lewis, *Between the Wire and the Wall*, p. 86

404 Ibid.

405 Ibid.

406 Van der Ross, *Say It Out Loud*, p. 146

407 Ibid., p. 88

408 Lewis, *Between the Wire and the Wall*, p. 82

409 *Eastern Province Herald*, 19 February 1920

410 Sheridan Johns, 'The Birth of the Communist Party of South Africa', *International Journal of African Historical Studies*, vol. IX, no. 3, 1976, p. 371

411 *Cape Times*, 14 January 1920

412 Lewis, *Between the Wire and the Wall*, p. 98

413 Jack and Ray Simons, *Class and Colour in South Africa*, p. 270

414 Sadie Forman and Andre Odendaal (eds.), *A Trumpet from the Housetops: The Selected Writings of Lionel Forman*, Mayibuye Centre, University of the Western Cape, 1992, p. 43

415 Ibid., p. 44

416 Jack and Ray Simons, *Class and Colour in South Africa*, p. 126 quoting from the *APO*, 1910–12

417 Baruch Hirson, *A History of the Left in South Africa*, I.B. Tauris, London, 2005, p. 2

418 Lewis, *Between the Wire and the Wall*, p. 94

419 Ibid.

420 *Cape Times*, 21 December 1918, quoted in P.L. Wickins, 'General Labour Unions in Cape Town, 1918–1920', *South African Journal of Economics*, vol. 40, no. 3, September 1972, p. 277

421 *Indian Opinion*, 20 June 1919

422 Van der Walt, 'Anarchism and Syndicalism in an African Port City', p. 150

423 Ibid., pp. 95ff

424 Ibid., p. 100

425 *APO*, 12 September 1919

426 Lewis, *Between the Wire and the Wall*, pp. 95–6

427 Ibid., p. 94

428 Abdurahman to Merriman, 9 January 1920, quoted in Walshe, *The Rise of African Nationalism in South Africa*, p. 71

429 *Cape Times*, 22 November 1919

430 *Cape Times*, 18 December 1919

431 *Cape Times*, 29 December 1919

432 *Cape Times*, 5 January 1920, letter signed by Z.R. Mahabane, president, Cape Province Native Congress

433 *Cape Times*, 13 January 1920; *Eastern Province Herald*, 16 January 1920

434 The chairman of the strike committee was J.H. Dean, who became secretary of the Cape Province Federation of Labour Unions by 1913 (*Cape Times*, 3 November 1913).

435 Lewis, *Between the Wire and the Wall*, p. 102

436 Allison Drew, *Discordant Comrades: Identities and Loyalties on the South African Left*, Ashgate, Aldershot, 2000, p. 74

437 Lewis, *Between the Wire and the Wall*, p. 102

438 Wickins, 'General Labour Unions in Cape Town', p. 297

439 Ibid.

440 Lewis, *Between the Wire and the Wall*, p. 102

441 Ibid., p. 103

442 Ibid., p. 103

443 https://www.sahistory.org.za/organisations/industrial-and-commercial-workers-union-icu

CHAPTER 10

444 Wessel Visser, *A History of the South African Mine Workers' Union, 1902–2014*, Edwin Mellen Press, Lewiston, 2016, pp. 14-17. Visser suggests that after the First World War Afrikaners made up the majority of union members, although the leadership was almost completely English-speaking.

445 *Cape Times*, 22 March 1922

446 Jeremy Krikler, *White Rising: The 1922 Insurrection and Racial Killing in South Africa*, Manchester University Press, Manchester, 2005, pp. 256ff

447 Ibid., p. 291

448 Geoffrey Wheatcroft, *The Randlords: The Men Who Made South Africa*, Weidenfeld and Nicolson, London, 1985, p. 251

449 Hirson, *A History of the Left in South Africa*, pp. 39–40

450 Ibid., p. 67

451 Ibid., p. 77

452 Ibid., pp. 81ff

453 *Cape Times*, 13 March 1919

454 *Cape Times*, 9 March 1922

455 *Eastern Province Herald*, 14 February 1922

456 R.E. van der Ross, *The Rise and Decline of Apartheid: A Study of Political Movements among the Coloured People of South Africa, 1880–1985*, Tafelberg, Cape Town, p. 60

457 *South African*, 17 February 1922

458 *Cape Times*, 10 March 1922

459 Ibid.

460 It was a process that had started to emerge a decade earlier: in the 1914 election the Labour Party had won the majority of the Transvaal seats in the Provincial Council, with even Krugersdorp and Pretoria West returning English-speaking Labour candidates. T.R.H. Davenport and Christopher Saunders, *South Africa: A Modern History*, 5th edn, Macmillan Press, London, 2000, p. 283

461 Ibid., p. 297

462 Lewis, *Between the Wire and the Wall*, p. 120

463 Ibid., pp. 120ff

464 Van der Ross, *Say It Out Loud*, pp. 80–1

465 Van der Ross, *The Rise and Decline of Apartheid*, pp. 71ff

466 Giliomee, *The Afrikaners*, p. 391

467 https://www.sahistory.org.za/topic/history-bulhoek-massacre

468 Maurice Hommel, *Capricorn Blues: Struggle for Human Rights in South Africa*, Culturama, Toronto, 1981, p. 60

469 Giliomee, *The Afrikaners*, p. 391

470 Ibid.

471 Van der Ross, *The Rise and Decline of Apartheid*, p. 75

472 Lewis, *Between the Wire and the Wall*, p. 122

473 Ibid., p. 123

474 Ibid., p. 124

475 The position of coloured people in the Free State was distinct and peculiar. Under the Free State Constitution of 1854 they were 'never' to be regarded as burghers, even if they owned property, but would be required to provide military service and serve in a commando if requested to do so. *Report of the Commission of Inquiry Regarding the Cape Coloured Population of the Union*, para 1077, p. 218. Hence, coloureds had responsibilities to serve the state as troops, but did not have the right to vote.

476 Lewis, *Between the Wire and the Wall*, p. 124

477 Giliomee, *The Afrikaners*, p. 391

478 Lewis, *Between the Wire and the Wall*, p. 125

479 Giliomee, *The Afrikaners*, p. 391

480 Lewis, *Between the Wire and the Wall*, p. 126

481 Ibid., p. 127

482 Ibid., p. 128

483 *Cape Times*, 11 June 1924

CHAPTER 11

484 Edgar, *The Travel Notes of Ralph J. Bunche*, p. 61
485 *Indian Opinion*, 23 June 1909
486 See, for example, *Indian Opinion*, 23 October 1912
487 Yousuf Rassool, *District Six – Lest We Forget: Recapturing Subjugated Cultural Histories of Cape Town, 1897–1956*, University of the Western Cape, Bellville, 2000, p. 19
488 See, for example, *Indian Opinion*, 7 April 1911
489 Ramachandra Guha, *Gandhi before India*, Allen Lane, London, 2013 provides an excellent overview of Gandhi's life and role in South Africa until he left permanently for India in 1914.
490 Ibid., p. 429
491 *Indian Opinion*, 22 October 1912
492 Corder and Plaut, 'Gandhi's Decisive South African 1913 Campaign'
493 Van der Ross, *Say It Out Loud*, p. 54
494 Guha, *Gandhi before India*, p. 527
495 J.E. Corbett, *A Study of the Cape Town Agreement*, MA, UCT, 1947, p. 17
496 M.K. Gandhi, 'Statement to the Press on Anti-Indian Campaign in South Africa', 14 February 1924
497 Goolam Vahed, 'Race, Empire, and Citizenship: Sarojini Naidu's 1924 Visit to South Africa', *South African Historical Journal*, vol. 64, no. 2, 2012, p. 332
498 *Lourenco Marques Guardian*, 27 February 1924, quoted in ibid., p. 332
499 Ibid., p. 333
500 Van der Spuy and Clowes, '"A Living Testimony of the Heights to Which a Woman Can Rise"'
501 Vahed, 'Race, Empire, and Citizenship', p. 339
502 Van der Spuy and Clowes, '"A Living Testimony of the Heights to Which a Woman Can Rise"'
503 G.A. Natesan, *Speeches and Writings of Sarojini Naidu*, G.A. Natesan & Co., Madras, n.d., pp. 432–3, cited in Vahed, 'Race, Empire, and Citizenship', p. 341
504 Lewis, *Between the Wire and the Wall*, p. 136
505 This was the Areas Reservation and Immigration and Registration (Further Provisions) Bill, which Malan introduced in Parliament in July 1925. Essop Pahad, *The Development of Indian Political Movements in South Africa, 1924–1946*, DPhil, University of Sussex, 1972, p. 44
506 Pahad, *The Development of Indian Political Movements in South Africa*, p. 45
507 G.H. Calpin, *Indians in South Africa*, Shuter and Shooter, Pietermaritzburg, 1949, quoted in Pahad, *The Development of Indian Political Movements in South Africa*, p. 46
508 Pahad, *The Development of Indian Political Movements in South Africa*, p. 53. See P.S. Joshi, *The Tyranny of Colour: A Study of the Indian Problem in South Africa*, Durban, 1942, p. 114 for a detailed description of the negotiations with Malan.
509 *Cape Argus*, 3 August 1925
510 Lewis, *Between the Wire and the Wall*, p. 136
511 British Library, IOR/L/E/7/1411, File 5215(ii), Department of Education, Health and Lands, Proceedings, Overseas – A; March 1926, Nos. 1-88, p. 21
512 Ibid., p. 22
513 Ibid., p. 57. Indians, including Gandhi, frequently referred to Dr Abdurahman

as Dr Abdu Rahman. It was a mistake, but often repeated.

514 Pahad, *The Development of Indian Political Movements in South Africa*, p. 54n. Gandhi described the delegation as consisting of Dr Abdurahman, 'a well-known Malay doctor from Cape Town. He has Indian blood too.' The others were 'James Godfrey, a barrister and son of an Indian Christian school teacher. The third is Sorabji, the brave son of the late Parsi Rustomji. He is a tried soldier and has been to prison. Those who have read the *History of Satyagraha in South Africa* will be familiar with his name. I pray that their visit and their efforts will meet with success.' *Collected Works*, Navajivan, 29 November 1925

515 Gandhi, *Young India*, 26 November 1925, in *Collected Works*

516 Northwestern University, Melville J. Herskovits Library of Africana Studies, Abdurahman Family Papers (hereafter NWU/AFP): General Correspondence 1919–1938 (Box 1, Folder 5): Letter to Mr. Coovadia, 12 November 1925

517 UCT, Manuscripts & Archives, BC506 Abdurahman Papers: Folder B2, Newspaper Clippings, Loose clipping undated, unsourced

518 UCT, Manuscripts & Archives, BC506 Abdurahman Papers: Folder B2, Newspaper Clippings, Loose clipping undated, unsourced; handwritten 'November 19'

519 Joshi, *The Tyranny of Colour*, p. 117

520 'K.K. Aziz, in his book *The Coffee House of Lahore: A Memoir (1942–1957)*, describes the vibrant life that surrounded the building, "In the two hall-size rooms of the Shahdin building was the Lorangs, the finest restaurant in town, patronised by the elite. Near it stood the Stiffles where the guests dined in dinner jackets, danced in the evening and lunched with their friends in as English an ambience as could be conceived."' See https://www.ghoomlo.pk/listing/punjab/lahore/city-sightseeings/shahdin-manzil-faisal-chowk/, accessed 15 September 2019

521 *Sunday Times* (India), 31 January 1926

522 Ibid.

523 Ibid.

524 Unnamed cutting, 6 February 1926, Dr Edgar Maurice Private Papers

525 *Sunday Times*, 31 January 1926

526 Charlotte Viall Wiser, 'Madam President' in the 'Chair in India: A Woman's Hands and her Fiery Words Guiding the Indian National Congress', *Asia Magazine*, New York, vol. 26, no. 7, July 1926, pp. 634–42

527 Presidential Address delivered at the 40th Indian National Congress by Sumali Sarojini Naidu, 26 December 1925, pp. 6–7, Dr Edgar Maurice Private Papers

528 Joshi, *The Tyranny of Colour*, p. 117

529 Wiser, 'Madam President', p. 635

530 Ibid., pp. 635–36

531 Extract from private letter from Lord Reading to Lord Birkenhead, 12 February 1925, British Library, IOR/L/PO/1/22, Folio 207 – 346, No. 246

532 Pahad, *The Development of Indian Political Movements in South Africa*, p. 54. Lord Reading was Viceroy from 2 April 1921 to 3 April 1926.

533 Ibid, p. 55

534 Indian Overseas Association, *The South African Indian: Helot or Citizen*, London, 1926, pp. 34–5

535 Ibid., p. 39

536   Viceroy to Secretary of State, Telegram No 369, 19 December 1925, British Library, MSS Eur E 238/19; see also British Library, IOR/L/PO/1/22, Folio 88–206

537   British Library, MSS Eur E 238/19

538   Ibid., Viceroy to Secretary of State, Telegram 390, 13 January 1926

539   Hansard, House of Lords Debate, 24 February 1926, https://api.parliament.uk/historic-hansard/lords/1926/feb/24/indians-in-south-africa

540   British Library, IOR/L/PO/1/22, Folios 2–87, no. 68

541   *Indian Opinion*, 12 March 1926, cited in Pahad, *The Development of Indian Political Movements in South Africa*, p. 56

542   Letter from Dr Abdurahman to Sarojini Naidu, 26 April 1926, Dr Edgar Maurice Private Papers

543   Meer, *I Remember*, p. 32

544   Ibid., p. 32

545   https://en.wikipedia.org/wiki/Mian_Muhammad_Shafi, accessed 23 September 2019

546   Vineet Thakur, 'Liberal, Liminal and Lost: India's First Diplomats and the Narrative of Foreign Policy', *Journal of Imperial and Commonwealth History*, vol. 45, no. 2, 2017, p. 236

547   https://en.wikipedia.org/wiki/Satyendra_Prasanna_Sinha,_1st_Baron_Sinha, accessed 23 September 2019

548   Thakur, 'Liberal, Liminal and Lost', p. 240

549   Ibid., p. 250

550   C.M. van der Heever, *General J. B. M. Hertzog*, A.P.B. Bookstore, Johannesburg, 1946, p. 206

551   Ibid., p. 210

552   Pahad, *The Development of Indian Political Movements in South Africa*, p. 60

553   Telegram from the Viceroy, 24 November 1924, British Library, IOR/L/E/7/1411, File 5215(ii)

554   Surendra Bhana, *Gandhi's Legacy: The Natal Indian Congress, 1894–1994*, University of Natal Press, Pietermaritzburg, 1997, p. 36

555   Ibid., p. 67

556   Telegram from the Governor General of the Union of South Africa to the Viceroy, 13 January 1927, British Library, IOR/L/E/7/1411, File 5215(ii)

557   See Pahad, *The Development of Indian Political Movements in South Africa*, and Corbett, *A Study of the Cape Town Agreement*, for a full description of how this took place.

558   Corbett, *A Study of the Cape Town Agreement*, p. 74.

559   'The Capetown Agreement bears the same relation to the South African scene as the Atlantic Charter bears to the world scene … If, in the years that followed, the hopes of Indians receded and the spirit of the Capetown Agreement was lost in new estrangements, it still shines as a beacon for all Indians in the country.' Calpin, *Indians in South Africa*, p. 67

560   *The Servant of India*, 24 February 1927

CHAPTER 12

561   Lewis, *Between the Wire and the Wall*, p. 128

562 Ibid., p. 19

563 Ibid., p. 128

564 Giliomee, *The Afrikaners*, p. 392

565 Lewis, *Between the Wire and the Wall*, p. 129

566 Ibid., p. 130

567 Ibid., p. 131

568 Ibid., p. 132

569 Ibid., p. 133

570 Ibid., pp. 134–5

571 Ibid., pp. 145–6

572 Ibid., p. 147

573 Ibid., p. 148

574 Haines, *Opposition to General J.B.M. Hertzog's Segregation Bills*, pp. 101, 35

575 Lewis, *Between the Wire and the Wall*, p. 137

576 Ibid., p. 139

577 *Umteteli wa Bantu*, 26 June 1926, cited in Haines, *Opposition to General J.B.M. Hertzog's Segregation Bills*, p. 101

578 Van der Ross, *Say It Out Loud*, p. 84

579 Ibid., p. 92

580 Lewis, *Between the Wire and the Wall*, p. 140

581 Ibid., p. 141

582 Ibid., p. 141

583 Richard John Haines, *The Opposition to General J.B.M Hertzog's Segregation Bills, 1925–1936: A Study in Extra-Parliamentary Protest*, MA thesis, University of Natal, 1978, p. 132

584 Brian Willan, *Sol Plaatje: A Life of Solomon Tshekisho Plaatje, 1876–1932*, Jacana Media, Johannesburg, 2018, p. 468

585 Van der Ross, *The Rise and Decline of Apartheid*, p. 91

586 Bhana, *Gandhi's Legacy*, p. 43

587 Tom Karis and Gwendolen Carter (eds.), *From Protest to Challenge: A Documentary History of African Politics in South Africa*, vol. 1, *Protest and Hope, 1882–1934*, Hoover Institution Press, Stanford, 1972, p. 386

588 Willan, *Sol Plaatje*, 2018, p. 468

589 Ibid.

590 Ibid., p. 424

591 Ibid., p. 65

592 Ibid., p. 431

593 Ibid., pp. 64–5

594 https://www.sahistory.org.za/archive/testimony-professor-d-d-t-jabavu-walter-rubusana-and-rev-abner-mtimkulu-cape-native-voters, accessed 28 August 2019

595 https://www.sahistory.org.za/archive/native-disabilities-south-africa-pamphlet-professor-d-d-t-jabavu-july-1932, accessed 28 August 2019

596 The author has been assured that there is no reference to this question in the Royal Archives.

597 Robert MacGregor Dawson (ed.), *The Development of Dominion Status, 1900–1936*, Frank Cass, London, 1937, p. 25

598 A former Foreign Secretary, by 1926 Balfour was Lord President of the Council, a senior government position.

599 http://www.nationalarchives.gov.uk/cabinetpapers/themes/dominion-sta-
tus-legislation.htm, accessed 28 August 2019

600 http://www.nationalarchives.gov.uk/cabinetpapers/help/glossary-s.ht-
m#Statute_of_Westminster, accessed 28 August 2019

601 As Balfour's secret report puts it: 'Consequently, it would not be in accordance
with constitutional practice for advice to be tendered to His Majesty by His
Majesty's Government in Great Britain in any matter appertaining to the affairs
of a Dominion against the views of the Government of that Dominion.'

602 Hertzog was exultant on his return to Cape Town after the 1926 Conference. 'No
declaration could be devised by which the country's liberty in a most unlimited
manner could be so clearly demonstrated as was done in the document as it
stood. No one need bother in future about South Africa breaking away from the
Empire. As a result of the Imperial Conference, the old Empire no longer exists.
The old Empire was a domination of States under which South Africa and other
Dominions had to, and did, submit for years. All that remains was a free alliance
of England and the six Dominions, co-operating as friends and, so to speak,
forming their own League of Nations.' *The Times*, 15 December 1926

603 Lewis, *Between the Wire and the Wall*, p. 154

604 Ibid., p. 155

605 Ibid., p. 155

606 Ibid., p. 158

607 Ibid., p. 158

608 Ibid., p. 167

609 *Report of the Commission of Inquiry Regarding the Cape Coloured Population of the
Union*, p. 230

610 Ibid., p. 242

611 Ibid., p. 242

612 Lewis, *Between the Wire and the Wall*, p. 169

613 Francois Cleophas, *Physical Education and Physical Culture in the Coloured
Community of the Western Cape, 1837–1966*, PhD, University of Stellenbosch,
2009, pp. 146, 154

614 Lewis, *Between the Wire and the Wall*, p. 169

CHAPTER 13

615 Alan Wieder provides this damning assessment: 'The APO and the Conferences
worked hard but accomplished little.' Alan Wieder, *Teacher and Comrade:
Richard Dudley and the Fight for Democracy in South Africa*, SUNY Press, New
York, 2008, p. 32

616 Walshe, *The Rise of African Nationalism in South Africa*, p. 255. Walshe argues
that 'it was not until 1936 when the Rev. James Calata became Secretary-General
that a gradual recovery began.'

617 Giliomee, *The Afrikaners*, p. 441

618 Wayne Dooling, 'Poverty and Respectability in Early Twentieth-Century Cape
Town', *Journal of African History*, vol. 59, no. 3, pp. 411–35

619 David Lewis, 'Trade Union and Class Stratification: A Preliminary Analysis
of the Role of Working Class Organisations in the Western Cape', in Hendrik
van der Merwe and C.J. Groenewald, *Occupational and Social Change among*

Coloured People in South Africa, Juta, Cape Town, 1976, p. 192

620 *The International*, 13 April 1923

621 Heidi Villa-Vicencio, *Colour, Citizenship and Constitutionalism*, MA thesis, UCT, 1995, p. 33

622 *Imvo Zabantsundu*, 20 May 1931, quoted in Haines, *The Opposition to General J.B.M. Hertzog's Segregation Bills*, p. 149

623 Everett, *Zainunnissa (Cissie) Gool*, p. 3

624 Ibid., p. 9; Gool, *The Gools of Cape Town*, vol. 1, p. 20, https://independent.academia.edu/SelimGool

625 Ibid., p. 10

626 Baruch Hirson, *The Cape Town Intellectuals: Ruth Schechter and Her Circle, 1907–1934*, Merlin Press, Cape Town, 2001, pp. 170–1

627 Lewis, *Between the Wire and the Wall*, p. 180

628 Intriguingly, the historian and senior Communist Party member Ray Simons has a vivid recollection of Cissie calling her onto a platform in Cape Town, during a visit by Sarojini Naidu in 1929 or 1930 at the Cape Town City Hall. Simons, *All My Life and All My Strength*, pp. 59–60. This visit by Sarojini Naidu is not recorded in the exhaustive *Gandhi Collected Works*. Patricia van der Spuy and Lindsay Clowes say they 'were unable to reconstruct a timeline that would have allowed Naidu to be in Cape Town on either date.' Patricia van der Spuy and Lindsay Clowes, 'Transnational Mentoring: The Impact of Sarojini Naidu's 1924 Visit to South Africa on Cissie Gool and Women's Leadership', in Francisca de Haan et al. (eds.), *Women's Activism: Global Perspectives from the 1890s to the Present*, Routledge, London, 2012, pp. 39–40

629 Wieder, *Teacher and Comrade*, p. 44

630 Doreen Musson, *Johnny Gomas: Voice of the Working Class*, Buchu Books, Cape Town, 1989, p. 62

631 Peter Abrahams, *Tell Freedom*, Faber and Faber, London, 1954, pp. 274–5

632 Programme of the National Liberation League of South Africa, in Allison Drew (ed.), *South Africa's Radical Tradition: A Documentary History, vol. 1, 1907–1950*, UCT Press, Cape Town, 1996, pp. 183, 257

633 Ibid. p. 183

634 Ibid. p. 179

635 Crain Soudien, *The Cape Radicals: Intellectual and Political Thought of the New Era Fellowship, 1930s–1960s*, Wits University Press, Johannesburg, 2019, p. 88

636 Ibid., p. 184

637 Ibid., p. 182

638 Bickford-Smith, Van Heyningen and Worden, *Cape Town in the Twentieth Century*, p. 84

639 It was a stand that probably resonated with many of her constituents. As one later recalled: 'I felt the theoreticians were integral so that others could understand, implement and expand on their ideas. However, an African cannot eat a theory, nor will it buy a person watered-down soup made from bare bones or a piece of scrap fat, if lucky.' Naz Gool-Ebrahim, with Donna Ruth Brenneis and Shahena Wingate-Pearce, *The Truth Is on the Walls*, David Philip, Claremont, 2011, p. 38

640 Everett, *Zainunnissa (Cissie) Gool*, p. 11

641 Ibid., p. 15. *The Liberator* only published five issues, the last in September.

642 Lewis, *Between the Wire and the Wall*, p. 184

643 Ibid., p. 185

644 Ibid., p. 187

645 Ibid., p. 28

646 Ibid., p. 28

647 Ibid., p. 29

648 Van der Ross, *The Rise and Decline of Apartheid*, p. 123

649 Ibid., p. 34

650 Ibid., p. 50

651 Lewis, *Between the Wire and the Wall*, p. 179

652 Ibid., p. 179

653 Ibid., p. 187

654 Lewis, *Between the Wire and the Wall*, p. 187

655 Ibid., p. 189

656 Ibid., p. 190

657 *The Sun*, 29 April 1938

658 *The Sun*, 10 June 1938

659 Lewis, *Between the Wire and the Wall*, p. 191

660 *The Sun*, 19 August 1938

661 *The Sun*, 5 May 1939

662 Dr Abdurahman continued: 'On the other hand, the APO would continue to function as vigorously if he died. There were sufficient men of personality for the APO to carry on.' In this he was incorrect. The APO was unable to continue without his leadership.

663 Lewis, *Between the Wire and the Wall*, p. 192

664 Ibid., p. 192

665 Ibid., p. 192

666 Ibid., p. 197

667 *Cape Standard*, 5 September 1939

668 *Cape Standard*, 12 September 1939

669 Lewis, *Between the Wire and the Wall*, p. 197

670 Ian Gleeson, *The Unknown Force: Black, Indian and Coloured Soldiers through Two World Wars*, Ashanti Publishing, Rivonia, 1994, p. 105

671 David Killingray with Martin Plaut, *Fighting for Britain: African Soldiers in the Second World War*, James Currey, Oxford, 2010, p. 71

672 Jack and Ray Simons, *Class and Colour in South Africa*, p. 528. For details of divisions on the left over whether to support the war effort or to back a campaign of passive resistance, see Van der Ross, *The Rise and Decline of Apartheid*, pp. 133–36.

673 Jack and Ray Simons, *Class and Colour in South Africa*, p. 529

674 Everett, *Zainunnissa (Cissie) Gool*, p. 45

675 Jack and Ray Simons, *Class and Colour in South Africa*, p. 536

676 Sarah-Jane Walton, *Remembering and Recollecting World War Two: South African Perspectives*, MA thesis, UCT, 2014, p. 69–70. These were of course not the only indignities the community suffered. Coloured veterans lost the homes built for them in Diep River when they were forced to leave for Lavender Hill when apartheid came into force. Ibid., pp. 108–9.

677 *Cape Times*, 21 February 1940

678 *Cape Standard*, Special Memorial Supplement, 27 February 1940

679 Mogamed Ajam, 'Dr Abdullah Abdurahman: Benefactor of the Bo-Kaap', *Kronos*, no. 17, 1990, pp. 48–58
680 *Cape Argus*, 21 February 1940
681 *The Sun*, 23 February 1940
682 Lewis, *Between the Wire and the Wall*, p. 198
683 *The Sun*, 1 March 1900
684 *Cape Argus*, 20 February 1940

CHAPTER 14

685 *Cape Times*, 21 February 1940
686 *The Sun*, 23 February 1940
687 Lewis, *Between the Wire and the Wall*, p. 200
688 Ibid., p. 200
689 *Cape Argus*, 20 February 1940
690 Ajam, *The Raison d'Etre of the Muslim Mission Primary School*, p. 198
691 University of London, Senate House Libraries, Institute of Commonwealth Studies: ICS2 Dr Abdurahman Papers, UOL/ICS2, Dr Hendrickse's Notes, n.d., p. 5
692 Wong, *Doctor of District Six*, p. 117
693 Edgar, *The Travel Notes of Ralph J. Bunche*, pp. 79–80
694 Denis-Constant Martin, 'The Famous Invincible Darkies', in Barnard Bel et al. (eds.), *Communication Process*, vol. 3, Sage Publications, London, 2010, p. 428. The doctor's son, A.E. Abdurahman, was chairman of the Western Province Jubilee Carnival Board until 1940. Ibid., p. 441
695 Raynard, *Dr A. Abdurahman*, pp. 79–80
696 Lewis, *Between the Wire and the Wall*, p. 89
697 Ibid., p. 203
698 Ibid.
699 Davenport and Saunders, *South Africa*, p. 365
700 Ibid., p. 365
701 Lewis, *Between the Wire and the Wall*, p. 268
702 Everett, *Zainunnissa (Cissie) Gool*, p. 79
703 Ibid., p. 97
704 http-://www.livingstonehighschool.co.za/?page=THE+HISTO-RY+OF+LIVINGSTONE+HIGH+SCHOOL&cat=ABOUT+US, accessed 12 September 2019
705 https://studentportal.org.za/western-cape/rahmaniyeh-mos-prim-zonnebloem-cape-town-information/, accessed 12 September 2019
706 Lewis, *Between the Wire and the Wall*, p. 314
707 Ibid., p. 328
708 In 1939 it was estimated that some 40,000 children were attending coloured schools in the Cape Province, many of which owed their existence to his persistent efforts. Ajam, *The Raison d'Etre of the Muslim Mission Primary School*, pp. 337–8
709 Ajam, *The Raison d'Etre of the Muslim Mission Primary School*, p. 341
710 Raynard, *Dr A. Abdurahman*, p. 87
711 Ibid., p. 33

712   Ibid., p. 32
713   Mohammed Adhikari, *Let Us Live for Our Children: The Teachers' League of South Africa, 1913–1940*, Buchu Books and University of Cape Town Press, 1993, pp. 180–1
714   Van der Ross, 'The Founding of the African People's Organisation in Cape Town', p. 37

Select bibliography

BOOKS

Adhikari, Mohamed, *Not White Enough, Not Black Enough: Racial Identity in the South African Coloured Community*, Ohio University Press, Athens, 2005

Adhikari, Mohamed, *Let Us Live for Our Children: The Teachers' League of South Africa, 1913–1940*, Bunchu Books and University of Cape Town Press, Cape Town, 1993

Adhikari, Mohamed (ed.), *Dr A. Abdurahman: A Biographical Memoir by J.H. Raynard*, Friends of the National Library of South Africa, in association with the District Six Museum, Cape Town, 2002

Bickford-Smith, Vivian, *Ethnic Pride and Racial Prejudice in Victorian Cape Town: Group Identity and Social Practice, 1875–1902*, Cambridge University Press, Cambridge, 1995

Bickford-Smith, Vivian, Nigel Worden and Elizabeth van Heyningen, *Cape Town in the Twentieth Century: An Illustrated Social History*, David Philip, Cape Town, 1999

Davenport, T.R.H., *South Africa: A Modern History*, 3rd edn, University of Toronto Press, Toronto, 1987

Davenport, T.R.H. and Christopher Saunders, *South Africa: A Modern History*, 5th edn, Macmillan Press, London, 2000

Difford, Captain Ivor D., *The Story of the 1st Battalion Cape Corps, 1915–1919*, Hortors, Cape Town, 1921

Drew, Allison, *Discordant Comrades: Identities and Loyalties on the South African Left*, Ashgate, Aldershot, 2000

Edgar, Robert R. (ed.), *The Travel Notes of Ralph J. Bunche, 28 September 1937 – 1 January 1938*, Ohio University Press, Athens, 1992

Giliomee, Hermann and Bernard Mbenga, *New History of South Africa*, Tafelberg

Publishers, Cape Town, 2007

Giliomee, Hermann, *The Afrikaners: Biography of a People*, Hurst, London, 2003

Grundy, Kenneth, *Soldiers without Politics: Blacks in the South African Armed Forces*, California University Press, Berkeley, 1983

Guha, Ramachandra, *Gandhi before India*, Allen Lane, London, 2013

Heartfield, James, *The Aborigines' Protection Society: Humanist Imperialism in Australia, New Zealand, Fiji, Canada, South Africa and the Congo, 1836–1909*, Hurst, London, 2011

Hirson, Baruch, *A History of the Left in South Africa*, I.B. Tauris, London, 2005

Hommel, Maurice, *Capricorn Blues: Struggle for Human Rights in South Africa*, Culturama, Toronto, 1981

Krikler, Jeremy, *White Rising: The 1922 Insurrection and Racial Killing in South Africa*, Manchester University Press, Manchester, 2005

Lewis, Gavin, *Between the Wire and the Wall: A History of South African 'Coloured' Politics*, David Philip, Cape Town, 1987

Morgan, Kenneth O., *Keir Hardie, Radical and Socialist*, Phoenix, London 1997 (first published by Orion Books, 1975)

Nasson, Bill, *Abraham Esau's War: A Black South African in the Cape, 1899–1902*, African Studies Series, 68, Cambridge University Press, Cambridge, 1991

Nasson, Bill, *WWI and the People of South Africa*, Tafelberg, Cape Town, 2014

Odendaal, Andre, *The Founders: The Origins of the ANC and the Struggle for Democracy in South Africa*, Jacana Media, Johannesburg, 2012

Plaut, Martin, *Promise and Despair: The First Struggle for a Non-Racial South Africa*, Jacana Media, Johannesburg, 2016

Rassool, Yousuf, *District Six – Lest We Forget: Recapturing Subjugated Cultural Histories of Cape Town, 1897–1956*, University of the Western Cape, Bellville, 2000

Ross, Robert, Anne Kelk Mager and Bill Nasson (eds.), *The Cambridge History of South Africa, Vol. 2: 1885–1994*, Cambridge University Press, Cambridge, 2012

Sherwood, Marika, *Origins of Pan-Africanism: Henry Sylvester Williams, Africa and the African Diaspora*, Routledge, London, 2011

Simons, Jack and Ray, *Class and Colour in South Africa (1850–1950)*, IDAF, London, 1983

Simons, Ray Alexander, *All My Life and All My Strength*, STE Publishers, Johannesburg, 2004

Soudien, Crain, *The Cape Radicals: Intellectual and Political Thought of the New Era Fellowship, 1930s–1960s*, Wits University Press, Johannesburg, 2019

Van der Ross, R.E., *Say It Out Loud: The APO Presidential Addresses and Other Major Political Speeches 1906–1940 of Dr Abdullah Abdurahman*, Western Cape Institute for Historical Research, Bellville, 1990

Van der Ross, R.E., 'The Founding of the African People's Organisation in 1903 and the Role of Dr Abdurahman', *Munger Africana Library Notes*, 28, 1975

Van der Ross, R.E., *In Our Skins: A Political History of the Coloured People*, Jonathan Ball, Johannesburg, 2015

Van der Ross, R.E., *The Rise and Decline of Apartheid: A Study of Political Movements among the Coloured People of South Africa, 1880–1985*, Tafelberg, Cape Town, 1986

Walker, Cherryl, *Women and Resistance in South Africa*, Onyx Press, London, 1982

Walshe, Peter, *The Rise of African Nationalism in South Africa: The African National Congress, 1912–1952*, C. Hurst, London, 1970

Wickins, P.L., *The Industrial and Commercial Workers' Union of Africa*, Oxford University Press, Cape Town, 1978

Willan, Brian, *Sol Plaatje: South African Nationalist, 1876–1932*, University of California Press, Berkeley, 1984

Willan, Brian, *Sol Plaatje: A Life of Solomon Tshekisho Plaatje, 1876–1932*, Jacana Media, Johannesburg, 2018

Worden, N., E. van Heyningen and V. Bickford-Smith, *Cape Town: The Making of a City*, David Philip, Cape Town, 1998

THESES

Adhikari, Mohamed, *Hope, Fear, Shame, Frustration: Continuity and Change in the Expression of Coloured Identity in White Supremacist South Africa, 1910–1994*, PhD, University of Cape Town, 2002

Ajam, Mogamed, *The Raison d'Être of the Muslim Mission Primary School in Cape Town and Environs from 1860 to 1980 with Special Reference to the Role of Dr A. Abdurahman in the Modernisation of Islam-Oriented Schools*, PhD, University of Cape Town, 1986

Corbett, J.E., *A Study of the Cape Town Agreement*, MA, University of Cape Town, 1947

Everett, Elizabeth, *Zainunnissa (Cissie) Gool, 1897–1963*, BA (Hons) dissertation, University of Cape Town, 1978

Gencoglu, Halim, *Abu Bakr Effendi: A Report on the Activities and Challenges of an Ottoman Muslim Theologian in the Cape of Good Hope*, MA, University of Cape Town, 2013

Grossman, Jonathan, *Class Relations and the Politics of the Communist Party of South Africa, 1921–1950*, PhD, Warwick University, 1985

Hendricks, Seraj, *Tasawwuf (Sufism): Its Role and Impact on the Culture of Cape Islam*, MA dissertation, University of South Africa, 2005

Laitila, Teuvo, *Soldier, Structure and the Other: Social Relations and Cultural Categorisation in the Memoirs of Finnish Guardsmen Taking Part in the Russo-Turkish War, 1877–1887*, University of Helsinki dissertation, 2001

Nicol, Martin, *A History of Garment and Tailoring Workers in Cape Town, 1900–1939*, PhD, University of Cape Town, 1984

Orakci, Serhat, *A Historical Analysis of the Emerging Links between the Ottoman Empire and South Africa between 1861–1923*, MA, University of Johannesburg, 2007

Pahad, Essop, *The Development of Indian Political Movements in South Africa, 1924–1946*, DPhil, University of Sussex, 1972

Paleker, Gairoonisa, *'She Was Certainly not a Rosa Luxemburg': A Biography of Cissie Gool in Images and Words*, MA, University of Cape Town, 2002

Ross, Barry Kennedy, *A Study of Politics in the Cape Colony from January 1908 to May*

1910, MA thesis, University of Cape Town, 1950

Ticktin, D., *The Origins of the South African Labour Party, 1888–1910*, PhD, University of Cape Town, 1973

Trapido, Stanley, *White Conflict and Non-White Participation in the Politics of the Cape of Good Hope 1853–1910*, PhD, University of London, 1970

Van der Ross, Richard, *A Political and Social History of the Cape Coloured People, 1880–1970*, Unpublished thesis submitted to the University of Cape Town, 1973, UCT Special Collections

Van der Spuy, Patricia, *Not Only 'the Younger Daughter of Dr Abdurahman': A Feminist Exploration of Early Influences on the Political Development of Cissie Gool*, PhD, University of Cape Town, 2002

Wong, Eve, *The Doctor of District Six: Exploring the Private and Family History of Dr Abdullah Abdurahman, City Councillor for District Six of Cape Town (1904–1940)*, MA, University of Cape Town, 2016

Index of names

We thank the following for their support in publishing this book:

Arthur Goldstuck

Ashwin Moyene

Ben Williams

Beverley Naidoo

Carolyn Raphaely

Catriona Jarvis

Corinne Rosmarin

Denis Hirson

Dianne Stewart

Gill Bolton

Glen Impey

Graeme Friedman

Helen Douglas

James Bissett

Karin Pampallis

Kevin Ritchie & Associates

Louis Gaigher

Maeve King

Mamma Jacqui

Mary Burton

Michelina Giacovazzi

Moira Levy

Roger Southall

Rona V van Niekerk

Ryan Childs

Sebastian Seedorf

Steven Dubin

Sue Grant-Marshall

Trisha Cornelius